FRANZ KAFKA
An Anthology of Marxist Criticism

FRANZ KAFKA

An Anthology of Marxist Criticism

Edited and translated by

KENNETH HUGHES

PUBLISHED FOR CLARK UNIVERSITY

BY UNIVERSITY PRESS OF NEW ENGLAND

Hanover and London, 1981

Copyright © 1981 by Trustees of Clark University
All rights reserved. Except for brief quotation in critical
articles or reviews, this book, or parts thereof, must not be repro-
duced in any form without permission in writing from the publisher.
For further information contact University Press of New England,
Hanover, NH 03755.

"Franz Kafka" by Hannah Arendt translated
and published by permission of Harcourt Brace Jovanovich, Inc.

"Franz Kafka in the Prague Perspective: 1963"
reprinted by permission of Eduard Goldstücker © 1965.

Library of Congress Catalogue Card Number 81-51611
International Standard Book Number 0-87451-206-9

Printed in the United States of America

Library of Congress Cataloging in Publication data
will be found on the last printed page of this book.

PREFACE

I have compiled this anthology for a number of reasons. First, Marxist criticism of Kafka is not well known in the West. Although a good deal has appeared in German during the past twenty years, it has been noticed only by the relatively small circle of Kafka specialists who follow the literature in German: in the numerous anthologies of Kafka criticism that have appeared in the United States, and that have translated some German work, one searches in vain for Marxist viewpoints on Kafka.[1] And even among those specialists who have read the German Marxist material, there is only a handful who are aware of the work done in the Soviet Union. As recently as 1974, one editor of an American anthology was capable of asserting that "from one corner of the globe to the other there is hardly a major language or literary culture that is without Kafka translations or commentaries (Russian is the one notable exception)."[2] Yet, as the selections in this anthology make clear, the debate about Kafka started in major Soviet literary journals as early as 1959, and he was translated and anthologized in the Soviet Union during the sixties: apparently, not only are Western critics unaware of the content of the Soviet material, they are unaware even of its existence. In his essay in this volume, Ernst Fischer calls for an East-West dialogue on Kafka's work, and that is

---

1. *The Kafka Problem*, ed. Angel Flores (New York: New Directions, 1946); *Kafka: A Collection of Critical Essays*, ed. Ronald Gray (Englewood Cliffs, N.J.: Prentice-Hall, 1962); *Franz Kafka Today*, ed. Angel Flores and Homer Swander (Madison: University of Wisconsin Press, 1964); *Twentieth Century Interpretations of "The Castle": A Collection of Critical Essays*, ed. Peter F. Neumeyer (Englewood Cliffs, N.J.: Prentice-Hall, 1969); *New Views of Franz Kafka*, ed. Kenneth McRobbie, *Mosaic*, 3 (1970), No. 4; *The Problem of "The Judgment*," ed. Angel Flores (New York: Gordian, 1976); *Twentieth Century Interpretations of "The Trial": A Collection of Critical Essays*, ed. James Rolleston (Englewood Cliffs, N.J.: Prentice-Hall, 1976); *Franz Kafka: A Collection of Criticism*, ed. Leo Hamalian (New York: McGraw-Hill, n.d.); *The Kafka Debate*, ed. Angel Flores (New York: Gordian, 1977). Of the 161 essays presented in these collections, I would say that only about five of them either approach Kafka from Marxist perspectives or deal with him in the context of Marxist literary theory. One must remember that, as the writers presented here frequently mention, Marxist occupation with Kafka began relatively recently.

2. Hamalian, p. 146.

certainly a worthy goal. But the Eastern material must first be made
as available in the West as Western criticism is in Eastern Europe and
the Soviet Union, and that is one of the aims of this collection.

Another is to dispel the mistaken notion that there is some sort of
uniform and monolithic Marxist literary criticism forever lockstepped
into an unswerving and undifferentiated ideology. This curious mis-
conception is no doubt based partly on "honest" ignorance, but it is
also partly a tenacious survival of the conscious distortions inherent in
the cultural politics of the cold war, and as such it has persisted into
the present—despite the fact that the West is fully aware of the debate
between the "dogmatists" and the "revisionists." The truth is, however, that there is as much disagreement—and agreement—among
Marxists as there is among bourgeois critics, and for bourgeois writers
to refer to "Marxist" critics in general is just as undiscriminating as it
is for Marxists to speak of "bourgeois" criticism *en gros*. This is why
I have not attempted to define what I understand to be Marxist criticism. Perhaps what unites all the essays presented here, and what
characterizes them as Marxist in their fundamental concerns, is their
commitment to the argument that "it is not the consciousness of men
that determines their being, but, on the contrary, their social being
that determines their consciousness."[3] If that position is as basic to
Marxist views as it seems to be, then it is appropriate that a picture
of Marxist criticism be allowed to emerge from the selections presented here, rather than that their inclusion be justified by reference
to a preconceived definition. In this regard, there is a clear advantage
to an anthology of Marxist criticism centered around a single author,
as opposed to a more general collection of essays dealing with a
variety of writers. If in a given Marxist collection Joyce and Proust
are rejected and Steinbeck and Thomas Mann accepted, that is en-
lightening, but it does not afford the reader nearly as good an opportunity to appreciate the divergence of Marxist opinions in a more
focused debate, from various sides, around the work of a single writer.

A third aim of this anthology is more specifically pedagogical. The
view that it is necessary to include Marxist perspectives in our literary
criticism has been gaining ground rapidly—and not merely for the
reason that such a vast part of the world's population currently lives

---

3. Karl Marx, Preface to *A Contribution to the Critique of Political Economy* in
Marx and Engels on Literature and Art, ed. Lee Baxandall and Stefan Morawski (St.
Louis: Telos Press, 1973), p. 85.

in societies predicated on Marxist principles (although that in itself is surely a compelling reason), but because of the growing conviction that Marxists have something important to say to us. This is reflected in the recent appearance of several anthologies of Marxist literary criticism.[4] But the usefulness of such collections in dealing with comprehensive problems of literary criticism and theory is distinctly limited, especially in the college and university curriculum: to read literary criticism is a frustrating exercise to people who are not familiar with the literature under discussion, and one can hardly presuppose a general acquaintance with the majority of primary works discussed in those anthologies. In fact, the idea for this volume came from practical experience that I have had over several years in teaching a seminar on "applied" literary criticism. The problem was how to enable students to read as many diverse methodologies of criticism as possible and yet to ensure that they were familiar with the literature being criticized. The solution I devised was to construct the course around Kafka, whose central oeuvre, so far as it is not already known to the students, is compact enough to be read in the first few weeks of a semester, and who has been treated from every conceivable critical angle, all of which but the Marxist were represented by readily available work in English. To fill that gap, I started translating German, Russian, and French material for my students, and this anthology is an extension of that effort.

It will be apparent that, in the selection of these essays out of the huge body of Kafka criticism, I have striven toward a principle of mutual illumination and commentary in order to communicate the sense of the very real debate, argument, and polemic in which these Marxist critics are engaged. I have purposely given the Soviets more room—not because I am convinced of their greater merit, but because their work is the least accessible and least known. Thus the very important views of Georg Lukács and Walter Benjamin, without which no picture of the Marxist reception of Kafka is complete, are not included here because they have been readily available in English for some time and are therefore among the few Marxist evaluations of

---

4. Such as *Marxism and Art: Writings in Aesthetics and Criticism*, ed. Berel Lang and Forrest Williams (New York: McKay, 1972); *Preserve and Create: Essays in Marxist Literary Criticism*, ed. Gaylord C. LeRoy and Ursula Beitz (New York: Humanities Press, 1973); *Marxists on Literature: An Anthology*, ed. David Craig (Baltimore: Penguin, 1975); and *Weapons of Criticism: Marxism in America and the Literary Tradition*, ed. Norman Rudich (Palo Alto, Calif.: Ramparts Press, 1976).

Kafka that have been taken into account by Western critics.[5] I have
not limited the selections to passages that are particularly and charac-
teristically "Marxist" in the antagonistic, bourgeois sense of the term,
for that would have been to distort the concerns of Marxist criticism.
Although it is true that the concentrated article on the aesthetic spe-
cifics of a single work is not a highly developed critical tradition in
the Soviet Union—for ideological and historical reasons—Marxist critics reguarly work also with the "text"; but perhaps it is precisely in
their refusal to limit themselves to an "intrinsic" explication that their
Marxism is most apparent. Nor have I sought to eliminate occasional
repetitions, which are the bane of all anthologies; most of what I have
deleted is material familiar in the West, such as biographical information and some of the better known quotations from Kafka's works.
There is, of course, much more of this in the Soviet criticism than in
the Western essays, because there Kafka was being introduced to a
readership which knew relatively little about him. I have also attempted not to tamper with terminology or phraseology at any point;
that these selections are relatively free of jargon is a fact that may
surprise some readers, but it is a reflection of the texts themselves and
not a product of the editor's hand.

The order of the selections is roughly chronological and divides
naturally into "initial positions," that is, those taken before the Prague
conference in 1963, those assumed at that meeting, and the subsequent
Soviet reaction. The major exception is Boris Suchkov's essay, which
I have placed out of order at the beginning of the Soviet reaction because it is the most comprehensive Soviet treatment of Kafka to date,
and because the other contributions are therefore best read against
that background.

Apart from Howard Fast's short piece, a version of Hannah Arendt's
essay, and the selections from Avner Zis and Yuri Barabash, none of
the material here has, to my knowledge, ever before appeared in English. As mentioned, all translations are my own. Since the majority
of Russian names referred to is already familiar to the Western
reader, I have retained the traditional style of transliteration throughout. Titles, deletions, and notes in brackets are mine; non-bracketed
titles, ellipses, and notes are those of the authors.

---

5. Georg Lukács, *Realism in Our Time: Literature and the Class Struggle*, trans.
John and Necke Mander (New York: Harper & Row, 1964); "Franz Kafka" and
"Some Reflections on Kafka" in Walter Benjamin, *Illuminations*, ed. Hannah Arendt,
trans. Harry Zohn (New York: Schocken, 1969), pp. 111-40 and 141-45, resp.

CONTENTS

Contents

INTRODUCTION

Probably no writer has more extensively and more deeply divided Marxist literary scholarship and criticism than Franz Kafka. Although Marxist appraisals of other modernists, such as Proust and Joyce, also sharply diverge, it is Kafka who, in terms of the sheer amount of attention that has been paid to him and in terms of the substantive ideological debates that have crystallized around discussions of his works, has replaced Balzac and Tolstoy and has become the literary watershed of contemporary Marxist opinion. There are obvious historical reasons for this: Kafka's work was becoming known at the same time that the quasi-official Communist aesthetic of socialist realism was being promulgated as an authoritative standard and model in the Soviet Union. Andrey Zhdanov's insistence, at the First All-Union Congress of Soviet Writers in 1934, on the primacy of that new concept as "the basic method of Soviet literature and literary criticism"[1] was bound to evoke sharp debate, especially in view of the vigorous creative and theoretical ferment which had characterized the Russian literary sphere at least since 1905. Since Kafka was in many ways the most fascinating and enigmatic new star on the horizon, he was naturally used as an example in the arguments that ensued. Moreover, the most significant Communist literary theoreticians of the time, Georg Lukács and Bertolt Brecht, not surprisingly based their theories on the literature most familiar to them, and they were naturally more closely tied to the German literary heritage from which Kafka came than to any other.

But there is more involved: Kafka deals much more directly than most writers with the kinds of alienation that become institutionalized in the capitalist social order on the one hand and in bureaucratic governmental hierarchies in general on the other, and his work is thus a two-edged sword which can be used both to dissect the specific evils of capitalism and to lacerate the vestiges of alienation which, in the

1. Quoted by Abram Tertz [i.e., Andrey Sinyavsky], *On Socialist Realism* (New York: Pantheon, 1960), p. 24.

opinion of some of these critics, still persist in socialist societies. This sounds much more like a political point than a literary one, but of course it is impossible, in the Marxist view, to separate aesthetics and politics, which are interdependent ideological phenomena. This is the crux of Kafka's particular divisiveness in the Marxist debate: more than that of other modernists, Kafka's literary work has lent itself to exploitation in the literary-unspecific ideological struggle between the dogmatists and the revisionists. As the Soviet scholar G. I. Safronov has polemically put it, in reference to Kafka and his positive assessment by certain Yugoslav critics, "the persistent attempts of the revisionists [. . .] to depreciate all the realistic classics in favor of modernism, to discredit the classical heritage, testify to the fact that it is not only a matter of literary questions, but also of an ideological and aesthetic struggle."[2] It is only in this context that the passion and heat generated by the Marxist discussion of Kafka can be understood, and only against this background that one can accurately evaluate the significance of such events as the Prague conference on Kafka in 1963, in which, as I have said elsewhere, "alienation was the issue; Kafka was the catalyst."[3]

Obviously, there are many questions. Is Kafka an "anti-realist," as he appears generally in the Soviet view and specifically in Zatonsky's phrase, or is he a "huge, monumental realist," as Alexej Kusák calls him? (And, indeed, what is realism?) Is his work relatively devoid of content and therefore merely a decadent display of empty formalism, or does it in fact capture a specific and characteristic content of our time? Is Kafka a "poet of alienation," as some writers presented here call him, and, if so, in what sense; that is, did he succumb to and accept alienation as an inevitable human condition, as the Soviets tend to believe, or is it not rather that, in Garaudy's words, he "awakens in people the consciousness of their alienation" and thereby implies an alternative? (Is Fischer correct in his contention that it is not the artist's responsibility to provide answers; or are the Soviets right when they imply that it is the artist's responsibility at least to suggest alternatives?) In general, did Kafka create a kind of existentialist "everyman" in his heroes, or was he aware that these were the representative

2. G. I. Safronov, "Rodstvenny li idealy F. Kafki i R. Domanovicha?" ["Are the Ideals of F. Kafka and R. Domanovich Related?"] Vestnik Leningradskogo Universiteta: Seriya Istorii, Yazyka i Literatury, No. 14 (1963), pp. 54-63.

3. Kenneth Hughes, "The Marxist Debate, 1963" in The Kafka Debate, ed. Angel Flores (New York: Gordian, 1977), p. 52.

products of a transitory and alterable historical stage? These and similar substantive questions are directed specifically to Kafka's works, but they imply and exemplify broader questions of critical method and social interpretation, which are never divorced in Marxist considerations: To what extent can Kafka's work be explained as the product of his social environment and to what extent is it aesthetically "autotelic," to use Paul Reimann's term? When the writer is most individual and subjective, is he therefore conversely least social and objective—or concomitantly *most* social and objective? Is alienation solely a product of capitalist society, which has been overcome in socialist society (and does Kafka therefore have nothing to say to the socialist world, apart from providing a little historical local color), or does alienation in fact persist in socialist society (and can Kafka therefore teach even socialists something)? The issues are doggedly complex, and like all complex issues, they give rise to abundant ironies. The complexities and ironies were underlined by Roman Karst when he pointed out that even in the Soviet Union the situation is basically so paradoxical that the excellently translated and edited Soviet Kafka anthology of 1965 is perhaps the only published collection of any writer's works prefaced with an introduction attempting to convince the prospective reader that he would be wasting his time if he actually went ahead and read the works collected.[4]

In view of this situation, it is clearly impossible, in the scope of an introduction to this volume, to discuss all the aspects of the debate, and in the following only some of the major questions, such as realism and decadence and their attendant secondary issues can be discussed.

Realism is a central touchstone in the Marxist evaluation of literature and of all art. It is through realism that the art work can most immediately exercise its cognitive function, an aspect that Marxists always insist on in contrast to the conception of art as entertainment and ludic distraction, which sometimes appears in bourgeois views. In general, realism implies a faithfulness to the accurate representation of the objective social reality that surrounds us and in which we live our daily lives—"truth of detail," as Engels put it in his famous formulation.[5] Thus Howard Fast insists that in "The Metamorphosis," "the

4. Roman Karst, "Kafka and the Russians" in *Perspectives and Personalities: Studies in Modern German Literature Honoring Claude Hill*, ed. Ralph Ley, et al. (Heidelberg: Winter, 1978), p. 186.

5. *Marx and Engels on Literature and Art: A Selection of Writings*, ed. Lee Baxandall and Stefan Morawski (St. Louis: Telos Press, 1973), p. 114.

equation of man and cockroach is a [. . .] confusion and distortion of the objective reality"—for truth to zoological detail must convince us that man and cockroach are wholly separate and unequatable species. Fast's extreme reductionism would banish metaphor and simile altogether from the realm of realist art, but few Marxists have been that extreme. Most have, however, insisted that realism is characterized by the artist's concentration on man in his social context, by the examination of man and society *together,* in their mutual relations. Dmitri Zatonsky maintains in "The Death and Birth of Franz Kafka" that Kafka cannot be considered a realist, for his extremely pessimistic view of man does not comprehend the optimism and the faith in the future that objectively is also an important part of our reality, and he argues in "Kafka Unretouched" that Kafka's tendency to exaggerate things to the point of absurdity is tantamount to a "derealization" of reality. And Knipovich believes that Kafka's "metaphysical absurdity" leads him to concentrate on unimportant aspects of reality, which also disqualifies him as a realist. Similarly, Boris Suchkov asserts that in *America* (which he and some others call *Lost Without a Trace* [*Der Verschollene*], in keeping with Kafka's original title) the fantastic elements gain the upper hand and finally overwhelm what may have started out as a relatively realistic presentation, and the result is that, disregarding "truth of detail," Kafka simply grafted his view of European conditions onto his fanciful idea of America and that the body of the work was right in rejecting the transplant. Moreover, the court in *The Trial,* he says, cannot be sufficiently correlated to anything actually existent and amounts to nothing more than an incomprehensible reality. Thus Kafka can never be included in the company of the great realists such as Gorky, Thomas Mann, Rolland, Hemingway, and so forth.

Another implication of realism is that the work of art contains a certain basic "content," a minimum of features, which we can identify as composing important parts of our socially shared reality. This "richness of content" (*soderzhatel'nost'*) is insisted upon, especially by Soviet critics, because it is a particularly important vehicle for the cognitive function of art.[6] Suchkov maintains that the aesthetic influ-

---

6. One must remember too that the Soviet critics approach Kafka and modernism in general from the point of view of the great realistic content of the nineteenth-century Russian novel, especially of Tolstoy, a tradition which reaches into the twentieth century in such writers as Sholokhov.

ence of literature on the reader is constituted as much by this "richness of content" as it is by the "strictly aesthetic properties" of the work. The social contexts of our lives, the "details" of reality to which the writer is enjoined to be true, are so extremely rich and various that they must be palpably present in any work which aspires to be a realistic representation. Suchkov finds Kafka's work to be generally lacking in such detail: the content, he says, is not definitive because the motivations behind the action are not clear; Kafka's portrayal of reality is "monotonous" because it is "limited to the twilight side of life." Conversely, Kafka's characteristic narrative form, the parable, is so extremely ambiguous and "polyvalent" that it amounts to a virtual lack of content (*bessoderzhatel'nost'*), that is, to a lack of incidents that reflect identifiable experiences in our normal lives. Jiří Hájek, on the other hand, views Kafka's parables as "infinitely saturated with reality."

Clearly, the solution to this problem lies in the definition of reality. It would be most unfair to tax the Soviet critics with having failed to define what they mean by reality—they have done so no more vigorously than anyone else—but it is true that they have not been so scrupulous in meeting this problem, at least in their views on Kafka and art, as some other Marxists have. Roger Garaudy has adopted an extremely elusive position: all art partakes of reality; therefore, all art is realistic; therefore, Kafka too is a realist. There is an undeniable persuasiveness in the logical progression: nothing can come from nothing; reality is all there is for something to come from; all art therefore comes from reality. But the syllogism breaks down in its intended conclusion: that all art is therefore realistic in any specific and serviceable use of the term. Garaudy's endeavor to loosen the circumscribed constraints on "realism" is understandable and perhaps even honorable, but in allowing the concept to expand beyond any limits at all, he has deprived it of any usefulness, and he has been roundly castigated for this.[7]

More helpful are considerations based on the Marxist view of reality itself. The fundamental premise of both philosophical and historical Marxism, the *sine qua non* of its existence altogether, is the perception that reality is dialectical, that the only thing stable is flux and

7. Most sharply by Hachik Momjan, head of the Department of Marxist-Leninist Philosophy of the Academy of Social Sciences of the USSR, in his *Marxism and the Renegade Garaudy* (Moscow: Progress, 1974).

the only permanent phenomenon is change. Fischer has used this foundation to argue that, since reality itself is constantly developing in a process of perpetual self-sublation (*Selbstaufhebung*), any definition of realism is perpetually provisional and open. If I may paraphrase Marx to capture his meaning: It is not the definition of realism that determines its appearance, but rather the appearance of realism that determines its definition—with the understanding that Fischer does not, like Garaudy, have an infinitely expandable view of what is realistic.

There are others, such as Alexej Kusák, who have maintained that since reality really *does* change, new forms really *are* needed to capture the new realities. Thus he argues that Kafka is *more* realistic for having used forms that are not traditionally associated with realism (based, as that usually has been, on traditional reality) and that Lukács, say, is therefore in gross error when he applies the criteria of nineteenth-century critical realism to Kafka in order to find him wanting in realism. Jiří Hájek similarly claims that *America* is not more realistic than *The Trial* or *The Castle* simply because it contains more of the social documentation and commentary common to critical realism than the other two novels do. Lukács' conservative effort to petrify realism in its nineteenth-century forms, and specifically to lionize Thomas Mann at Kafka's expense,[8] was persuasively met by Brecht, who argued that "one cannot take the form of one single realist (or of several) and call it *the* realist form. This is not realism. Otherwise one comes to the conclusion that *either* Swift and Aristophanes *or* Balzac and Tolstoy were realists."[9]

The opposite of realism has been called a number of things by Marxists, but, as realism implies not only an artistic method but also the world view which that method expresses, the best term for its opposite would seem to be "decadence," which similarly implies both world view and artistic method. Both Zatonsky ("Remarks on Kafka's Journals") and Barabash point to this opposition, the latter citing

---

8. Lukács' unswerving, and sometimes apparently irrational, allegiance to Thomas Mann has been called "one of the most remarkable critic-author relationships in modern German literature." See Hans Rudolf Vaget, "Georg Lukács, Thomas Mann and the Modern Novel" in *Thomas Mann in Context: Papers of the Clark University Centennial Colloquium*, ed. Kenneth Hughes (Worcester, Mass.: Clark University Press, 1978), p. 37.

9. Quoted by Werner Mittenzwei, "The Brecht-Lukács Debate" in *Preserve and Create: Essays in Marxist Literary Criticism*, ed. Gaylord C. Leroy and Ursula Beitz (New York: Humanities Press, 1973), p. 112.

Horst Redeker's view that realism and decadence exist in an inverse ratio: when realism declines, it is decadence that gains ground, and vice-versa. The most characteristic phenomenon of decadence in the literary work is an excessive attention to artistic form at the expense of content, that is, "formalism."

The relation of content and form is a fundamental problem in Marxist aesthetics, one we can only touch on here. The Marxist critic is committed to viewing form and content as coexisting in an indissoluble dialectical unity, namely, the work itself. However, in analyzing the way in which the economic base exercises its influence on the superstructural phenomenon of art, most Marxists, including Marx and Engels themselves, have concentrated on the aspect of content. Stefan Morawski is unquestionably right in calling the aesthetics of Marx and Engels a *Gehaltästhetik*.[10] But that is not necessarily true of Marxist aesthetics as a whole. The fact that the concept of "form" seems somehow less concrete, less palpable—in a word, less "materialistic" and therefore more "idealistic"—than "content" has led some aestheticians into the belief that Marxist aesthetics as a whole is a *Gehaltästhetik*, that the base exercises its influence on the form of art (as the relatively "idealist" aspect) primarily through the vehicle of content (which is seen as the relatively "materialist" aspect). Thus Henri Arvon writes that "Marxist esthetics, which considers the work of art to be intimately related to social life as a whole, is left no choice with regard to the relation between content and form. It is forced to admit the priority of content, which then creates the need for an appropriate form."[11] Similarly, Terry Eagleton states that "Marxist criticism [. . .] wants to assert in the end the primacy of content in determining form."[12] Such arguments do not seem to confront fully the fact that the base, as well as conditioning the contents of our lives and art, also conditions their form; in a dialectical view, there is perhaps less reason than has generally been thought to assign so exclusively to content the role of mediator between base and artistic form. This is not to excuse the excesses of formalism, either in art or critical method, whose view of form is indeed idealistic, as it is largely detached from the conditioning factors of the base. There is, of course,

10. *Marx and Engels on Literature and Art*, p. 18.
11. Henri Arvon, *Marxist Esthetics*, trans. Helen Lane (Ithaca, N.Y.: Cornell University Press, 1973), p. 41.
12. Terry Eagleton, *Marxism and Literary Criticism* (Berkeley: University of California Press, 1976), p. 23.

an alternative line of Marxist aesthetics which has posited that it is in fact form that is "the truly social element in literature"[13] and that has borne its best fruit in the "genetic structuralism" of Lucien Goldmann, which is genetic and structural in the sense that Goldmann is interested in investigating the sociohistorical genesis of structures of thought that determine the structures and forms of literature.

In any case, those critics who charge Kafka with a lack of "richness of content" therefore simultaneously chide him for what they see as the formalism of his work. Thus Suchkov states that Kafka's parables are an appropriate form in which to clothe his peculiarly ambiguous contents, for they are rather bloodless "constructions," and he argues that "the polyvalent character of Kafka's symbolism turns out to be a lack of full content and turns into a purely formal-logical structure." In general, what is objected to as formalism in Kafka's work is his devices of "de-realizing" (Zatonsky) reality, two of which are most frequently commented on. One is the "encoding" into "chiffres" or "hieroglyphs" that the Soviets point to. The implication is that Kafka, not having really very much to say, essentially played a formalist game with his readers by creating a kind of code that is left to his readers to break or "de-code"—rather than operating in the more conventional and comprehensible tradition of the symbol, which is always grounded in concrete reality. This interpretation is repudiated by many critics, including Hájek, who insists that Kafka's creative method is not a gratuitous encoding, but that it is absolutely necessary as a device to destroy the pseudoconcrete (a point to which we shall return below).

The second device putatively inimical to realism is Kafka's use of the fantastic, which, according to Suchkov, overwhelms whatever realistic elements might be in the fiction, especially in *America* and *The Castle*. Neither he nor other Soviets have anything against the fantastic per se. He specifically credits fantasy as "a means of analyzing reality"—provided that it be used cautiously. The Romantics, he says, who also created "phantasmagorical works which largely scorn external verisimilitude," were careful not to "cut the threads which united their creations with the maternal soil of reality," and so in their works one can still recognize "the contours of the real world and its authentic conflicts." But in Kafka, he believes, the fantastic

---

13. Georg Lukács, *The Evolution of Modern Drama*, quoted in Eagleton, p. 20.

becomes excessively formalist, whereas it is only "the freedom of fantasy from formalization" which "opens a space for true creativity and understanding of the world." Zatonsky ("Kafka and Problems of Modernism") comes to a similar conclusion when he compares "The Metamorphosis" not with a Romantic work, but with H. G. Wells's short story "The Man Who Could Work Miracles." Ernst Fischer implies, however, that the Soviet point is ahistorical: the Romantics, with the fine anticipatory antennae peculiar to writers, felt the shudder of dehumanization, of reification, and captured their feeling in the marionettes, automata, and other fantastic phenomena of which they were so fond. But Kafka, he maintains, was the first to feel such things in the *everyday*—and that surely implies an historical difference.

It seems to me that Alexej Kusák has very accurately defined the situation when he says with only apparent paradox, that Kafka had to use a relatively "de-realized" form of the parable in order to "grasp more reality, because he was a greater realist than those who castigate him." And Hájek too maintains that Kafka's fantastic elements are not gratuitous, but a means of encompassing a greater reality. Both Kusák and Hájek refer to Karel Kosík's concept of the "destruction of the pseudoconcrete" in this regard, and Hájek quotes the relevant passage: the everyday world is *not* the one we know best, precisely because it is everyday, because of its "intimately fetishized familiarity"; in order to *see* it—not simply to *recognize* it—we must gain distance from it, it must be divested of its quality of "*seeming* known" through a fictional device similar to Brecht's principle of the "alienation effect" in drama. It is not entirely accidental that this point should have been voiced so strongly by three Czech writers, but it is also not unique to recent Czech criticism. The Cultural Theory Panel of the Central Committee of the Socialist Workers' Party of Hungary has also admitted the usefulness of the kind of estrangement which Kafka has been criticized for: "socialist realism does not exclude, it even presupposes a certain aesthetic abstraction which serves the better recognition of the essential reality and which therefore always maintains a functional connection with it."[14]

"Artistic device," "estrangement," "seeing" as opposed to mere "recognizing"—such terminology necessarily recalls critical categories of Russian Formalism, and an interesting, if somewhat peripheral, as-

---

14. "Of Socialist Realism" in *Radical Perspectives in the Arts,* ed. Lee Baxandall (Baltimore: Penguin, 1972), p. 263.

pect of these essays is the manner in which Russian Formalism has continued to exert an influence on both Soviet and non-Soviet Marxist critics, although these have largely rejected the major Formalist concerns as ahistorical and idealistic. Viktor Shklovsky was apparently correct when he found in 1926 that "even while our theories are being attacked, our terminology is generally accepted, and . . . our errors are somehow finding their way into the textbooks on literary history."[15] When the Soviet critic Zatonsky entitles a section of his book on Kafka "Not a Matter of Literary Devices," he is implying that Kafka's artistic aberrations lie not only in the formal and stylistic techniques to which the Russian Formalists tended to limit their attention, and that their methods are therefore inadequate. However, it is impossible in contemporary criticism written in Russian to use the word "device" (*priëm*) without automatically recalling Shklovsky's seminal 1917 essay "Art as Device" (*"Iskusstvo kak priëm"*), which, virtually founding the Russian Formalist school, predicated its method on the investigation of the device as the heart of the literary work and posited the techniques of estrangement (*ostranenie*) and "defacilitation" (*zatrudnenie*) as absolutely fundamental to art—that is, just those methods of complication and bewilderment which the Soviets have rejected as gratuitous and unserious in Kafka's work. Nor is it difficult to recognize, in Kosík's, Kusák's, and Hájek's interest in Kafka's "destruction" of the "pseudoconcrete," a continuation of Russian Formalist concerns mediated by Roman Jakobson when he went to Prague, which were quickly adapted by him, Jan Mukařovsky, and others to Czech literary concerns, and which have remained a far stronger critical convention in Czechoslovakia than in the USSR.

But formalism is only the literary expression of decadence, which is ultimately a matter of world view. To Zatonsky ("Remarks . . ."), "Kafka's attitude toward the world is a decadent one typical of a crisis situation," for he "didn't believe in society and didn't believe in man." Suchkov taxes Kafka with decadence because the writer was ignorant of the true social nature of the forces which subjugate man, and he generalized them into absolutes. The implication is that Kafka can be of little interest in a society that has understood those forces and subjected them to a Marxist analysis and to reform. Other Marxists have attempted to rescue Kafka's paradigmatic value, and that of

15. Quoted in Victor Erlich, *Russischer Formalismus* (Frankfurt am Main: Suhrkamp, 1973), p. 88.

decadent literature in general, by arguing, as Fischer and Garaudy do, that Kafka's depiction of alienated man in a hostile environment forces us to ask ourselves the right questions about our own lives and to consider whether or not they are subject to the same conditions as are the lives of Kafka's heroes. Hájek contends, for example, that "Kafka's entire work has no other purpose than to awaken and stimulate [the] consciousness" that one cannot go on living as his characters do; Hájek calls Kafka's work a "darkly negative" vision, but one in which it is not hard to read the positive message out of the negative. In implying that Kafka's work is a negation of the negation, in the best dialectical tradition, Hájek is able to see the signs of hopefulness behind the general hopelessness. This is not true, says Yuri Barabash, who takes a harder line against decadence. In his view, decadent literature cannot be excused simply because it voices a protest against capitalism, for such an attitude cannot nurture a "wholesome" art. He maintains that the mere depiction of alienation does not automatically engender an awareness of alienation, and it is awareness that is necessary to overcome it.

Alienation is a fundamental category of Kafka criticism, and virtually all the writers here, as well as many bourgeois critics, discuss it. In a truly dialectical way, the concept of alienation is what simultaneously most closely unites and most sharply divides Kafka's commentators. Probably no one would deny that Kafka has created a most poignant picture of alienated man. But bourgeois critics tend to view alienation as an immutable and permanent characteristic of our existence; in fact, in nonreligious bourgeois viewpoints, alienation has sometimes replaced the "fall" of man as an explanation of why we inhabit a less than paradisaical reality. To the Marxist, however, alienation is a very specific and concrete historical phenomenon, a product of the way in which people organize the material reproduction of their lives, and, like all historical phenomena, it is subject to change and even elimination. Most Marxists agree that Kafka felt and portrayed alienation without having any idea of how to overcome it, or even that it could be overcome; that, in other words, he regarded it ahistorically, in the bourgeois manner, as part of the human condition (although Hájek, for example, claims that Kafka's statement is not that man is "unalterably predestined to loneliness" and insists that Gregor Samsa's metamorphosis has a "completely concrete meaning"). Suchkov writes that Kafka has in effect created a myth, for he "abstracted from the actual, really existing conditions which determine the movement of history and man's relationship to it."

Those who agree argue that Kafka's work is of no cognitive value: Avner Zis rejects Kafka because he did not reveal the sources of alienation and "work out ways for overcoming it," and Paul Reimann, contrasting Kafka with the experience of his Communist contemporaries, who did escape from alienation, concludes that, although Kafka "struggled for new perceptions," he is of little use today in socialist society, which has overcome alienation without Kafka. Revisionists might generally agree that if there were no alienation to fight, then Kafka, at least in so far as he portrays it, would be only of historical interest to us. But Eduard Goldstücker, Ernst Fischer, Kusák, and Hájek all maintain that alienation has not yet been completely eliminated in socialist society, and Kusák even says that Kafka's treatment of alienation is what makes him so particularly relevant today. This is one of the debates in which one can see how closely politics and literary criticism are connected in Marxism. Evgeniya Knipovich and Zatonsky ("Kafka Unretouched") are correct when they point to the almost infinite expansion of the definition of alienation and to its far too broad application to Kafka, which ultimately deprives the concept of meaning, as Garaudy's overextension of the term "realism" severely inhibits its usefulness. But they may well be going too far when they deny that alienation has any relation to socialist society and that Kafka therefore has no "direct educational meaning."

When Zis chided Kafka for not taking a stand against alienation, he did so on the ground that "the artist's task is not merely to diagnose; he cannot stand outside good and evil." This partisan behest is something quite foreign to bourgeois views, which frequently locate the "edifying" and "elevating" qualities of literature precisely in its putative position above good and evil, in its sociopolitical, if not moral, "neutrality." Marxists neither believe that literature, as ideology, can be neutral, nor do they wish it to be. Rather, since it inevitably expresses ideology, they wish it to be ranged on the side of progressive ideology. This is the "tendency" about which Marx and Engels wrote (and which, in his celebrated letter to Minna Kautsky, Engels said "must spring forth from the situation and the action itself, without explicit attention called to it"[16]) and that characterizes what bourgeois

---

16. *Marx and Engels on Literature and Art*, p. 113.

critics have called *littérature engagée.* In the theory and practice of socialist realism, it has been elaborated and codified into various "allegiances": *partiinost'* (party allegiance, *Parteilichkeit*), *klassovost'* (class allegiance), *narodnost'* (allegiance to popular national values), etc. They all imply that, since art unavoidably exercises an educational effect, it should be directed toward raising party, class, and national consciousness. This is a view which has been more insisted on by Soviet critics than by other Marxists. Suchkov therefore agrees with Zis when he rejects Kafka because he only echoed the social temper of his time, without pronouncing judgment on it: "Limiting itself to that task, [art] becomes flat and loses its opportunity truly to evaluate the real condition of the world, and the battle of history ceases to be audible to it." Fischer and others, however, flatly state that it is not the responsibility of the artist to suggest alternate social orders or in any other way to attempt to provide solutions to the world's dilemmas. In this they are closer than the Soviets to Engels' position, stated further on in the letter quoted above, that "the writer is not obliged to offer to the reader the future historical solution of the social conflicts he depicts."[17]

Such considerations lead us away from the specific evaluation of Franz Kafka to the more general issues of critical method raised by these selections. Here we shall discuss only the two most central: the issue of "vulgar sociologism" and the relation between individual, subjective experience and social, objective experience, as that relation is embodied in the literary work.

It is unfortunate, but not completely accidental, that bourgeois conceptions of Marxist literary criticism and scholarship have generally been informed by, and generally have taken as their objects for refutation, methods which can at best be called pseudo-Marxist. One must remember that Marxism developed dialectically from bourgeois ideology and that the dialectical method itself arises in our age (although not, in its original form, in classical antiquity) as an antithesis to a dominant metaphysical tradition. It is not an easy thing to shift from metaphysics to dialectics, and early Marxist critics did not always wholly succeed in liberating themselves from the metaphysical conventions in which they had been educated. One consequence of that is the "mechanical materialism" which is one aspect of "vulgar-

17. *Ibid.*

ism" in Marxist critical method. It consists in being overly enamored of the Marxian perception that the economic base exercises a determining influence on the cultural superstructure and in forgetting, on the one hand, that the superstructure also dialectically influences the base and, on the other, that there is a constant dialectical interaction between spheres of the cultural superstructure themselves. Thus to say that a literary work is completely determined by the sociohistorical factors of its creator's environment is "mechanical" and undialectical.

None of the writers here is vulgar in that sense; their insistence that they are not and their polemic against this distortion of their method bespeak an awareness of vulgar sociologism as an "infantile disorder" of their critical procedures which is inimical to the development of genuine Marxist criticism and which has been seized upon by antagonistic bourgeois opponents as representative of Marxist criticism as a whole. A limitation to that kind of investigation, Goldstücker says, would result only in "working out general theses in which the uniqueness, the very special character of Kafka's work would be lost." But Goldstücker immediately warns his Marxist colleagues that their aversion to vulgar sociologism should not inhibit them from investigating the sociohistorical genesis of the work and in concentrating, as he puts it, on the "Prague perspective." Kusák has chided him for this view and has, I believe unfairly, compared it with Willy Haas's opinion that Kafka can be understood *only* from the point of view of his geopolitical roots in Prague. In this regard, Kusák is being extremely rigorous in admitting only a macrosociological view as scientific: he rejects as unscientific not only Kafka's microsociological and local roots, but also his statements in letters and diaries, which Kusák says are subject to the "mystification of self-stylization and self-interpretation"; for if we wish to arrive at an objective evaluation of a person, we will not uncritically accept his opinion of himself.

Reimann too, who is generally closer to Soviet views than the other Czech writers, defends the relative autonomy of the artistic form from the vulgar view that would forget that art has its specific laws which are relatively independent of the economic base, and he maintains that "only through these laws does art really become art and literature really become literature." In this there is agreement between the Soviets and the other Marxist critics, as is exemplified in Zatonsky's points ("Kafka Unretouched") that artistry is not really confronted in any superficial examination of an artist's political sympathies, nor can uniqueness be explained by environmental influences alone.

Another area in which there is general agreement about method is in the Marxist view of the relationship between a writer's personal and public experiences. Zatonsky ("Kafka Unretouched") calls attention to the opinion that it is the "intersection of certain significant 'lines of force' in human culture" which produces the phenomenon of a great writer, "of his uniquely individual and at the same time his typical existence." Zatonsky is using the concept of the "typical" not in the sense of the statistical average, but in the Marxist sense, which refers to quality rather than to quantity. This Marxist sense retains a close semantic connection with the word "type"; when Engels speaks of realism as "the truthful reproduction of typical characters under typical circumstances"[18] he is speaking in this qualitative sense. Thus he can praise the characterization in a novel, for "each person is a type, but at the same time a distinct personality."[19] In this view, the great writer is capable of creating figures who are at once both individual and typical because his own individual experiences are highly typical. As Ernst Fischer puts it, "it is a characteristic of the great writer that his fundamental experiences are representative of the basic problems of an age"—they are not numerically, but qualitatively typical: "out of a fullness of details he [the writer] is able to grasp those which are essential to a still undiscovered and still fragmentary new reality." Similarly, Reimann states that "if the writer is a great one, the subjective experience is closely meshed with [. . .] the historical development of a whole age." Thus the source of the disagreement that arises when such principles are applied to Kafka is clear: these critics all refer to the "great" writer and artist, but for the Soviets Kafka cannot be such, for he is not a realist. Suchkov agrees with the principle, but he does not believe that Kafka fulfills its basic requirements: "with realist writers the peculiarities of their personal perception of the world do not usually obscure the objective picture of the world," as, in his view, Kafka's do.

18. *Ibid.*, p. 114.   19. *Ibid.*, p. 112f.

In this introduction, I have attempted to give only a brief survey of the issues raised in the articles collected here. But the texts must finally be allowed to speak for themselves. Ernst Fischer pleads with the socialist world to grant Kafka a "permanent visa," and it is to be hoped that Western Kafka critics will also no longer ignore the vigorous debate and the perceptions of their Eastern colleagues.

INITIAL POSITIONS

Franz Kafka

HANNAH ARENDT

[. . .]

When K. notices that, despite their senselessness, such trials [as his] do not necessarily have to come to no result, he hires a lawyer who explains to him in long speeches how one can adapt oneself to the existing circumstances and how unreasonable it is to criticize them. K., who does not want to adapt himself and dismisses his lawyer, meets with the prison chaplain, who preaches to him about the hidden grandeur of the system and advises him not to inquire about the truth, for "one does not have to consider everything true, one must only consider it necessary." In other words, if the lawyer was only intent on demonstrating "Thus is the world," the clergyman, who is hired by this world, has the task of proving "Thus is the order of the world." And since K. considers this a "melancholy opinion" and replies that "The lie is turned into the world order," it is clear that he will lose his trial. But since this was not his "final judgment" and he tried to slough off the "unusual trains of thought" as "unreal things" that at bottom had nothing to do with him, he not only loses the trial, he loses it in such an ignominious way that at the end he has nothing to oppose to his execution but his shame.

The power of the machine which seizes and executes K. is nothing other than the appearance of necessity, which can realize itself through people's admiration of necessity. The machine gets started because necessity is considered something elevated and because its automatism, which is interrupted only arbitrarily, is considered the symbol of necessity. The machine is kept in motion by lies in behalf of necessity, so that a man who does not want to subordinate himself to this "world order," this machinery, is regarded, in all its consequences, as a sinner against some kind of divine order. Such subordination is

Excerpted from "Franz Kafka" in Hannah Arendt, *Sechs Essays* (Heidelberg: Lambert Schneider, 1948), pp. 128-49.

3

achieved when the question of guilt and innocence is silenced and replaced by the decision to play whatever role in the play of necessity
arbitrariness dictates.

In *The Trial*, subordination is not achieved through force, but
rather through the growing feeling of guilt that is evoked in the defendant K. by the unfounded and empty accusation. Naturally, this
feeling ultimately rests on the fact that no man is free of guilt. In the
case of K., who, as a busy bank officer has never had time to torture
his head with such generalities, this guilt feeling becomes his actual
fate: it leads him into a confusion in which he mistakes the organized
and malicious evil of his surroundings for the expression of that general human guilt which is harmless and actually innocent in comparison with the evil will that turns "the lie into the world order" and
that can use and abuse man's justified humility for this world order.

The functioning of the malicious bureaucratic machine in which
the hero has innocently been caught up is therefore accompanied by
an inner development that is released by the guilt feeling. In this development he is "educated," changed and formed until he fits into the
role which has been forced onto him, until he is ready to take his
place, come what may, in the world of necessity, injustice, and the
lie. This is his manner of adapting himself to the ruling circumstances.
The hero's inner development and the machine's functioning finally
come together in the last scene of the execution, when K. allows himself without resistance or even contradiction to be led off and killed.
He is murdered for the sake of necessity and in the confusion of his
guilt feelings he subordinates himself. And the sole hope which flashes
like lightning across the very end of the novel is "it was as if the
shame would outlive him." The shame, naturally, that this is the
world order and that he, Joseph K., even if its victim, is its obedient
member.

It was immediately apparent upon its publication that *The Trial*
implied a criticism of the bureaucratic government of old Austria,
whose numerous and mutually fighting nationalities were ruled by a
uniform hierarchy of bureaucrats. Kafka, an employee of a workers'
accident insurance agency and a friend of Eastern European Jews,
for whom he had to obtain residency permits in Austria, knew the
political conditions of his country very accurately. He knew that, if
one were once caught up in the bureaucratic machinery of the apparatus, one was already sentenced. The rule of the bureaucracy in-

sured that the interpretation of the law became an instrument of lawlessness, and the chronic incapacity of the law's interpreters was compensated by a senseless automatism in the lower parts of the bureaucratic hierarchy, to which all the real decisions were left. But since in the twenties, when the novel first appeared, the real essence of bureaucracy in Europe was not sufficiently recognized, or had become fateful to only a small and disappearing stratum of Europeans, the horror and the terror expressed in the novel seemed inexplicable and not correlated to its actual content. One was more shocked at the novel than at the thing itself. And so one started to look for different, and apparently more profound interpretations, and they were found in a cabalistic representation of religious realities, something like a satanic theology.

That such errors were possible—and this misunderstanding is no less fundamental, if less vulgar, than the misunderstanding in the psychoanalytic interpretations of Kafka—is naturally rooted in Kafka's work itself. Kafka really does describe a society which considers itself the representative of God on earth, and he describes people who regard the laws of such a society as divine commandments, unalterable through human will. The evil of the world, in which Kafka's heroes are caught up, is precisely its deification, its presumption of representing a divine necessity. Kafka is intent on destroying this world by exaggerating the contours of its horrible structure and thereby juxtaposing reality and presumption. But the reader of the twenties, entranced by paradoxes and confused by the play of the opposites as such, did not want to listen to reason. His interpretations of Kafka revealed more about himself than they did about Kafka; in his naive admiration of a world that Kafka in his extreme clarity had represented as intolerably awful, the reader revealed his own suitability for the "world order," he revealed how closely the so-called elite and avant-garde were tied to this world order. Kafka's sarcastic and bitter comment about the mendacious necessity and necessary mendacity which together comprise the "divinity" of this world order, and which are so clearly the key to the novel's construction, were simply overlooked.

Kafka's second great novel, *The Castle*, leads us into the same world, but this time it is not seen through the eyes of a man who has never concerned himself about his government and other questions of a general nature and is therefore a helpless prey to the appearance of necessity. Rather, it is seen through the eyes of a different K., who comes to it voluntarily, as a stranger who wants to realize a particular design in it: to settle there, to become a citizen, to make a life, marry, find work—in short, to become a useful member of human society.

Characteristic of the action of *The Castle* is the fact that its hero is interested only in the most general things and fights only for things which actually seem guaranteed to man by birth. But whereas he demands no more than the minimum of human existence, it is clear from the very beginning that he demands this minimum as a right and will accept nothing less than his right. He is prepared to supply all the documents in order to obtain his residency permit, but he does not want it as a gracious gift; he is ready to change his job, but he cannot dispense with "regular work." All of this depends on the decisions of the Castle, and K.'s difficulties begin when it turns out that the Castle dispenses rights only as gracious gifts or as privileges. And since K. wants rights and not privileges, wants to be a citizen of the village and be "as far as possible removed from the lords in the Castle," he declines both the gift and the privileged relationship to the Castle: in this way he hopes that "all at once all of the ways will open to him which, had it depended only on the lords up there and their grace, would not only have been forever closed to him, but would have remained invisible."

At this point the villagers enter the center of the action. They are shocked that K. simply wants to become one of them, a simple "village laborer," that he declines to become a member of the ruling society. Again and again they try to explain to him that he lacks general worldly wisdom and experience, that he does not know what life is all about, that it is essentially dependent on favor and disfavor, curse and blessing, and that no really important and decisive event is more comprehensible and less accidental than fortune and misfortune. K. cannot understand that for the villagers justice and injustice, or being right or wrong, is still a part of the fate that one must accept, that one can fulfill but not change.

From this point on, the strangeness of the immigrant surveyor K., who is not a villager and not a Castle official and therefore outside of the relations of dominance in his surroundings, appears in its actual significance. In his insistence on human rights, the stranger demonstrates himself to be the only one who still has a concept of a simple human life in the world. The specific experience of the villagers has taught them to view all of this—love and work and friendship—as a gift which they may receive "from above," from the regions of the Castle, but over which they themselves no longer have any control. And so the simplest relationships have been shrouded in a dark mystery; what in *The Trial* was the world order appears here as fate, as a blessing or a curse which one interprets and to which one subordinates oneself with fear and reverence. K.'s intention of gaining and creating what is necessary to a human life on the basis of the rule of law therefore does not appear at all self-evident, but is completely exceptional in this world, and as such a scandal. And so K. is forced to fight for a minimum of human requirements as if they were an insane maximum of human desires, and the villagers distance themselves from him because in his demand they are capable of suspecting only a hubris that threatens them all. K. is strange to them not because as a stranger he is deprived of human rights, but because he comes and demands them.

In spite of the villagers' fears, which every moment expect a catastrophe, nothing actually happens to him. Of course he does not achieve anything, and Kafka's orally communicated ending envisioned his death from exhaustion, that is, a completely natural death. The only thing that K. achieves, he achieves unintentionally: through his attitude and his judgment of the things happening around him, he succeeds in opening the eyes of some of the villagers, one of whom says to him:

You have an incredibly comprehensive view of things . . . sometimes you help me with just a word. That must be because you come from outside. But we, with our sad experiences and our constant fears, take fright at every snapping of a twig, and if one gets scared, the other gets scared right away too and doesn't even know the reason. In that way you can't come to any proper judgment. . . . What good luck for us that you have come.

K. defends himself against this role; he has not come as a bringer of good luck; he has no time and no extra strength to help others; whoever demands that of him "confuses his path."[1] He doesn't want to do anything but get his own life in order and keep it in order. In the execution of this design, as opposed to the K. of *The Trial*, he does not

1. See the appendix to the third edition of *The Castle* (New York: Schocken, 1946).

subordinate himself to the apparently necessary; it is not shame, but the recollections of the villagers that will outlive him.

Unquestionably, Kafka's world is a terrible world. No doubt we know better today than we did twenty years ago that it is more than a nightmare, that, on the contrary, its structure is uncannily equivalent to the reality that we have been forced to experience. The greatness of this art lies in the fact that it can have just as convulsive an effect today as it had then, that it has lost none of its immediacy through the reality of the gas chambers.

If Kafka's writing were really nothing more than a prophecy of impending horror, it would be just as cheap as all the other prophecies of doom which have plagued us since the beginning of our century, or rather since the first third of the nineteenth century. Charles Péguy, who himself often had the dubious honor of being counted among the prophets, once remarked that "Determinism, in so far as it can be imagined at all, is perhaps nothing but the law of residues." There is a very precise truth in this. In so far as life is always inevitably and naturally terminated by death, its end can always be prophesied. The way of nature is always the way of decline, and a society which blindly turns itself over to the necessity of the laws inherent in it can only decline. Prophets are not necessarily always prophets of doom simply because the catastrophe can always be predicted. The miracle is always salvation and not doom, because salvation and not doom depends on man's freedom and his capacity to change the world and its natural course. The delusion, widespread in Kafka's time as well as in ours, that man's job is to subordinate himself to a process predetermined by whatever powers, can only accelerate the natural decline, because in such a delusion man and his freedom come to the aid of nature and its tendency to decline. The words of the prison chaplain in *The Trial* reveal the secret theology and the most intimate belief of the bureaucrats as a belief in necessity per se, and the bureaucrats are in the final analysis the functionaries of necessity—as if functionaries were ever needed to make decline and doom function. As a functionary of necessity, man becomes a highly superfluous functionary of the natural law of ephemerality, and since man is more than nature, he thereby degrades himself to an instrument of active destruction. For as surely as a house built by men according to human laws will decay as soon as man leaves it and abandons it to its natural fate, just as surely will the world built by men and functioning according to human laws once again become a part of nature and be abandoned to cat-astrophic doom as soon as man decides to become himself once again a part of nature, a blind tool of natural laws, but one which works with utmost precision.

In this context it is relatively unimportant whether the man ob-sessed by necessity believes in doom or in progress. If progress were really "necessary," really an unavoidable and superhuman law which equally embraced all the epochs of our history, then one could cer-tainly not describe the power and the course of progress better and more exactly than the following lines from Walter Benjamin's "The-ses on the Philosophy of History":

The angel of history . . . has turned his face to the past. Where a chain of events appears before *us*, there *he* sees a single catastrophe which piles rubble on rubble and throws it before his feet. He would surely like to stay, wake the dead, and put the shattered pieces back together again. But a storm is blowing from paradise, and it has caught in his wings, and it is so strong that the angel can't fold them any more. This storm is heading irresistibly into the future, to which he has turned his back, while the pile of rubble before him towers into the skies. What we call progress is *this* storm.[2]

[. . .]

[In the story "An Everyday Confusion"] Kafka's technique of construction is almost too clear. First of all there are all the essential factors that usually come into play in an appointment which is planned but missed: overzealousness—A. leaves early and is nevertheless in such a hurry that he doesn't see B. on the stairs; impatience—the road becomes terribly long for A., so that he worries about it more than about his goal, which is, namely, to meet B.; anxiety and nervous-ness—which prompts A. to the thoughtless hyperactivity of going back, when he could simply have awaited B.'s return. And all this finally prepares that well known trickiness of the object [*Tücke des Objekts*], which always accompanies complete failure and always in-dicates and seals the final rupture between the person who has been annoyed and the world. Since there is no reality that stands in the way of the construction and has, as it were, a mediating effect, the

2. The "Theses on the Philosophy of History" are the last work of the writer Walter Benjamin, who in 1940, on his way into his second emigration, to America, was driven into suicide on the Spanish-French border.

individual elements can assume their inherent comic and gigantic dimensions, so that at first glance the story looks like one of those fantastic Baron Münchhausen stories that sailors like to tell. The impression of exaggeration does not disappear until we stop reading the story as a report of an actual event, as a description of some occurrence that was born of confusion, and see it rather as a model of confusion itself, the grandiose logic of which our own limited experiences with confused events desperately attempt, as it were, to imitate. This extremely bold reversal of model and imitation, in which, in spite of a tradition of a thousand years, the fiction suddenly appears as the model and the reality as the imitation, is one of the essential sources of Kafka's humor, and it makes this story so indescribably humorous that it can almost provide us comfort for all of the appointments that we have already missed and will yet miss in our lives. For Kafka's laughter is a direct expression of that human freedom and levity which understands that man is more than his failure—simply because he can think up a confusion that is more confused than all real confusions.

From what has been said it should be apparent that Kafka is not a novelist in the classical sense of the nineteenth-century novel. The foundation of the classical novel was a feeling of life that basically accepted the world and society, that subordinated itself to life as it was and that sensed the grandeur of fate as being beyond good and evil. The development of the classical novel was parallel to the slow decline of the *citoyen* who, in the French Revolution and in Kantian philosophy, had attempted for the first time to rule the world with laws invented by men. Its bloom was accompanied by the full unfolding of the bourgeois individual, who regarded the world and life as the showplace of events and who wished to "experience" more sensations and happenings than the narrow and secure frame of his own life could afford him. All of these novelists, whether they painted a copy of the real world or dreamed up different ones, were in constant competition with reality. This classical novel ended in a form of the reportage-novel, which has become extraordinarily highly developed in America—and this makes sense if one just stops to think that virtually no imagination can enter into competition with the reality of today's events and destinies.

[. . .]

What makes Kafka seem personally so modern and at the same time so strange among his contemporaries and in his context of Prague and Viennese writers is precisely the fact that he so obviously did not want to be a genius or the embodiment of some kind of objective greatness, and that on the other hand he so passionately refused simply to subordinate himself to whatever fate was at hand. He was in no way in love with the world as it is given to us, and his opinion of nature was that even its superiority over man exists only so long as "I leave you in peace." What was important to him was a world constructed by people, in which the actions of man depend on nothing but himself and his own spontaneity and in which human society is ruled by laws established by men, and not ruled by arcane forces, whether they are interpreted as higher or lower forces. And it was in such a world, not one dreamed up but directly to be constructed, that he, Kafka, wanted in no way to be an exception, but rather a citizen, a "community member."

That naturally does not mean that he was modest, as is frequently assumed. After all, he once did remark in his diary that every sentence was already perfect the way he happened to write it down—which is the simple truth. Kafka was not modest, but humble.

And in order to become at least provisionally a citizen of such a world liberated from bloody spooks and murderous magic—such as he tentatively tried to describe in *America,* the happy ending of *America*—he necessarily had to anticipate the destruction of the present world. His novels are such an anticipated destruction, through whose ruins he carries the elevated portrait of man as a model of good will, who can truly move mountains and build worlds capable of withstanding the destruction of all false constructions and the rubble of all ruins because the gods have given him an indestructible heart—if only he be of good will. Since Kafka's heroes are not real people, with whom it would be hubris to identify—since they are only models and at rest in their anonymity, even when they have names—it seems to us as if each of us could be called and chosen. For this person of good will can be anyone and everyone, perhaps even you and I.

"The Metamorphosis"

HOWARD FAST

Very near the top of what I have, in the past, rather indelicately called the "cultural dung heap of reaction" sits Franz Kafka, one of the major Olympians in that curious shrine the so-called "new critics" and their Trotskyite colleagues have erected. Mr. Kafka is treasured as well as read; in a dozen literary quarterlies and "little" magazines, joss sticks are burned to him, and his stilted prose is exalted as a worthy goal. Worthy or not, that goal is certainly interesting, for in the creation of a shadow world, a world of twisted, tormented mockeries of mankind, Mr. Kafka holds a very high place. It is worth examining the substance of that throne.

Perhaps the most widely read of Kafka's work, here in America, is a tale called *Metamorphosis*,[1] which narrates in great detail how a German traveling salesman woke up one morning and discovered that he was a cockroach.

Now, although there is satirical intention in Kafka's tale, he departs from the satirists of the past in the absolute literal presentation of his point. It is much as if, having once proceeded to put down his idea upon paper, he was carried away by a conviction of the reality of the situation he had conceived. Let me quote the first two paragraphs of the story to make this plain:

As Gregor Samsa awoke one morning from a troubled dream, he found himself changed in his bed to some monstrous kind of vermin.

He lay on his back, which was as hard as armor plate, and, raising his head a little, he could see the arch of his great brown belly, divided by bowed corrugations. The bed-cover was slipping helplessly off the summit of the curve, and Gregor's legs, pitiably thin compared with their former size, fluttered helplessly before his eye.

From Howard Fast, *Literature and Reality* (New York: International Publishers, 1950), pp. 9-12.
1. Franz Kafka, *Man into Beast* (New York, 1947).

Just this will give you a sense of the horror Kafka evokes in this story, and the evocation of horror is precisely the result of the literal presentation of the situation. Whatever Kafka intended, his product is not satire; satire is a means whereby irony, ridicule, and sarcasm are used to expose tyranny, vice, folly, and stupidity; and thereby satire becomes a shortcut to reality. But in this story, Kafka does not direct himself toward such exposure; he is concerned only with proving that a certain type of human being is so like a cockroach that it is entirely plausible for him to wake up one morning and discover a natural metamorphosis has taken place. And throughout the remainder of the story, with a world of intricate detail concerning the various problems of a man who is a cockroach, Kafka reiterates his thesis.

Horror and nausea are the effects Kafka's tale have on the reader, but what is the purpose? We know that men do not turn into monstrous cockroaches overnight, and we also know that the German petty bourgeois, for all the despicable qualities he may exhibit, is far, far indeed from a cockroach. It was no army of cockroaches that devastated half the civilized world—what then is Kafka's purpose? In his mind, he has performed the equation; man and roach are the same; they are each as worthy as the other; they are each as glorious as the other; they cancel out—and thereby we have the whole miserable philosophy of the "new critics," of the "new poets," of the "avant-garde" of the *Partisan Review*, a philosophy which, to quote Milton Howard, in the periodical *Mainstream*, preaches

to the "educated classes" of contemporary America, confronted by the enormous inhumanity of capitalist society, that their sole cultural recourse lies in a literature which is presumably in the great "modern tradition" because it is based on helplessness, disgust, self-loathing, mysticism, and contempt for social action.[2]

But helplessness, disgust, self-loathing, mysticism, and contempt for social action do not arise spontaneously. The equation of man and cockroach is a part of an enormous process on the part of the ruling class which may be quite simply defined as a confusion and distortion of the nature of the objective reality. In literature, schools arise, and charming names are given to what is by no means a charming process; but the method is essentially no different from that of Mr. Bullitt, former ambassador to France, who, testifying before the House Com-

2. *Mainstream*, Winter, 1947.

mittee on Un-American Activities, stated that he suspected that Russians, when they were particularly hungry, ate their children.

Both Mr. Bullitt and Mr. Kafka, though they belong to different generations and cultures, and though they might, if Kafka were alive, disapprove of each other heartily, have separated themselves from reality, and however different their motivations, they are politically a part of the same thing, and each contributes in his own way to the debasement of American culture. Whether the product of either is art cannot be determined in a narrow frame of stylistic precision or emotional response; we must apply to their products a broader yet more accurate set of standards, using truth as a gauge within the context of culture in its broadest sense, that is, seeing culture as it is defined by the British anthropologist Grahame Clark. According to Mr. Clark, "Man has achieved his present status through the medium of his culture. Man and culture are, indeed, coincident; it is impossible to conceive of man at however low a level without culture, and there is no culture apart from man."[3]

If, therefore, we keep in mind the intimate relationship of human beings to culture, we can approach standards in terms of people; and thus we can examine art in the light of the reality of human beings. As a matter of fact, there are no other means whereby it may be examined.

3. Grahame Clark, *From Savagery to Civilization* (London, 1946).

The Death and Birth of Franz Kafka

DMITRI ZATONSKY

"The Kafka wave is inundating the countries of the West"—with these words, Franz Weiskopf began his 1945 article "Franz Kafka and the Consequences." And at present it is difficult to find another writer whose work so strongly attracts the attention of bourgeois literary scholarship.

[. . .]

That the legacy of this writer should have had such a fate is not accidental.

Up until World War I (and for some time even after that), a frank agnosticism dominated in bourgeois philosophy, in its neo-Kantian or positivist expressions. This was a period when under a thin crust of outward (although very problematic) "well-being" more and more the irreconcilable contradictions of the system were being aggravated. The present was still in the hands of the bourgeoisie, but on the horizon was rising the clear outlines of a frightening future. Hence the sharp narrowing of philosophical interests and empirism, the timid eschewing of generalizations. The bourgeoisie still hoped to hide its incurable sickness; it announced that the laws of reality were unknowable.

But gradually, starting with the twenties, the situation becomes different. The Great October Revolution, and then World War II and the rise of the powerful camp of the socialist countries—those bring a decided change into human life. The bourgeoisie is no longer able to hide the faults in capitalism and consequently it must "proclaim" in order to excuse. In proportion as Marxist-Leninist ideas become more widely disseminated, the ideologues of imperialism feel

Excerpted from D. Zatonsky, "Smert' i rozhdenie Frantsa Kafki," *Inostrannaya Literatura*, No. 2 (1959), pp. 202-12.

more urgently the necessity of opposing them with a whole system of world views. And thus decadent philosophy turns to broad generalizations and tries to create various "universal theories."

Mystical intuition is proclaimed the fundamental instrument of cognition, and the myth is raised to the fundamental form of generalization—that is, the arbitrary, subjective, and irrational perception of reality.

The historical-concrete is brushed aside as the "accidental," "superficial," "formal"; the philosophical argonauts of imperialism set out in search of a "higher reality," as if it were hidden behind some deceptive veil.

As a result the map of the world turns into an absurd one, unalterable in its disorderly chaos through which, relying only on his instincts and intuition, runs a savage dressed in the costume of contemporary man.

Similar phenomena are found in bourgeois literature also. One of the most characteristic features of contemporary modernism and its aesthetics is an unresolvable contradiction: a pretense of understanding certain "timeless," "universal" truths on one hand, and on the other hand fear of the truth of life. The only escape from such a contradiction is the perpetual destruction of the map of reality.

All this partially explains the strange fate of Kafka's creative legacy, his "renaissance" today—and not only his, but Joyce's too.

Their works contain fundamental elements of those ideological and formal principles which later are laid down as the basis of contemporary reactionary bourgeois aesthetics. In Joyce's *Ulysses*, for example, the day merges with eternity, reality is dissolved in an endless stream of accidental associations and recollections of the characters. However, all this linguistic and compositional "uproar," completely determining the structure of the novel, does not all appear to be literary tricksterism from Joyce's point of view. On the contrary, it is called upon to "facilitate" the understanding of "timeless," "general," "sacred" forms of being—that is, to give the reader the idea that man is a filthy and dumb creature (let us recall Bloom's delirious visions in the iniquitous den of Bella Cohen), to demonstrate that nothing has changed on this flat, bare, and lewd earth since the days when Odysseus, the legendary tsar of Ithaca, departed on his years-long voyage.

[. . .]

Franz Kafka too strove to locate some definitive "truth" at the limits of abstraction—a "truth" that, formulated succinctly, amounts to the belief that man is sick and powerless and the world around him is horrible and unalterable. Kafka proceeded to his goal as if it were on a path completely different from that of Joyce: he "destroyed" reality from within, pushing everyday life situations to absurd and grotesque forms, to a condition in which reality takes off as if on its own power. Objectively, however, efforts of both writers have always been directed to one side—to the debasement of humanity, the obliteration of its reason, the negation of general progress. These traits of Joyce's and Kafka's works made them into supports for the contemporary aggressive bourgeois aesthetic, that aesthetic which strives to desecrate the whole world, to spit on everything sacred so that against the background of this gloomy scene the foulness and depravity of bourgeois conditions does not stand out so clearly.

However, to say only that Kafka and Joyce appeared "too soon" would be to follow the route of vulgarization. In order to explain this phenomenon, it is necessary to answer two essential questions: First, why do the principal, problematic works of these artists appear just at the beginning of the twenties? Second, why is it that sated snobs are enraptured at the poetic puzzles of the dadaists and the canvases of abstract painters sell at fabulous prices, at the same time that Joyce's publisher is subjected to legal prosecution and innumerable copies of Kafka's novels gather dust on booksellers' shelves?

The Great October Socialist Revolution opened a new era in the history of humanity. The secular foundations of the bourgeois world crumbled, the deeply hidden contradictions were exacerbated and came out into the open, and the historical mask wore thin. In this situation the books of Kafka and Joyce (and not only theirs) appeared as original attempts to draw the sum of all the preceding development of bourgeois culture, a culture that was already degraded and dying. But to the extent that the authors of the books themselves were of the same flesh and blood as that culture, to the extent that they were marked by all the faults and delusions characteristic of their dying class, it was not possible for them to make the reckoning. Each succeeded to some degree in expressing a part of the truth of the antihuman order of capitalistic relations. And that grain of truth was so bitter that, even clothed in symbolic-abstract forms, it frightened the bourgeoisie, which had already adopted many other schools of modernism.

And when in the forties and fifties Joyce and Kafka were solemnly resurrected, the resurrection was accompanied by barefaced falsification. They were called "forerunners" and their works were called avant-garde. Meanwhile, reactionary criticism tried to smooth out all the "rough edges" of their works and adapt it to fashionable philosophical-aesthetic styles.

In this way, Kafka's legacy (and, further, that of the bourgeois decadents of the twenties) is far from being simply a subject for literary history; rather, it is a question relevant to contemporary ideological and asthetic struggles.

[. . .]

In Kafka's temperament can be heard an echo of Schopenhauerian pessimism, his notorious "sympathy with death." A heady aroma of the deepest spiritual decline blows from these lines, filled with fear and sickness: "I was sent like the Biblical dove," he wrote to Milena, "I found no green, I return to the dark ark." "There is a goal," he wrote, "but no path; everything we call a path is a hesitation."

In this way, the "mysterious essence of the dialectic of human history" consists in the fact that man, a pitiful and lonely creature who is a stranger to everything around him, is thrown into life without being asked, thrown onto a thousand troubles and bitter paths which lead to the one senseless but, at the same time the only appropriate goal, his death.

This theory, laid down in its general outlines already by Kierkegaard, and brought into an "orderly system" by contemporary existentialists, is convenient to the ideologues of reaction: it (so it seems to them) clearly "liberates" man from the "necessity" of striving toward a better future; it (as they would like it to seem) provides, if not a scientific, then at least an emotional argument against Marxism-Leninism.

Kafka contributed fundamentally to the construction of this theory; however it did not cheer or satisfy him. And what bitter jealousy, what suicidal mockery speaks in the writer's words when he compares himself to the literary giants of the nineteenth century—with those artists for whom courage and will were enough to surmount the prejudices of their class, to brand that class: "Balzac carried a cane with the motto 'I crush all obstacles'; my motto would sooner be 'all obstacles crush me.' "

The basis of the majority of the reactionary legends about Kafka seems to be the assertion that the writer's method and worldview did not undergo any change from his first story to *The Castle*. Interpretations of Kafka are based chiefly on the analysis of *The Castle* as the last of his works. However, even a superficial acquaintance with the other writings of this artist exposes such a conception as an obvious and conscious falsification.

[. . .]

Kafka's artistic method changed along with the evolution of his thinking. He came from expressionism, specifically from Austrian expressionism, which was largely infected by irrationalism. He belonged to the circle of Franz Werfel and Max Brod; his immediate predecessors were G. Meyrink, A. Kubin, and P. Siebardt, writer-mystics who filled their works with secret nightmares and allegorical visions. Here Kafka partly borrowed the technique of depicting the fantastic (although the influence of Kleist and Hoffmann is very palpable also). Later however, Kafka departed from expressionism, retaining an interest only in several specifically expressionistic themes—for example, the conflict of generations (*America* and the story "The Judgment").

[. . .]

The artistic manner, subject, and composition—these do not come from life in Kafka's work, but rather from a preconceived idea. Most characteristic in this regard is the novella "The Metamorphosis." The traveling salesman Gregor Samsa, awakening in his bed one morning, discovers that he has turned into a disgusting insect, something like a giant centipede. When, in this guise, he appears in the living room in order to go to work, his father, filled with loathing, drives him back into the bedroom with a stick. From then on, the centipede-Gregor lives there alone. He crawls around the walls and ceiling, lies for a long time on the window sill and languishes. One day his father, in a fit of rage, breaks his soft back with an apple, and the unfortunate Gregor quietly dies in a dark corner of his own dirty, empty room.

In developing this more-than-strange subject, Kafka is attempting to demonstrate that the ties between the individual and the outside world are a fiction, that the essence of human existence consists in absolute loneliness, complete isolation, tragic impotence, desperate defenselessness. For the figurative embodiment of such a thought it is not sufficient simply to distort reality or to depart completely from its representation; possibly the individual does appear lonely, powerless, and defenseless, but *outside* the public order, and not *within* himself. Only one thing remains: the artistic cutting of the ties, the "destruction" of reality while at the same time not leaving its borders.

That is the way Kafka proceeds: he turns the hero into a centipede, but leaves him in the original (family) environment. Something similar happens to the heroes of *The Trial*, *The Castle*, and "The Judgment."

[. . .]

The goal of all creative power consists, as Kafka believes, in reaching the "Archimedean point," that is, a condition "in which life to be sure hides its natural and ponderous rhythm of ups and downs but at the same time, and with no less expressiveness, reveals itself as a nothing, a dream, a puff of air."

In these words of the writer is the key to his candidly antirealistic method directed toward the "destruction," the "razing" of reality.

The intentional mixing, on principle, of the real and the fantastic, the objective and subjective, leads not only to the "self-destruction" of things, but also to the obliteration of character.

For Kafka, "character" as such does not exist, for he does not recognize the psychological motivations of human conduct; the writer believed that explanations of the actions of people (in principle absurd) are introduced only post-factum by a series of "excuses." His hero is not an individual (and even more so not a social human being), but an abstract "I," bound in his universal, philosophical relation to being.

Both Kafka's characters and the circumstances in which they find themselves—and the interaction of the characters and circumstances—are all symbols, symbol-signs, symbol-hieroglyphs, forms; and the inward content of them exists only in accidental, arbitrary connections between them. Moreover, the figures and situations, the vehicles of the symbols, do not possess any independent content. But with Kafka—in contrast to the "pure" symbolists—these figures and situations simulate the presence of an independent content. In this way, Kafka's method is rather a revised, "modernized" form of symbolism.

In his works Kafka not only presented a number of reactionary philosophical and aesthetic ideas; he also developed the technique of embodying these ideas in art in complete harmony with contemporary bourgeois culture and with the concrete political problems which the ideologues of reaction were posing.

Therefore, his influence on modernist art of the forties and fifties is not accidental. Many writers have followed directly in Kafka's wake and copied his method, but as a rule these are insignificant figures like the West German novelist Hermann Kasack (*The City Beyond the Stream*) or the Austrian writer Ilse Aichinger (*The Bound Man*). But the connection with the tradition of Kafka is apparent also in the works of Albert Camus, Samuel Beckett, and Eugène Ionesco. The first follows after Kafka in his manner of seeing and representing man, in his use of pseudorealistic linguistic and stylistic means. Beckett and Ionesco, on the other hand, are closer to Joyce in their language, borrowing from Kafka the conception of "frozen time," that is, depicting the world as arrested in a mute and motionless chaos (Beckett's *Waiting for Godot*, Ionesco's *Chairs*).

And the main thing in this is that the majority of contemporary modernists strive in their work for that "ideal" universal objectlessness so characteristic of Kafka, for a symbolic, metaphorical interpretation of the world which presupposes the hermetic isolation of the object of their representation from each and every geographical, historical, and social connection.

Thus all the most reactionary elements, all those most hostile to realism in contemporary bourgeois literature, are related in one way or another to Kafka's name.

[. . .]

Kafka's *America*

KLAUS HERMSDORF

If one looks at the characters of *Lost Without a Trace* [*Der Verschollene*; also called *America*] as a whole, one must conclude that they provide an aesthetic mirror of the world. The spectrum of social life which Kafka encompasses through the choice of his characters is quite extensive: we see people of the "upper crust" of modern capitalist society; there are numerous representatives of the petty bourgeoisie; and a third social sphere is that of the "Proletariat," which is most widely represented. The path of Karl Rossman's fate becomes a real journey through the modern world: he is a guest of both the great and the insignificant; from the steel palaces and country estates of the rich he is thrown into the power of petty superiors and foremen, and finally into the quarters of the lowest strata, of those who have been forced out of society. Kafka grasps the central conflict of contemporary society; in the figures of the capitalist grand bourgeois and the proletariat he embodies its "heroes," its chief antagonists. This representation of society in its totality, the expansion of the fictional horizon beyond the bourgeois class by including the working class as its foil, is an artistic design which is rarely presented so decisively in late bourgeois literature. It is the design of a great social novel, of an epic of modern times, and it is highly significant even in its failure.

Kafka's relationship to individual social levels, his appraisal of the different social forces, and his aesthetically partisan evaluation can be seen in whether the characters appear aesthetically "beautiful" or "ugly," and especially in their objective behavior toward the hero. It turns out that Kafka's aesthetically expressed sympathies are almost always on the side of the characters from the lower social classes: on

From Klaus Hermsdorf, *Kafka. Weltbild und Roman* (Berlin: Rütten & Loening, 1961), pp. 57-61, 121-29, and 146-50.

the side of the chief cook, a simple woman of the common people; of the student in his hopeless fight for higher education; of the stoker, the working-class girl Therese, or the helpless little elevator boy Giacomo. These characters are weak, but they are just and of good will, and the writer arouses our sympathy for them by making us feel and suffer along with them. The arousal of sympathy is in fact Kafka's chief method of expressing aesthetic partisanship for them. The writer's aesthetic partisanship is clearly on the side of the disfranchised and exploited; only in them can Kafka represent positive values of goodness and the struggle for justice. His relationship to the hero is, conversely, a measure of the writer's aesthetic partisanship. But the characters who appear in a negative and deprecatory light are the "powerful." Karl's opponents come mostly from the ruling class, but they are not as a whole unambiguously classified. Characters from all social classes are Karl's "enemies," for "each exploited his power and humiliated the lower."[1] For Kafka the "powerful" are *everyone*. Both the obscure and unfathomable advice of his uncle and Green's meanness turn out to be hostile; both the perfidious bureaucratic souls of Isbary and the head porter as well as the pitiful tramps Delamarche and Robinson are characterized negatively— in general, Kafka's world is filled by nameless and countless "enemies." But chiefly it is a world divided in two: into the "powerful" and the subordinate "lower elements." Kafka's humiliated people are those who have been truly humiliated in the social struggle, figures from the plebeian levels of society. But the "powerful" surround the hero as hostile forces on all sides; his opponents arise from all classes and levels. However, exactly in what the power of the powerful consists, and why the enemies behave as enemies—this decisive question is left unanswered by the novel, which contains the concept of the powerful primarily as an abstract and subjective idea.

When one questions further if the characters in Kafka's novel parallel the objective essence of the real social phenomena which are indicated through their individual profiles, one sees that they may be called typical characters only in a limited sense. Surely, individual and typical traits of the underlying social phenomenon of the imperialist grand bourgeoisie are accurately portrayed in the figure of the uncle. But in general this figure is more of an indication and a design: whereas

1. Franz Kafka, *Amerika* (*Gesammelte Werke in Einzelbänden*, ed. Max Brod, Frankfurt am Main: Fischer), p. 355.

his dangerous social effectiveness as an exploitative industrial magnate is "asserted" with semiclarity, even if not really portrayed, his most decisive action, his rejection of Karl, is not motivated as an expression of his social being. Even more than the uncle, Green, Pollunder, and other secondary characters from this sphere are incomprehensible shadows rather than artistically portrayed figures. These unrealistic traits manifest themselves in the proletarian figures too. On the one hand their complete helplessness is emphasized, and on the other hand their moral laxity and corruption. Clearly, that is no picture of the real prewar working class, whose best forces were well organized and clearly knowledgeable and went about changing their situation and the situation of all of society. The aspects which Kafka emphasizes in his proletarian characters are not the historically characteristic and essential ones; and where historically characteristic traits of the modern proletariat are mentioned—such as strikes and the organization of the hotel workers—they remain insignificant and outside the sphere of individual action. It is with the petty bourgeois and the bureaucratic-administrative figures that the objective essence of a social class is most strongly grasped. In the individual characterization of such figures as the head waiter, Kafka truly and critically exposes important and typical aspects of the petty bourgeois class.

In addition, the artistic significance of the figures is narrowed by peculiarities of Kafka's method of characterization, which are expressed most clearly in the inadequately objective portrayal of the characters. For example, who Isbary or Green, who have such a decisive effect on Karl's life, "really" are, and why and with what intentions they act as they do—this we cannot discover. We learn only that at some arbitrary moment and for some unfathomable reasons they do the things that Karl experiences. The reason for such vagueness and ambiguity in the characters lies primarily in the fact that Kafka, especially in his secondary figures, can make only fragments of a character come alive for us, only traits which are taken out of context and the presuppositions of which are left in the dark. The incomprehensibility of many of the characters lies primarily in their incompleteness. In this way, even the characterization in *Lost Without a Trace* reveals the two lines of Kafka's manner of representation, which cross in this novel: Kafka's realist designs lead to three-dimensional and rounded figures when—as in Therese's case—the isolation of human characteristics can be derived from their individual and social connection. Conversely, the fragmentary grasp of the characters, the abbreviation of the richness of their specific individuality, leads to a metaphor and to an allegory of their real being—to forms of epic portraiture which are characteristic of decadent art.

[. . .]

THE AGE OF IMPERIALISM

Kafka grew up at a time when a new development was appearing in the leading industrial nations of the world. It is the "transition from the capitalist socioeconomic order to a new one" which presents itself as "transitional capitalism or, more accurately, as dying capitalism."[2] The general characteristic of this imperialist period is an extraordinary intensification of the existing socioeconomic contradictions and the birth of new ones: "This sharpening of the antitheses is the most powerful motor of the transitional period . . ."[3] The effects of these processes on cultural and artistic life are permanent and profound; they do not express themselves uniformly, but rather in a multilayered, contradictory, and unequal way. Since comprehensive scientific investigations of this problem are lacking, we can point here only to some phenomena which are particularly important in respect to Kafka.

It is apparent that in the imperialistic period the social division of labor has assumed particularly crass forms. The specialization of work has become entrenched, and the division between mental and manual labor has become unbridgeable. The intellectual worker, too, has become increasingly a specialist in one narrow area, and even his view of the neighboring specialty has become lost. This division, which is rooted in economic development, goes far beyond the sphere of labor. Among other things it produces a separation of the individual and the individual sphere from the living whole [*Lebensganze*], which, especially after the unsuccessful bourgeois revolutions in Germany and Austria, reacts in turn on the entire living experience of the individual. It separates the intellectual from the life of the people and alienates him from the socially and politically important decisions of society. This results primarily in the threat that the intellectual and

2. Vladimir Ilich Lenin, *Der Imperialismus als höchstes Stadium des Kapitalismus* (Berlin, 1952), pp. 133, 137.
3. Ibid., p. 135.

writer may decline from an actively experiencing and codetermining participant in the social process to a merely observing and passively reflecting contemporary. That the jurist Goethe could be a statesman and administrative lawyer, an economic organizer and cultural politician, a broadly educated scientist and theater director, and also a writer who was able to subsume the entire knowledge and experience of his age in his art, while the jurist Kafka became at best a passable insurance specialist whose art was not in harmony but rather in contradiction to his professional work—this difference lies less in Goethe's "universality" and in Kafka's incapacity than in changed social circumstances which no longer admit the universality of life and knowledge.

In that the bourgeois artist is thus more or less pushed off from the central areas of social development, from the centers of real political and economic power as well as from the life of the people altogether, an extraordinarily reduced experience of reality is available to him, reduced primarily to the knowledge of his most personal subjective and individual experience. These conditions effect a latent tendency toward individualistic subjectification of art; in some respects they destroy the presuppositions of a broad realism directed to representing the totality of reality. It is surely indicative that with the beginning of the age of imperialism the problem of the separation between art and life becomes increasingly a general theme of late bourgeois literature itself. The extent to which Kafka felt this contradiction is demonstrated by his unsuccessful and touching attempts to overcome the one-sidedness of his existence through his interests in the natural health cure movement, horticulture, and manual activity: "Intellectual work tears one out of the human community. But manual labor leads one to man," he once mentioned in conversation with Gustav Janouch.[4] This feeling of having broken entirely out of the context of life is a central content of Kafka's art.[5]

In addition, it is not only the situation of the intellectual in society that has changed, but above all society itself. The internationalization

4. Gustav Janouch, *Gespräche mit Kafka. Erinnerungen und Aufzeichnungen* (Frankfurt am Main, 1951), p. 17.

5. This feeling is particularly palpable in an aphorism in the *Er* series; see Franz Kafka, *Beschreibung eines Kampfes. Novellen, Skizzen, Aphorismen aus dem Nachlass* (*Gesammelte Werke*, Frankfurt am Main: Fischer), p. 295. In this respect see especially the stories "First Pain," "A Hunger Artist," and "Josephine the Singer."

of monopoly capital, the anonymity of the industrial and financial oligarchy, the coupling of national and colonial exploitation, the external separation but internal amalgamation of political and economic power, the enormous extension of economic spheres of influence—all this makes social development appear even more inscrutable. But in any case the complexity of modern imperialist social relations can no longer be fathomed through spontaneous and individual judgments gained from personal experience in a subjective field of view. And this circumstance alone effects a general acceptance of irrationalistic ideologies in the period of imperialism. This happens because from the subjective impossibility of grasping the social processes rationally on the basis of one's own experience comes the view that it is impossible to grasp them rationally *at all*. And conversely, the feeling of being confronted by an undecipherable and chaotic social condition inevitably evokes a heightened need for clarification and interpretation, for elucidation of the increasingly murky obscurity. The history of modern philosophy clearly reflects this general "need for a world view" in the imperialist period, especially in the tendency to fetishize and inflate individual perceptions taken out of their context, and to generalize the deductions from individual phenomena and elevate them to the level of principles and "essentials."

Moreover, it is also naturally the fact of the general intensification of all contradictions in the imperialist age that creates a new situation for the bourgeois intelligentsia. The "negative of my time," as Kafka expressed it, consisted precisely in the constantly more apparent crisis situation, which to be sure had its roots in the intensified economic contradictions, but which extended to all areas of human existence and could not be denied even by bourgeois critics. The crisis in philosophy, the crisis in art, the crisis in interpersonal relations—such formulas even became clichés in intellectual circles, and one flirted with them. The "negative" of this time, the general crisis, must have been perceived particularly because the new development was manifesting itself more and more obviously as the opposite of the progressive and positive traditions of the bourgeoisie. Moreover, the monopolistic development in the major industrial nations was leading to a growing parasitism of the bourgeois classes, to the development of a class of unproductive people living on investment income—a circumstance which found expression "in all the social and political relations in the countries concerned"[6] and which obviously also put its stamp on bourgeois ideology. The morbid mood of decline, parallel to parasitic capitalism, increasingly gained the upper hand—those phenomena for which the concept of decadence was quickly found. In Kafka's work, to be sure, there is no justification of the crisis, no public apology for the imperialistic age; nowhere is there an affirmation of inhumanity and ruthless misanthropy. Kafka's art does mean, however, an inner avowal of crisis, a lifelong persistence in the crisis situation. And wherever one can neither overcome the crisis situation nor wish to become an apologete of the new age, negation is the logical consequence. Extreme scepticism and nihilism, in the most varied forms and nuances, are the necessary reaction of the honest writer; and the tendency toward sceptical nihilism is therefore a general phenomenon particularly in the realm of decadence. The absence of an exit, and of perspective in the judgment of the age, are of course necessary expressions of the perspective-less age itself; but they are necessarily so only when the bourgeois writer late in this age is not in a position to see, at the same time, the transition to a higher social order. This perception was closed to Kafka.

Such general latent tendencies are naturally modified, eliminated, or strengthened in each case through national, social, and individual circumstances. In Kafka's case it is apparent that strengthening circumstances are at work, and that latent tendencies become dominant. Kafka was educated during the last years of the Austro-Hungarian monarchy; he was a member of one of the strangest and certainly the most contradictory national formations before the First World War. Whereas imperialist development in Germany proceeded very vigorously and thereby communicated an activist character to many aspects of national life—even if in the most grotesque forms—a condition developed in its southern neighbor that resembled the gradual disintegration of the state apparatus. Its contemporaries had the feeling of living in a state "which was itself just barely getting along; one was negatively free in it, constantly sensing the insufficient reasons for one's own existence."[7] In Austria-Hungary the contradictions and problems of the imperialist age were intensified by the contradictions left over from past historical conditions. Here highly developed economic forms of monopoly capitalism confronted semifeudal and feu-

6. Lenin, p. 110.
7. Robert Musil, *Der Mann ohne Eigenschaften* (Hamburg: Rowohlt, 1952), p. 35.

dal ones; along with the decline of the old capitalist modes of production, the decline of the feudal economic forms was still in progess. On one hand, cartelization and monopolization had reached a high level,[8] and even imperialist capital export was not insignificant, especially the export to the Balkan states, which were largely in economically semicolonial dependency on Austria.[9] On the other hand, Austria was itself in semicolonial dependency. Although at first France had been the primary bankroller, after the war between Germany and France German capital began increasingly to penetrate the land.[10] On the whole, Austria-Hungary remained an agrarian country, and industrial development on the grand modern scale proceeded within limits: it was one of the most backward countries of the modern world and the most helpless of the "great powers," without, to be sure, wanting to relinquish its inherited feudal presumption of being a great power.[11]

Kafka's childhood and youth were at a time of relative equilibrium among the antagonistic forces of the Kaiser state, during the administration of the conservative cabinet of Taaffe (1879-1893, a very long administration for Austrian conditions), in what Taaffe himself called a "condition of well tempered dissatisfaction."[12] Refined feudal traditions united with bourgeois wealth, and lighthearted "muddling through," which had become habitual, developed into that feeling of

8. Shortly before the First World War there were in Austria approximately seventy cartels, which dominated the most important branches of industry; the six iron and steel monopolies controlled 99% and 92% of production. See "Geschichte Österreichs" in the *Grosse Sowjet-Enzyklopädie* (Berlin, 1953), p. 40.

9. Eva Priester, *Kurze Geschichte Österreichs* (Vienna, 1949), pp. 487 and 489.

10. See ibid., pp. 489 and 491; and "Geschichte Österreichs," p. 40.

11. Friedrich Engels concisely summarized the situation of Austria-Hungary before the turn of the century thus: "Industry in strong development but, in consequence of years of high protective tariffs, generally still working with backward forces of production (the Bohemian factories I have seen prove that to me); the majority of the industrialists . . . themselves interconnected as much with the stock market as with industry itself; in the cities a politically rather indifferent philistinism which above all wants its peace and pleasures; in the country rapid indebtedness or absorption of small property holdings; as the really ruling class, the owners of large estates, who are quite satisfied with their political position, which guarantees them a more indirect dominance; and also a grand bourgeoisie, not very extensive *haute finance*, closely tied to that major industry whose political power is expressed *much more indirectly,* but which is quite satisfied with that; among the leading classes, the powerful have no desire to turn their indirect domination into a direct and constitutional one, and the dependents do not seriously strive toward active participation in political power; result: indifference and stagnation which is disturbed only by the national struggles of the various aristocrats and bourgeois among themselves and by the development of the union with Hungary." (Engels' letter to Viktor Adler, October 11, 1893, quoted in Albert Fuchs, *Geistige Strömungen in Österreich 1867-1918* [Vienna, 1949], p. 89.)

12. Priester, p. 439.

cultural resignation and melancholy acceptance of decline and fall that found its literary expression in Viennese neo-romanticism.[13] But as an adolescent Kafka experienced the intensification of the contradictions at the end of the Taaffe administration. The political crisis became permanent; the cabinets changed; the grotesqueness of public politics became increasingly apparent. With respect to foreign policy Austria became more and more dependent on the German Empire and so was drawn closer to military adventurism; its own attempts at Balkan annexation added to this. Sharp economic crises led to a hitherto unknown intensification of the class conflict. Within this general crisis of the Austro-Hungarian state at the beginning of the age of imperialism, there were in particular two aspects that affected Kafka and that found direct or indirect expression in the writer's work.

In 1911, the year of the conception of *Lost Without a Trace*, a world-wide economic crisis was ripening, one which shook vast parts of the capitalist world and provoked a serious state crisis in Austria-Hungary in particular. In England, France, Spain, and Belgium also it led to strikes and demonstrations on the part of the proletariat, which in Spain even moved the ruling police regime to declare martial law. In Austria-Hungary on September 17 there occurred in Prague and Vienna the most powerful mass demonstrations of workers in the whole history of the Austrian labor movement. After the huge political demonstrations which had been called by the Social Democrats, and in which tens of thousands of people participated, there were spontaneous riots against the state. The government sent in police and the army, and there was ruthless shooting. In Vienna there were outright street battles between military forces and demonstrators that lasted the whole day. In Prague too there were forceful demonstrations and proclamations against the inflation.[14] Even large segments of the petty bourgeoisie were radicalized by the effects of the economic crisis; in fact, the crisis reached all the way to Kafka himself. His situation is reflected in his correspondence with the workers' accident insurance office, which he was constantly approaching with petitions for a raise in salary. These were founded on the extraordinary increase in prices; in a monstrous letter of seventeen pages, he says that

13. The feeling of life and the consciousness of that period are incomparably expressed in Hofmannsthal's prologue to *Anatol*.

14. Based on news reports in the contemporary press. See especially the *Neue Freie Presse*, 1911, No. 16909.

"the inflation of all factors necessary for the maintenance of life has for several years already been reaching a degree which is now felt to be most oppressive," and he speaks of the "generally reigning conditions of inflation which have become intolerable."[15] There can be no doubt of the close connection between the socially critical tendencies of *Lost Without a Trace* and the intensified crisis situation of the years in which the novel was conceived and written. One must regard the socially critical consciousness of this novel as an expression of the heightened economic and social situation of the world economic crisis before the First World War, which necessarily turned the writer's attention to the social struggles of his time.

The only halfway permanent element in this torn and deteriorating nation of many nationalities was, externally regarded, the Austrian bureaucracy. It was this which actually kept the nation together—not through any particular activity, to be sure, but through a certain viscous passivity, through "despotism moderated by sloppiness," as Viktor Adler so accurately described the old Austrian manner of government.[16] And so the structure of the Austro-Hungarian state insured that the bureaucracy, here as nowhere else, was on the one hand of extraordinarily real importance; but on the other hand, through its uniting of feudal-*gemütlich* and modern-imperialist traits, it had an exceedingly negative effect. Moreover, Kafka did not himself have to be a bureaucrat to feel the paralyzing power of the Habsburg governmental hierarchy as a specific and essential problem of his surroundings. The theme of paralyzing bureaucratic power, which has such a large place in Kafka's work, is in some measure an indirect and distorted reflection of the Austrian administrative bureaucracy—in other words, of specifically national conditions.

To experience the development of the imperialist age precisely in the atmosphere of Austria-Hungary meant in any case to suffer it in an atmosphere of undisguised decay and visible decline. It was just through the backwardness of this country that the sense of no-exit and the social contradictoriness were driven to extremes. The decline of the capitalist social order was accompanied by the decline of the feudal social order; the economic and political crises came together in a permanent national crisis. Here in Austria-Hungary, as perhaps nowhere else in Europe, the decay of the traditional orders could be

15. Kafka's letter of December 11, 1912.
16. Quoted in Fuchs, p. 103.

grasped with one's hands. Undoubtedly the lack of perspective on this state, of which Kafka was a citizen, fostered the lack of perspective in his world view. At twenty-one, Kafka wrote to his youthful friend Pollak: "So much power in me is tethered to a stake, from which a green tree might grow, whereas if it were liberated it could be useful to me and the state."[17] It is the only time that Kafka considered that a job in the service of the national community might be possible. To be sure, only the very young Kafka could be of the opinion that the Austro-Hungarian state could give him an essential, human job. Later, Kafka no longer expressed any such hopes: the opposition between individual and society in the national context was for him already largely unbridgeable.

[. . .]

[KAFKA'S FAMILY POSITION]

The German speaking population of Prague was of course not at all a socially undifferentiated unity. On the contrary. To be sure, grand bourgeois strata predominated, and it was precisely the German-speaking Jews who had important positions in industry, commerce, and finance;[18] and to be sure there was virtually no German proletariat. But there was a petty bourgeoisie which itself contained many strata, reaching from intellectual circles and the bureaucracy through petty merchants and artisans down to a not inconsiderable semiproletariat consisting of traveling salesmen and apprentices, employees and petty officials, that is, of all the lower echelons of the administration, an infinite army which feudal Austria-Hungary mobilized into petty activity. The narrowness of the Prague German conditions, the unnatural concentration of wealthy and parasitic strata led to extremely sharp social differences: it was almost impossible to cross over the borders between the individual "castes."[19] Kafka came from the better situated mercantile petty bourgeoisie of Prague; he himself called his social background the "Jewish middle class," according to whose "value judgments" he had been educated.[20] And it is manifest that this

17. Franz Kafka, *Briefe 1902-1924* (*Gesammelte Werke*, Frankfurt am Main: Fischer), p. 21.
18. See Pavel Eisner, *Kafka and Prague* (New York, 1950), p. 22.
19. Ibid.
20. Franz Kafka, *Hochzeitsvorbereitungen auf dem Lande und andere Prosa aus dem Nachlass* (*Gesammelte Werke*, Frankfurt am Main: Fischer), p. 203. Subsequent references in the text are to *H* and page number.

social and class position was a determinant in Kafka's world view. Indeed, in the context of previously mentioned contradictions in the life of the writer, this must surely be regarded as the main contradiction of his existence. Kafka's fate is in a highly typical way the expression and mirror of the modern situation of the petty bourgeoisie and its problems.[21]

21. The situation of the petty bourgeois class in modern society is that of a differentiated interstratum that on one hand is in constant decline and on the other hand is constantly gaining new numbers. Through the development of large-scale industry and commerce embracing broad areas and organizations, the actual economic foundation of the petty bourgeoisie, that is, artisanship and petty commerce, is dissolved; especially the extensive monopolization in imperialism destroys the economic basis of the petty bourgeoisie to such an extent that the existence of the class is constantly threatened. Whereas this process in the developed countries had already taken on a significant scope, in backward countries such as Austria-Hungary it proceeded with tortuous slowness. That is why an opposite development could continue there to a significant extent: the economically productive petty bourgeoisie was increased by numbers from the proletariat, the peasantry, and its own lowest strata, so that new small-scale factories, retail outlets and enterprises could be founded and maintain themselves for shorter or longer periods against the competition from large-scale capitalism. Of course, such an ascent was possible only through the most extreme diligence and application. The "interest of the business" had to rule the life and thought of everyone connected with the enterprise. Nevertheless, even the most extreme energy was sharply limited. The lack of capital and credit kept the business activity within the frame of petty conditions; the activity itself had to remain uniform and limited; the narrow capital basis forced one to caution and fearful timidity. The greatest fear of the petty bourgeois was that unfavorable circumstances could throw him back again into the despised lack of property; security was therefore a major requirement, and he was therefore ready to follow whoever promised him the greatest security.

It is of course clear that such a social situation had to evoke simultaneously a consciousness and a class mentality appropriate to this situation. The petty bourgeoisie developed specific political and ideological views and its own morality, which differed radically from proletarian morality but which also manifested specific characteristics vis-à-vis bourgeois morality. It also created particular cultural and aesthetic tastes, which provided endless material for several generations of caricaturists and satirists. It is not necessary to portray the individual forms of petty bourgeois consciousness in greater detail; their narrowness and pettiness have become proverbial in later times. The German petty bourgeoisie—the Austrian type differed from it only in gradations—was basically the pillar of modern philistinism [*"Spiessbürgertum"*], the lamentable appearances of which can be appraised only as the products of a long and complicated sociohistorical development. "In Germany, philistinism is the fruit of an unsuccessful revolution, of an arrested and retrograde development, and it received its particular and abnormally developed character of cowardliness, narrowness, helplessness, and lack of initiative from the Thirty Years' War and the following period, when practically all the other great nations were rapidly working themselves higher. This character remained with it, even when historical movement again gripped Germany. . . . German philistinism is therefore not a normal historical phase, but rather an exaggerated caricature." (Friedrich Engels, letter to Paul Ernst, June 5, 1890; quoted in Marx and Engels, *Über Kunst und Literatur*, ed. Michael Lifschitz [Berlin, 1953], p. 30.) One must not forget that the petty bourgeoisie at the same time also preserved essentially positive moral values such as diligence, tirelessness, and persistence, which were simply ham-

As the son of a typical petty bourgeois family, Kafka grew up in the ideas and ideals of this class. Later, according to the "standardized general treatment of sons of the Jewish middle class, or at least according to the value judgments of this class" (H, p. 203), he ascended from the stratum of the economically productive petty bourgeoisie into the stratum of the intelligentsia attached to the petty bourgeoisie. But from this more elevated position he had to come to terms with the burdensome petty bourgeois consciousness, without having ever really gotten out of his connections with petty bourgeois life. This confrontation never took place on an intellectually conscious level, though; rather, it remained on a personal level. It assumes the external form of a permanent and conflicted confrontation with the family; one could say that it is concentrated in Kafka's astonishing, principled, and stubborn confrontation with his father. No matter how much this father-son conflict took on an almost neurotically exaggerated and purely individual character in the writer's life, it can be completely understood only if one regards it as the subjective expression of a phenomenon which also goes beyond the accidental and personal.

Kafka's father Hermann perfectly embodied the type of the mercantile petty bourgeois who through tireless labor, tenacity, energy, and unending pains has worked himself up from semiproletarian conditions to a certain wealth.[22] And the essential traits of his class had been formed in just such an exemplary way: excellent business sense, niggling frugality, self-glorifying presumption, intellectual narrowness, the drive to dominate, close sense of family—such characteristics obviously completely obscure his surely excellent capabilities.[23] But from the father's person an extremely powerful influence went out to the young Kafka. According to the descriptions of the writer, he was

---

pered in their productive development; on the other hand, it is irrefutable that the petty bourgeois ideology had adopted numerous negative traits of the bourgeois ideology without taking part in its progressive traditions.

22. Kafka's father was born the son of a poor butcher in Wossek near Strakonic. Upon his death he left behind a wholesale textile business and a multi-storied tenement house in the center of Prague. See Max Brod, *Franz Kafka, eine Biographie* (Berlin-Frankfurt am Main, 1954), p. 9, and Klaus Wagenbach, *Franz Kafka. Eine Biographie seiner Jugend 1883-1912* (Bern, 1958), p. 16ff.

23. Kafka sketches the following picture of him: "Strength and contempt for the other, health and a certain lack of moderation, eloquence and inadequacy, self-confidence and dissatisfaction with everyone else, worldly superiority and tyranny, knowledge of people and mistrust of most, then also qualities without any disadvantages, like diligence, persistence, presence of mind, fearlessness" (H, p. 219f.; See also H, p. 169).

oppressive in the literal sense: crushing and suffocating the independence and even the personality of the boy, so that even in the recollections of the adult the figure of the father has retained an almost mythical size. Only from the great power of this influence can one explain why Kafka attempted to regard all his anxieties, his guilt feelings, and his lack of vitality as the results of the paternal upbringing. ". . . all of your pedagogical methods," he wrote in the *Letter to His Father*, the main document of his confrontation with his petty bourgeois family, were "perfectly aimed; I did not escape from a single one. The way that I am, I am (apart from basics and the influences of life) as the result of your upbringing and my obedience." But from Kafka's characterization of his father it appears that it was just the typical petty bourgeois traits that he objected to. What repelled him were the distortions of a natural human countenance that were necessarily developed by a specific class situation. That the struggle against the parents is really a completely unconscious struggle for a humane conception of man is seen when Kafka describes a character which seems positive to him and different from that of his parents: one which is free of petty bourgeois distortions. Thus he describes his sister Ottla: she "sometimes seems to me to be a mother the way I would like to have her: pure, truthful, honest, consistent, humble and proud; receptivity and aloofness, devotion and independence, shyness and courage in certain balance. I mention Ottla, because my mother is in her too, but of course completely unrecognizable." And a much more decisive reason for Kafka's dislike for his father must, beyond that, have come from his business activity: as a little businessman the father did, after all, embody even economically the essence of the petty bourgeoisie in an exemplary way.

In many respects Kafka developed beyond the sphere of his parents' family. At the gymnasium and university he received a broad education, and he became prominent in a local environment of the grand bourgeoisie at a time when petty bourgeois ideals were in any case discredited: thus inevitably he had to come into conflict with his family's ideas. This conflict expressed itself in rejection and deep hatred—mixed with love—of the family.[24] But a deeper reason for such

24. In a letter to his fiancée, the thirty-one year old Kafka says that he has always "in all my meanness, rudeness, egoism and lovelessness trembled before them [his parents, *Ed.*], and really I still do it today, because one cannot stop that, and if they, father on the one side and mother on the other, necessarily almost broke my will, then I want them at least to be worthy of that. I was deceived by them, and I cannot

unusual and no doubt also infantile hatred, for being stuck in such personal feelings, lies also in the fact that Kafka never really succeeded in intellectually rising above his parents' petty bourgeois sphere.[25] To a considerable extent that was because of the weakness and fragility of his mental and physical constitution and his lack of assertiveness, but more essential reasons were also decisive. To be sure, Kafka had risen above his parents' position in respect of education, but his development had really only elevated him from one sphere of the petty bourgeoisie into another. The conditions of his own life had not removed him objectively and in principle beyond the class borders of his background. He had not gained in knowledge of life, experience of reality, or in philosophical-ideological perception—which would have made it possible for him to come to terms with the ballast of his petty bourgeois background from a new and qualitatively higher standpoint. In addition, circumstances had put Kafka not only in an apparent disadvantage vis-à-vis his father, but in a factual one. From the productively active sphere of the petty bourgeoisie, Kafka had gone over to an unproductive, bureaucratic-intellectual one. Externally, his path was smooth and simple: he had had little difficulty in school, and therefore a dawning recognition, which later became class consciousness aiming at more elevated activity, prevented him from going into his father's business. After hesitant and tentative attempts to define a real "occupation" that would have given his life a decisive direction—Kafka studied chemistry for two weeks and German literature for a semester—he chose law, without any real predilection or definite goal (see H, p. 207). He had hardly ever left Prague or come into contact with a life style different from his own. Finally he landed "at the bureaucrat's desk" (H, p. 188). From the standpoint of the practical experience he had gained—too conflicted in respect to his psychic development but too free of conflict in respect to his confrontation with living reality—the figure of his father must indeed have seemed overwhelmingly superior to him. His father possessed true superiority in his energy, his proven strength and experience, and

---

rebel against a natural law without going crazy, so: hatred and nothing but hatred" (Franz Kafka, Tagebücher 1910-1923 [Gesammelte Werke, Frankfurt am Main: Fischer], p. 515; subsequent references in the text are to T and page number). At another place he speaks about how "the beginnings of hatred" developed from insignificant events of his youth, hatred which determined his "life in the family" and "in a certain sense his whole life" (H, p. 229).

25. At best in the last years before his death, especially through his stay in Berlin.

in the accomplishments of a disciplined life. Kafka's objective inferiority vis-à-vis his father was the objective inferiority of the intellectual and bureaucratic petty bourgeoisie of the twentieth century in comparison with the productive petty bourgeoisie in a time which still knew how to mobilize bourgeois virtue and energy. This productive petty bourgeoisie had developed in secure and orderly social circumstances which seemed guaranteed for millennia, but the intellectual and bureaucratic petty bourgeoisie was experiencing a time in which the hitherto concealed contradictions of the end of the era were becoming generally visible. The former was caught in his harmless errors and narrow horizons, but the latter was helpless in the face of reality—only now the helpless started to rebel against the narrow. Against this background, Kafka's apparently completely private conflict with his father manifested itself as an expression of the conflict of two generations of the petty bourgeoisie; and this conflict of the generations reflected to some extent the historical opposition between the bourgeois-capitalist and the imperialist ages, in which the generational conflict was objectively founded. It is therefore not accidental that it played a central role in the literature of the time, especially in expressionist writing: in it the vaguely felt but not understood historical opposition was concentrated in the rebellion of the sons against the fathers, but even more it was reductively distorted.[26]

26. In this way the opposition of generations is constantly found in Kafka's artistic work, especially in the story "The Judgment." However, it differs in content from the creations of the expressionists, for in Kafka the son does not actually rebel against the father, and the son is always the subordinate. His appraisal of Hasenclever's play *Der Sohn* and of Synge's *The Playboy of the Western World* is interesting and characteristic of Kafka's position. See Janouch, p. 34f.

Kafka's Early "Conversations"

HELMUT RICHTER

[. . .]

If this work results, in comparison with many other interpretations, in a sober, surprisingly simple, and clear picture of Kafka, that is expressly its intention. Such an examination is necessary in order to paint a clear and unprejudiced portrait of the writer and his work after a long period in which Kafka's work was examined under literary-unspecific aspects, freighted with various interpretations, and primarily glorified. This examination is not possible without a firm yardstick of literary criticism, and it will therefore be necessary to investigate in each case the extent to which Kafka succeeded in making a significant statement about man and the world artistically convincing. Such a statement must be comprehensible and must develop from inner necessity out of the work itself. It cannot be the task of an interpretation to try to discover a meaningful content when a direct and convincing statement is lacking.[1]

The critical method of the study determines the omission of Kafka's historical and biographical circumstances, his surroundings, and his literary and philosophical educational experiences, even when such references seem to suggest themselves directly.[2] The same is true of points which his journals and letters might contribute to our understanding.[3] The goal here is to provide an objective view of Kafka's

From Helmut Richter, *Franz Kafka: Werk und Entwurf* (E. Berlin: Rütten & Loening, 1962), pp. 32f. and 39-50.

1. This method has been abused *ad nauseam* almost everywhere. It has not promoted, but rather hindered, access to the work and its realistic evaluation. Of course works and fragments which are at first obscure can be explained by reference to relationships outside the work, but that is sensible only if there is a minimum of *direct* comprehensibility and convincing statement.

2. A scientifically valid Kafka biography is not yet available. A first step in that direction has been made by Klaus Wagenbach's investigation of Kafka's youth until 1912. For the subsequent years we must still use the very subjective and fragmentary biography by Max Brod, but Kafka's letters provide valuable additional material.

3. Only in a few cases do the notes refer to passages which amplify, but in no way can be used as points of departure for interpretation.

works, to demonstrate that they are artistically autonomous represen-
tations of a concrete social and individual reality—a procedure which
was postponed at first by the indifference and the bewilderment of
the literary public, then by the zeal of the interpreters, and finally by
the delinquency of literary criticism. This does not in principle deny
the correctness of interpretations which see more general questions,
even of a philosophical and theological nature, reflected in Kafka's
works. Rather, it is a matter of natural priorities: first the artistic nucleus of each work, the represented reality, must be clearly worked
out before one can discuss the potential philosophical interpretations
which may be drawn from it. An unprejudiced and comprehensive
examination of such influences and tendencies will undoubtedly bear
interesting results; this is indicated by even a cursory look at Kafka's
personal notes, which register an abundance of formative impressions.
One must agree with Manfred Seidler's thesis and also recognize his
conclusion when he writes, in reference to the many-voiced and often
heterogeneous echo to Kafka's works, that Kafka must have "felt and
touched in his writing a very general situation." It is therefore "at
least thoughtless, no matter from what perspective—including the
philological and literary—to explain that this or that thing has nothing to do with Kafka."[4] But this perception should not be allowed to
lead to the complete dissolution of the concrete contents, and it is
therefore necessary to proceed from the essence of the art work, the
reflected reality, and only then to examine the possibility of further
interpretations.

[. . .]

"CONVERSATION WITH THE SUPPLICANT"

If the terse title indicates that an essential and isolated conversational situation is to be depicted, then the beginning of the story further strengthens this impression. Place, time, and preceding history
remain unconcrete: "There was a time when I went to a church every
day, because a girl with whom I had fallen in love prayed for a half
an hour on her knees there in the evenings, and I could watch her in
peace."[5] When repeatedly the girl does not come and the narrator

4. Manfred Seidler, *Strukturanalysen der Romane "Prozess" und "Schloss,"* Diss.,
Bonn, 1953, p. 122.
5. Franz Kafka, *Erzählungen* (Frankfurt am Main: Fischer, 1946), p. 9. Subsequent
references are in the text and are to *E* and page number.

waits in vain, his attention falls on a young man who says his prayers with great fervor and so attempts to draw attention to himself. The narrator is angry about that, for he considers such a manner of praying inappropriate and importunate, and he decides to confront the man. Although the relationship to the girl was only an occasion for meeting with the young man, we are astonished by the peculiar form of this "love" which apparently proceeded without any personal contact, for the narrator limited himself completely to watching his beloved silently. And at first it is difficult to start a conversation with the young man too, because he seems to have noticed the intention and avoids a meeting. Not until a later occasion, after waiting for three hours, can the narrator force a confrontation. He carefully observes the man's behavior: "He walked cautiously, and his feet first gently touched the floor before they set down. When we had gone down the stairs he said with a very tremulous voice, 'Good evening, dear, dear sir. Please do not be angry with me, your most devoted servant' " (E, p. 11). Even his appearance and his first words testify to a great weakness and, initially, a hardly comprehensible consciousness of guilt. And for the narrator too the conversation obviously means extreme inner stress: "I distorted my mouth, as I always do in preparation for speaking firmly" (E, p. 9). But he asks questions with a passionate interest while the supplicant tries to escape. The latter feels himself to be pitiable, for he must bear a "vacillating misfortune, . . . a misfortune balancing on such a fine point, and if one touches it, then it falls down on the questioner" (E, p. 11). Some inner connection, which still remains uncertain, causes the narrator to have the young man tell him his story. " 'No,' I screamed into the noise of the passing streetcar, 'I won't let you go. I like stories just like that. You're a lucky find. I congratulate myself' " (E, p. 11). After both, upon the wish of the young man, have selected a stairwell as the place for their conversation, the narrator asks him why he prays so conspicuously. The answer is that his purpose in life is "to be looked at by people" (E, p. 13). To the narrator's own astonishment and consternation, this answer sets a previously hidden string in his heart resonating; he believes he is familiar with the condition of his interlocutor. He believes the latter has forgotten the true names of things and now is giving them constantly changing titles. A direct relationship between this characterization and the answer of the young man is not recognizable, and so the man answers that he did not understand what was just said. But in the tone of this assertion there lies something that indicates a deeper understanding. That is a confirmation for the narrator, after he had been disturbed by his partner's apparent lack of understanding. "I was a bit dismayed when he said, 'I am glad that I didn't understand what you said'" (*E*, p. 13).

With that the conversation has gotten into trouble. The narrator seeks confirmation of his interpretation of the young man's problem: the unnatural purpose of his life is supposed to be "to be looked at by people," but he himself does not want to talk about this problem. The remarkable thing is that the narrator, from some inner connection, seems to have found a correct interpretation. The supplicant is forced to admit this: "To be sure I showed it, sir, but you too spoke strangely" (*E*, p. 13). Now the conversation takes a surprising turn. Suddenly the narrator does not want to have anything more to do with what he said; the strange things which he said in his interpretation and which the supplicant now points out to him, he feels to be an attack, a dangerous subversion, and he now wishes to distance himself from them. This also brings about a change in the external situation of the conversation. "I laid my hands on an upper step, leaned back and asked in this almost unassailable position, which is the last resort of wrestlers: 'You have a funny way of saving yourself by presupposing your situation in others'" (*E*, p. 13). Now this is once again remarkable, because in doing that he is characterizing much less the young man's behavior than his own intuitive interpretation. And the supplicant immediately understands the real situation. "Thereupon he became courageous" (*E*, p. 13). Now, apparently because he feels some connection his partner has to his own fate, he takes up the question the latter posed at the beginning and wants to explain why he needs the attention of the people in the church. But that no longer has any value for the narrator; the situation has changed so much for him that now he even feels himself to be an unwilling partner in the conversation: "I hadn't even wanted to come here, I said to myself then, but the man had forced me to listen to him" (*E*, p. 14). But he cannot summon up the energy to break off the conversation, and the young man recounts: "There has never been a time when I have felt convinced of my life through myself. I comprehend things around me with such inadequate conceptions that I always think the things were once living, but now are declining. Always, sir, have I wanted to see things the way they are before they appear to me. They must be beautiful and peaceful. It must be so, for I have often heard people speak about them in this way" (*E*, p. 14).

The loss of a solid connection to the things of his surroundings makes the supplicant doubt himself and also the existence of external reality, which for him still represents an unsurveyable and frivolous mass of invisible and vacillating phenomena. He asks his partner if *he* can still believe in natural, self-evident things and connections. As an example of that he tells about an experience from his childhood: ". . . when as a child I opened my eyes once after a nap, still half asleep, I heard my mother asking, in a natural tone, from the balcony, 'What are you doing, my dear? It's so hot.' A woman answered from the garden: 'I'm having my lunch outside.' They said that without thinking about it, and not too clearly—as if everyone must have expected it" (*E*, p. 15). As if under the influence of an *idée fixe*, the narrator answers that he too cannot believe in the possibility of such uncomplicated events.

With that, the young man's heart opens itself to him; he believes he has found a kindred soul. The feeling of not being alone in having a problematic relationship to the world gives him the strength to speak openly about what at first he had not dared to say. Now his longing for communication and understanding breaks forth: "Oh, it is good that you agree with my opinion, and it was unselfish of you to have stopped me to tell me that. Right? Why should I be ashamed— or why should we be ashamed—that I don't walk upright and firmly, that I don't bang my cane on the sidewalk and don't examine the clothing of the people who loudly walk by. Should I not rather justly and defiantly be allowed to complain that like a shadow with square shoulders I hop along the houses, sometimes disappearing into the glass panes of the show windows" (*E*, p. 15). He does not feel himself a secure citizen of the city, but rather hops in an apocalyptic mood through a world in which man is no longer worth anything and not even death is noticed. Everywhere he feels the incalculable effect of things which have been built by men blindly in gigantic dimensions and which have made themselves independent. Nowhere can he find a foothold, primarily because he thinks that this anxiety at life is peculiar to him alone. Other people let themselves be carried along by the storm which things have whipped up; they do not resist and are content. They do not recognize the problems of their lives. "Of course they have to hold their hats on tight, but their eyes sparkle merrily, as if the weather were fine. Only I am afraid" (*E*, p. 17). The last means of avoiding this fear was the attempt to create a sensation, to be pinned down, as it were, by the looks of other people and to see oneself confirmed at least as a physical existence by the attention of others. His partner in the conversation has listened with sympathy and above all with understanding, for he feels himself "mistreated" (*E*, p. 17) by the young man's openness. Only now does he recognize the whole problem of his own existence, which previously he had instinctively shied away from, and, as if at the same time he could remove this problem from the world, he takes back his answer, which had prompted the supplicant's self-portrait: "The story that you told earlier, about your mother and the woman in the garden, I don't find remarkable at all. Not only have I heard and experienced many such stories, I have even participated in many. This is a completely natural thing" (*E*, p. 17). In the final paragraph, Kafka succeeds masterfully in summarizing the whole thing with ironic humor. After the reversal the young man apparently attempts the salvation of the narrator, who himself feels the questionable character of this agreement: "When I had said that, he seemed very happy." In a tone which is at once sober, patronizing, and ironic, the supplicant produces empty formulas about his partner's exterior, as if he wants to take back the more intimate acquaintance with his interior and thereby confirm also the unproblematic existence of the things. "He said that I was dressed nicely and that he liked my tie very much. And what nice skin I have." But the ruthlessly clear conclusion suddenly produces the original situation once again: "And confessions become clearest when one retracts them" (*E*, p. 17).

The first impression which suggests itself after reading this "conversation" is probably that it is not a real conversation at all, if one understands by that an open questioning, answering, and exchange of experiences. Here there are no clear antitheses or happy agreements, but only a reluctant admission of characteristics which are apparently felt to be unnatural, connected always with the attempt to impute similar things to the partner. The conversation is supported by an awareness of community between them, but it is constantly complicated by the fact that they are aware of the abnormality of this community and would both like to be different, that, in order to live, they both absolutely need faith in the possibility of being different. The anomie common to both is the loss of a direct connection to the world, the inability to realize themselves in it. This leads to fear of the world, which can no longer be conceived as objective and sensible, but which appears as a collection of momentary subjective ideas, and it leads finally to the destruction of the human personality which, left entirely to itself and cut off from the world, is condemned to a shadowy existence without the possibility of integration and sensible activity.

This tenuous position in life seems to rest on subjective lack of ability, on personal failure; but the text shows that the subjective weakness and lack of relatedness is determined by real social factors which have here become peculiarly concentrated in the emotional reflection. The social determination is indicated by the course which the supplicant chooses to overcome his lack of relatedness to people and things, which has also deprived him of his belief in himself. Through his theatrical behavior in the church he alienates himself from his own nature, in order to make at least the external impression of a significant, integrated personality—that of the religious zealot. He makes himself into an object of his surroundings. In that we see that he adapts himself to the essential trait of reality, as he has learned to see it. In his picture of life, which is filled with apocalyptic anxiety, the basic premise is the recognition that things rule over people; things are what determines life, and man loses his value before them.

Frequently people fall down in the street and lie there dead. Then all the merchants open their doors, which are covered over with merchandise, and they nimbly run up, bring the deceased into a house; then they come out, smiles around their mouths and eyes and say: "Good afternoon—the sky is pale—I'm selling a lot of kerchiefs—ah yes, the war." I bound into the house and, after having several times anxiously raised my hand with the finger crooked, I finally knock on the concierge's little window. "Dear sir," I say amicably, "a dead person was brought to you. Please show him to me, I beg you." And when he shakes his head, as if he were undecided, I say firmly: "Dear Sir, I am a secret police officer. Show me the deceased immediately." "The deceased?" he now says and is almost insulted. "No, we don't have any dead man here. This is a decent house." I say goodbye and leave. (*E*, p. 16)

The supplicant follows this characteristic tendency of a capitalistic society by setting a market value on himself, which is the only thing that makes him an object of general attention. In order no longer to be invisible behind the merchandise, the man too reifies himself; the purpose of his life becomes "to be looked at by people" as an interesting object like the merchandise. The turn in the supplicant's complaint, which was incomprehensible at first, becomes clear from this point of view; it was that "like a shadow with square shoulders I hop along the houses, sometimes disappearing into the glass panes of the show windows."

In view of such a crystal clear perception of the determining powers of society, the simple truths of human life are hardly believable any more. In the view of the young man, who senses life as a chaos subject to the inexplicable domination of human creations which have become autonomous, humanity becomes incomprehensible; he no longer has any faith or any trust in it. But the recognition that most people apparently don't know about this problem and that things may therefore still be felt as peaceful and beautiful, determines the desperate situation of the conversants. They know that they are exceptions, and at the same time they feel a powerful objective compulsion forcing them into this exceptional position. They cannot master this divided situation in their lives. On the one hand, it leads them to defend their particular feeling of life as the only correct and humanly appropriate reaction to the inhumanity of the world, and on the other hand to a desperate belief in the normality of life—for a life feeling which on principle considers the world to be chaotic, incomprehensible, and uncontrollable, must be directed against man and his existence.

The kernel of this feeling is an unusually sensitive feeling for the reality of everyday bourgeois life; its determining characteristics are perceived with such intensity that there is no room in the consciousness for anything else, and a rational processing of the perceptions is no longer possible. Reality, and the inhuman events in it, are in addition experienced by a character which cannot oppose these frightening impressions with any foothold in the human world: "There has never been a time when I have felt convinced of my life through myself." And so these feelings must decisively determine the position in life: fright, experienced by an unstable character, leads to horror at the world, in which no place can be found for man any more. In that lies the danger that destroys every true perception. Correctly perceived or sensed individual traits of the surroundings are taken to be life itself and so are given a false presumption of totality, which must have a destructive effect and condemn man to helplessness. The human standpoint which, in a direct examination of the world, must lead to a clear differentiation between good and evil, which must stamp the human as true and the inhuman as corrupting, manifests itself only as anxiety and fear of what is perceived and in the consciousness of its own state of anomie. The dead end that perception then gets caught in shows itself in the juxtaposition of two possibilities of "truth" which are placed in conflict. The lost connection to the sur-roundings, the destruction of the personality, and the reification of life are on one hand generalized as a chaotic picture of the world, and on the other hand the presence of simple everyday truths is supposed to prove the fundamental order and beauty of the world. In this un-resolved juxtaposition one can see the limits of a perception which starts out from immediately felt experience and cannot attain to any more distant or total perspective. The dividedness and inner uncer-tainty which result cannot lead to adopting a position against society or any of its individual phenomena; the weakness of his position drives the lonely person to a subjectively understandable, but—despite correct elements—an objectively false, contradictory, and life-denying position toward his surroundings.

Another important problem central to Kafka's overall development is indicated here: the impossibility and necessary dishonesty of an op-positional stance, to which everything is questionable and to which the world seems fundamentally a senseless chaos. Whoever adopts such a position, if he does not prefer death to such an existence in permanent chaos, and because of the lack of differentiation in his *theoretical* negation, must accept *practically* the fact that society is this way, even if this fateful dialectic causes him discomfort and a bad conscience. The "oppositional" person then disappears back into the mass of the average, which in principle allows itself to be driven along by the events of the surroundings; his suffering in the world remains without result, and his complaint does not lead to a trans-forming act.[6] Dissatisfaction and opposition therefore also can be-come a noncommittal intellectual game.[7]

Kafka created the complexity of this content in a conversation, a

6. The cycle *A Country Doctor* culminates in the final piece, "A Report to an Academy," in a similar stance, and, in modified form, so does "Josephine, the Singer," the concluding piece of the cycle *The Hunger-Artist.*

7. In the posthumous story "Description of a Struggle," this conversation is put together with other episodes and appears with them under the remarkable title "En-tertainments, or Proof that it is Impossible to Live."

form which made the problematics of such a life-feeling very apparent. People who can find no general relation to their environments are not capable of a real conversation, no matter how much they may strive toward communication and understanding. Just that which they have in common, their problematic relation to reality, prevents comradeship. A connection between them could lead only to a synergistic and deeper recognition of their inevitable incapacity for life. They cannot confirm one another in their humanity, which was the unconscious wish of both; they can only rob one another of any belief in objective values.[8] Their relationship destroys itself or can at best find a possible continuation in an ironic stance. From the intuition or perception of this problem comes the supplicant's fear of the conversation, the narrator's withdrawal, and his final reinterpretation of the actual situation. And so the life-denying character of the world view is reflected in the impossibility of arriving at true community; thus, the artistic form has a particular quality which strengthens the statement. Content and form create a unity which, to be sure, becomes accessible to the reader only after he has completely grasped the problematics of the content.

"CONVERSATION WITH THE DRUNK"

This second prose piece is about the vain attempt to protect oneself through fictions from the environment's presumption of dominance. The opening of the story shows the relationship to reality which we have already seen: "As I was taking a small step out the house door, I was attacked by the sky with the moon and stars and its huge arch and by the Ringplatz with the city hall, the Mary-Column, and the church" (E, p. 17). The man feels himself to be a victim of the world of nature and of things, which has come alive. He responds to that with a desperate attempt to oppose this attack with inner calm and a transforming imagination, to master it through thought.

Yes, it is true, you are still superior to me, but only when I leave you in peace. Thank God, Moon, you are no longer Moon, but perhaps it is negligent of me that I am still calling you, who are called Moon, Moon. Why is it you are no longer so haughty when I call you "Forgotten

8. See the action and end of the communal walk, the "struggle," in the "Description of a Struggle."

Paper Lantern with a strange color." And why do you almost withdraw when I call you "Mary-Column"; and I do not recognize your threatening stance any longer, Mary-Column, when I call you "Moon throwing yellow light." It really seems that it does not do you good when one thinks about you; you lose courage and health. (*E*, p. 18)

Here is an example of that tendency indicated in the first conversation to forget the "real names of things" and to give them "accidental names"; but at the same time its psychological foundation becomes understandable. The narrator attempts to rescue his tenuous individuality from the superior power of a firmly established environment by mastering it with the subjectivity of his imagination. To be sure, he recognizes the superiority of the things, but since he tries to avoid their presumption, he tries to believe that it is people's passivity toward external appearances and traditional ideas that constitutes the foundation of that superiority, that the power of the things is dependent on their recognition, on the concept that one forms of them—if one changes and humanizes the concepts, then the objects lose their old strength and thus become toys of thought.

As a model of such a position regarding the surroundings the narrator considers a drunk who meets him and who, in his intoxication, seems really to have forgotten ordinary, everyday concepts. He wants to learn from the drunk how the world can be mastered: "God, how salutary it must be when the thinker learns from the drunk!" (*E*, p. 18). True to his method, he sees a Parisian nobleman from the time of Louis XVI in the reeling tavern visitor, and through enthusiastic gushing about Paris tries to draw him into the conversation he wishes, which will overcome reality through the free play of the imagination, and which will confirm his subjective world view. "Good evening, gentle nobleman; I am twenty-three years old, but I still do not have a name. But you no doubt come from this great city of Paris with an astonishing and even singable name. The very unnatural aroma of the eccentric court of France surrounds you" (*E*, p. 19). Paris is named as a catchword for the transformation of nature according to human ideas in the absolutist eighteenth century. But the drunk has no intention of getting involved in this fiction; he is too much occupied with his own cares and his intoxication. He "belches" now and then and finally allows himself to be brought home by the narrator, who maintains his tragicomical self-deception.

Most immediately, the piece seems to be a humoresque, in which the changing of the roles is cleverly exploited. The thinker, through the manner of his thought, is in reality the drunk, whereas the latter is completely clear about his real situation and at least tries to think. And the comical impression is additionally strengthened by the fact that the "pupil" in the end becomes the leader of his "teacher." In this piece too there arises no real conversational situation. But what is fundamental, beneath the foreground comedy, is the failure of a serious attempt to master life with the help of reflective constructions—whereby the action must be taken as more exemplary than literal. The lonely person who can not come into any genuine relationship with the world and master it tries to deny objective reality independent of man and, conversely, to make the environment dependent on him by arbitrarily equating it to the world of his imagination. Thereby he hopes to be able to stand up to the almighty and hostile reality. From the building blocks of reality he creates an unreal dream world. But reality proves to be stronger and refers him again to the necessity of a sober confrontation.

In his first prose pieces, Kafka sketches the situations of people who have lost their relationship to the environment, their ability to recognize it, and who, limited by that, have also lost their faith in themselves. The major content of their lives is the attempt to save themselves from the attack of the incomprehensible world, from which they feel cut off. These pieces content themselves with establishing a certain inner situation; they do not suggest any way that could lead out of it. But Kafka shows very clearly which ways are not viable. A fundamentally chaotic world view or subjective whimsy vis-à-vis the surroundings cannot liberate one from the obligation of striving toward an objective perception of the world and toward integration of the personality. Both conversations end with the failure of unrealistic attempts at rescue; they challenge us to find a more appropriate answer. The incomprehensible cannot just be accepted; rather, it demands mastering. Kafka's first theme is thus the question of how the individual can live in a world which is felt to be inhuman but which is not recognized in its foundations. Thereby he establishes the genuine problem of a social order in which all the power relationships operate not directly, but in concealed and primarily reified forms, and the analysis of which is not possible through mere observation from outside. Kafka rejects the three most comfortable ways of avoiding this difficulty: the thesis of an environment which is chaotic in prin-

ciple; the illusion that everything is in order; and the subjective cor-
rection of the situation. The question of reality remains unanswered.

Although Kafka's question goes beyond the personal, the manner of
his dealing with it is completely determined by personal experience,
by the heavy atmosphere of a personally painful problem. Therefore,
it can be understood only through empathy with this very personal
world. Such pieces may either be empathically entered into or may
remain wholly incomprehensible, according to the reader's nature.
These documents, which have no answers to the questions they pose,
above all serve the self-comprehension of the writer. Therein surely
lie the reasons for Kafka's particular antipathy toward the publication of his first works, of which he destroyed a great quantity. In his
eulogy (in the Prague newspaper *Bohemia* on March 20, 1911) after
the end of publication of *Hyperion* (1910), in which these conversations had been published, he writes in the same sense that this journal
lacked *necessity*:

It was supposed to give those who live on the borders of literature a living
representation, but it did not respect them, and at bottom they didn't
want to have it either. People whose nature isolates them from the community cannot, without losing something, regularly appear in a journal
where, between the other works, they must feel as if they are placed in
the limelight and must look stranger than they are. They also do not
need any defence, because misunderstanding cannot hurt them, for they
are obscure and love finds them everywhere. . . . (*E*, p. 317)

These lines[9] confirm the suspicion that the "Conversations" are above
all a matter of a confession, a personal problem of Kafka's.

9. Brod's material in the afterword to the *Erzählungen* (p. 319f.) is amplified by
Wagenbach, *Franz Kafka, Eine Biographie seiner Jugend* (Bern, 1958), p. 235.

REVISIONISM AND THE
PRAGUE CONFERENCE

Kafka and the Present

PAUL REIMANN

[. . .]

We do not want to celebrate Kafka. He himself, who considered his work a failure and therefore wished it to be destroyed, would, if he were alive today, disapprove of such a celebration. But we want to honor him as a great writer who, in the chaos of his time and his life, struggled for new perceptions; we want to discuss his work critically and critically decide what in his life and work was successful and what was unsuccessful.

With such a position, we return to the stance which our communist movement in the ČSR[1] adopted during the writer's lifetime and which was also expressed in a short eulogy for Kafka which the official newspaper of the KPČ,[2] *Rudé právo*, printed on August 17, 1924, a month after the writer's death:

A German poet has passed away, a delicate and pure spirit, who abhorred this world and dissected it with the sharp knife of reason. Kafka has insight into the mechanism of society; he sees the misery of some, the power and wealth of others. In his very visual works, he satirically attacks the powerful of the world. His beautiful prose piece "The Stoker" was published by Neumann[3] in *Červen*. He wrote "The Penal Colony," the "Country Doctor," and other works.

That was written at a time when Kafka was not yet fashionable, when the only part of his work that was known was the part he had published himself. And if we honor Kafka today as a man and a writer who honestly strove, we do not wish to ignore what separates our world view from the concept of life which appears in his work.

Paul Reimann, "Franz Kafka und die Gegenwart," previously published in *Franz Kafka aus Prager Sicht 1963* (Prague, 1965), pp. 13-21.
[1. ČSR: Czechoslovakian Socialist Republic. *Ed.*]
[2. KPČ: Communist Party of Czechoslovakia. *Ed.*]
[3. Stanislav Kostka Neumann: a communist journalist and editor. *Ed.*]

53

Against the despair over the capitalist present, to which Kafka suc-
cumbed, we oppose our optimistic insight into the happy communist
future of our country. But our position shall not be that of those critics who in a few general sentences damn and demolish an excellent
writer's work, born out of spiritual pain. It shall be a gentle criticism
which will strive to understand and to comprehend the motifs even
when we cannot follow Kafka into the deepest abyss of human despair. If we honor Kafka this way, then we are aligning ourselves with
the motto of our teacher K. Marx: *Nihil humani a me alienum puto.*[4]
The time of harsh criticisms, which was born out of the atmosphere
of dogmatism and the personality cult,[5] which left many traces in our
thinking too, is definitely gone in our country. The path to serious
critical evaluation of prominent literary figures is now open. We do
not want to portray Kafka as someone he was not. The number of interpreters who mystify him, who put what they themselves think
into his work, is large enough without that. [. . .]

The way to understand every great writer leads through his work,
through the confrontation of his work with the circumstances of the
time and the life that gave birth to the work. Much in such a life work
is determined by personal factors, by unique subjective experiences;
but if the writer is a great one, the subjective experience is closely
meshed with larger contexts, which are determined by tendencies of
the historical development of a whole age—even when the creative
subject is not fully conscious of these contexts. The criticism we
mean, a serious but at the same time understanding criticism, cannot
pass over certain questions: to what extent did Kafka inwardly digest
the contexts of things he absorbed as a writer, things which tortured
and oppressed him in his life? To what extent was he able to arrive at
a synthesis, a harmonious artistic grasp of reality in the face of the
multitude of contradictory impressions which assail everyone in the
twentieth century? We do not hesitate to assert that he did not succeed in this. The bitter lament that human life is governed by laws
which we cannot comprehend characterizes Kafka's entire life work;
it is an essential motif in his writing. But at the same time this lament
honors him: the awareness of his own inadequacy pushed him to rec-

[4. "Nothing human is foreign to me." *Ed.*]
[5. "Personality cult" is the usual euphemism for Stalin's administration in the
USSR, when government authority proceeded from the "personality" of the dic-
tator. *Ed.*]

ognize what he could not understand; and even if he did not solve the problems of contemporary life, even if he finally capitulated before the difficulty of the problem he had set, nevertheless there are many pages in his works that indicate that—at least in fragments, for his work was a fragment, an unsolved puzzle—he was on the trail of many essential connections.

In many considerations of Kafka the question has been posed whether it is possible to judge Kafka's work from a sociological point of view. [. . .]

As adherents of the Marxist-Leninist world view, we are opposed to that vulgar-sociological procedure which derives the work of a writer only directly from his social position and ignores the fact that the aesthetic form of our perception of the world and of people, which comprises a determining factor in every artistic work, has its specific laws; that only through these laws does art really become art and literature really become literature. A vulgar-sociological proce-dure would be particularly inadequate to deal with Kafka: Kafka was not, as is frequently maintained, the son of petty bourgeois parents. His father was, even if to the modest extent of the middle bourgeoisie, a capitalist exploiter. Kafka's letter to this father is evidence that he hated his father not so much as a person as in his social function. But Kafka's honest hatred of what it was that he condemned in his father, his hatred of many repulsive characteristics of the capitalist world, did not result in the perception of new paths for social development. Whoever knows Kafka even a little will not doubt that this work was born out of a humanistic foundation; that Kafka's despair was genuine and not affected, that he found much to hate in life that we as adherents to a socialist world view also hate.

Whoever doubts Kafka's humanistic relationship to the working class should read his letter to Max Brod from the summer of 1909, which was written in the Workers' Accident Insurance office:

The things I have to do! In my four administrative districts—apart from my other responsibilities—people fall like drunks from the scaffolding into the machines; all the beams tip over; all the slag heaps loosen up; all the ladders slip; whatever people raise falls down, whatever people put down they fall over themselves. And one gets headaches from these young girls in the china factories, who are constantly falling down the stairs with mountains of dishes.[6]

6. Franz Kafka, *Briefe 1902-1924* (Frankfurt am Main, 1958).

This humanistic position also determines Kafka's attitude toward the Czech people at a time when German chauvinism was deepening the animosity between the peoples in our countries. Progressive Czech literary critics in the time before the First World War reckoned Kafka, along with E. E. Kisch, Max Brod, Rudolf Fuchs, Franz Werfel, and R. M. Rilke, in that group of Prague German writers who kept themselves free of all chauvinistic prejudices. Kafka's contact with that group of Czech writers who were in sympathy with anarchism before the war has been documented; S. K. Neumann's personal favoritism toward Kafka's work, even when Neumann had already embraced communism, is evident in the fact that he published Kafka's story "The Stoker." All those are contradictions—not invented contradictions, but real contradictions of life. A vulgar sociology is doomed to fail with them. But without that genuine, scientific sociology, which is our permanent inheritance from Marx and Lenin, without deep perception of the connections between reality and art, as even Chernyshevsky demanded, Kafka would remain a closed book for us. There are opinions that Kafka regarded the world from a religious point of view. We do not want to argue about Kafka's religiosity or irreligiosity. What is certain is that it is not the religious questions which are at the center of his work. What pained and oppressed him, what drove him to the edge of despair, were real life phenomena which he could not master. All this we want to investigate in order to understand Kafka as a man and an artist, in order to mark off the place which he deserves in the literature of the twentieth century.

Allow me to mention another German writer whose tragic fate recalls Kafka's in many respects: Hölderlin. In one of his best poems he complains that the Germans of his time were rich in thoughts and poor in deeds. And Hölderlin asked if upon the books the deeds would not soon follow. Indeed: rich in thoughts and poor in deeds—that is the proper word to express Kafka's deep tragedy, the failure of a life work grandly conceived but left as a fragment.

Kafka experienced the great turn of the world, which began in 1917 with the socialist revolution in Russia, as a gravely ill and dying man. The hope which could give his life a new direction could no longer reach him. It reached other writers of his generation, who had matured with him and next to him in similar circumstances. To the circle of close friends who were with him in the last years belonged the communist writer Rudolf Fuchs, whom Kafka appreciated and loved. And many of them who grew up next to Kafka raised themselves above the hopelessness to a new insight into the joy in the world: E. E. Kisch, Franz Weiskopf, Louis Fürnberg—they all, who came from a sphere like Kafka's, went on from where he, forced by life, had to stop. The magic circle from which Kafka could not escape was broken. The time of a new literature, a new poetry, ripened: rich not only in thoughts, but also in deeds. It ripened through difficult battles, through crises and confrontations, on paths that were not easy, often struggling against lack of understanding even in its own ranks. We cannot fail to mention that the vanguard of this new literature, in so far as it knew Kafka, was among the first to support a just, understanding appraisal of his work. In his last letter Louis Fürnberg asked me to write about Kafka the way we understand him from the Prague point of view, familiar with the circumstances of his life. And at the same time he wrote in his "Krankengeschichte": "Only future generations will appreciate that we became distrustful of the morbid, negative hero who was affected by decay and sickness, that we were not charmed by destruction, that we avoided decay, rot, and corruption."[7]

And in this spirit we want to appreciate Kafka's legacy. Whoever has really understood Kafka must irreconcilably hate everything that broke his great talent: not unfulfillable humanistic dreams, but deeds of true humanism—that is what Kafka's tragic fate calls us to. If today we reject much of what claims to be in Kafka's tradition, we have good reasons. We no longer believe that a tragedy such as Kafka experienced is a predetermined fate from which there is no escape: the path that Kafka sought in the dark has been found and no matter what troubles and struggles may be ahead of us, we will never abandon this path, neither in life nor in literature.

Yes, at this conference on Kafka I would like to emphasize Louis Fürnberg's humanistic thought that decay and corruption cannot be the program and perspective of our literature and art. Our literary criticism cannot limit itself to investigating Kafka's complicated character and work historically in connection with the conditions of his time—its task is also to pronounce a judgment.

And I wish to speak to that as a member of the generation which

7. Louis Fürnberg, "Krankengeschichte," in *Das Jahr des vierblättrigen Klees.*

entered active life in the time between the two World Wars and which had to seek and find its place in life in that time.

Franz Kafka was about twenty years older than we; he belonged to the generation directly preceding ours and which we had to confront both politically and literarily. All our concepts of the world in which we lived and in which we grew up collapsed in the flames of the First World War. And at the same time the event of the century, the socialist October revolution, gave us a new goal for life. We read Kafka for the first time during the great convulsions and conflicts which led to great changes in the world and the life of our country. We came to know him as a writer who convincingly revealed the decay and inhumanity of the capitalist order. At first we read his primarily satirical short prose pieces and only later, after his death, the novel fragments which Max Brod edited from his literary remains. And so Kafka, who often relentlessly criticized what we too hated in life, frequently reminded us of a mouse running about helplessly, seeking a way out of the trap until it finally collapses, exhausted. But we did not want to resemble such a mouse; we could not accept Kafka's melancholy conclusion that there is no salvation and no rescue. We sought and found something that he was not able to see: that there is a real and secure path to freedom, a path which he sought and could not find. We did not remain, like that man from the country whom Kafka introduced in his well-known parable, before the mysterious doors of an unknown Law; we pushed the guard aside and, filled with the excitement of attack, pushed on to the laws of life which Kafka had never learned. And in the very struggle we saw the world from a new side and overcame Kafka by finding what he had only sought. And therefore we pushed Kafka, whose artistic power in representing the contradictions of life we recognized, aside, and we rejected him. To be sure, he helped us to see the world; but he prevented us from entering on the path to which Marx and Lenin called us, the path toward changing the world. He prevented us from solving the problem which had become the life problem of our whole generation: of how to take the laws of life into our own hands and arrange the world so that people can live and work in it.

[. . .]

I feel all the more justified in speaking of the ways in which we parted and part from Kafka because we read and appreciated him while he was still unknown. Of course we cannot force our concept of life on anyone who does not have an optimistic faith in life, who, like Kafka, does not achieve an inner harmony. But I do not believe that Kafka's position can be the normal feeling of a person who is actively participating in building the new socialist society, who has before him a perspective on life. We appreciate Kafka as a writer who honestly sought the truth; but in the fight to build a new society [. . .] we follow the path of life and of joy.

Surely we do not need a literature which conceals the real conflicts of life; we need a literature which penetrates to the complicated conflicts in the inner life of men. In this direction we can learn from Kafka. For that reason we will again publish and attentively read his work. But at the same time we are decidedly against every kind of defeatism: we do not believe Kafka when he tells us that the laws of life cannot be recognized; nor do we believe in insuperable conflicts. Life itself, the decades-long experience of our struggle, has convinced us that new and higher forms of life regularly arise from the conflict of opposites. The conflicts which defeated Kafka are already largely part of the past. And we will overcome the new conflicts too, which are arising today from the construction of socialism, for we will never again allow the ship of our life to be driven without navigator or compass wherever the waves of the sea may take us. We have had storms; often our ship has pitched dangerously in heavy seas; but our course is sure, and we sail straight to the shores of tomorrow!

Franz Kafka in the
Prague Perspective: 1963

EDUARD GOLDSTÜCKER

[. . .]

I [. . .] want to consider the situation of Kafka research today, here and in the world. The situation is the following: whereas for almost a quarter of a century Kafka has been the object of intense interest on the part of bourgeois literary critics, Marxist research in this area began just a few years ago. In the time before that there were only separate and very sporadic approaches, such as the inquiry of the journal *Action* in 1946, under the title *Faut-il brûler Kafka?*[1] And in 1950 Georges Bataille wrote an article called "Franz Kafka devant la critique communiste,"[2] whose content did not fulfill the promise of its title. It is a fact that Marxist research into Kafka's work, as I have said, has begun only in the last few years. The impulse for that was certainly contributed by the results of the Twentieth Congress of the Communist Party of the Soviet Union and its conclusion that the antagonistic systems in the world today, in order to exist, must coexist. It was only this principle which created the presuppositions for the development of a real struggle, whose first presupposition is that the struggling sides, in contrast to the earlier mutual ignorance and isolation, now take cognizance of one another and try to prove, with the results of their efforts, which intellectual foundation can better meet the demands of today's world and awakens more trust as a point of departure for the world of tomorrow.

[. . .] Franz Kafka, whom the whole world attributes to us in Czechoslovakia, became with us—but not only with us—a victim of the consequences of what is called the personality cult. Among these

Eduard Goldstücker, "Über Franz Kafka aus der Prager Perspektive 1963," previously published in *Franz Kafka aus Prager Sicht 1963* (Prague, 1965), pp. 24-43.
[1. "Should we Burn Kafka?" *Ed.*]
2. "Kafka and Communist Criticism," *Critique*, 1950, No. 41, pp. 22-36.

consequences are a dangerous black-and-white simplification of the world view, doubt in the strength of the idea of socialism, and through that the replacement of discussion by administrative measures.

We can no longer abandon ourselves to the illusion that on the intellectual map of today's world, which has been shrunk so much by modern communications, any area can be covered up or in the long run simply ignored. We cannot use the comprehensive and indefinable term "decadence" to condemn summarily all artistic movements that develop from presuppositions different from ours and that produce works counter to our method and our spirit. Instead of a summary condemnation and dismissal, we must attain, through thorough study and analysis, to well-founded judgments that are convincing by virtue of their universal arguments. And above all, artistic creation based on our presuppositions must produce works that will decide the global competition in our favor.

Whatever has been written in recent years from our standpoint has reflected this spirit. If I may be allowed such an analogy, I will refer to Lenin's statement in *"Left-Wing" Communism: An Infantile Disorder*, in which he affirmed that the Workers' and Peasants' State, after the successful revolution, cannot sidestep a single problem that needs a solution, that it cannot be spared the necessity of solving every single question that life brings with it. In the non-socialist part of the world, Kafka's work became the object of extraordinary attention, of a burning interest, which proves that a large number of people found in his work an expression of their life's feelings and problems. We know that not all these people lived, and live, outside the socialist camp or within the boundaries of the socialist *Weltanschauung*. Even this obvious social fact should have forced us to consider Kafka's work and not just to dismiss it smugly with the catchall phrase "bourgeois-decadent tendencies." A scientifically executed analysis would have uncovered the causes and shown us what our contemporaries find in Kafka's work. That would have led us to study this work; we would have fathomed its essence, the manner of its statement, the secret of its emotional power, and its place in the contest between progress and regression.

[. . .]

It is not my task to evaluate the work of these or other critics, but rather to present for discussion a few questions which have recently arisen among us in Czechoslovakia. I suspect—and I hope that this suspicion will not remain a wish motivated by local patriotism—that some of the questions about Franz Kafka's life and work can be best answered from the vantage point of Prague.

I

The first problem that confronts us when we turn our attention to Kafka is the problem of the method of Kafka research. In order to be clear on what we are talking about, we must point out that the course of Kafka research already has a relatively long history and has assumed enormous proportions, whereas Marxist research is still in its infancy. So it is obvious that the breadth and weight of bourgeois Kafka literature are factors which everyone who sets out to do a thorough study of Kafka must reckon with. If we include the perfectly legitimate antipathy which the excesses of a vulgar sociologism has nourished especially among our younger literary critics and scholars—excesses which in the recent past have again and again crept into Marxist literary criticism and scholarship—then we will understand that many different opinions about the methodology of Kafka research have developed. Frequently one is warned against applying the so-called sociological method with reference to Kafka. In the light of what I just said, I find it understandable that such warnings are motivated by a sincere concern for not being satisfied only with determining the social conditions in Kafka's life and interpreting his work exclusively from them. That way we would undoubtedly get no farther than working out general theses in which the uniqueness, the very special character of Kafka's work, would be lost. That's one side of the coin. The other has to do with the question of the goal that we pursue in studying Kafka's work. What is our aim really? Understanding Kafka's work by explaining the history of how it was written, or understanding what Kafka's work meant and means for the reader? In order to answer these questions, or in order to decide if they are the right questions, we have to say—I hope it will not be considered an inadmissible generalization—that bourgeois Kafka research interprets his work primarily either from the individual psychological disposition of the author, or from his religious or existential speculations—that is, freed from the historical and social factors which formed his life and his work, and, in the final analysis, helped to determine his individuality. But the investigation of any work whatsoever, no matter how detailed, how sharp, or how scientifically pedantic it is, if the work is torn out of its historic and social context—that is, if it is investigated metaphysically (in Engles' sense)—then it cannot come to any scientific (in the true sense of the word) results, even if certain perceptions of details do turn out to be true. Recently, repeated warnings against such a one-sided method have been heard in the ranks of non-Marxist scholars. Let me refer at least to the objection of Wilhelm Emrich, who states that "the officials in *The Trial* and *The Castle* reflect not only the ceaseless inward reflection and dream consciousness of man, but also the external social life of our times."[3] Jean-Paul Sartre says in his famous Moscow speech with reference to Kafka: "The depth of a work arises from the national history, the language, the tradition, the special and often tragic questions which are put to the author by the epoch and the region and through the living community of which he is a part."[4] R. M. Albérès and Pierre de Boisdeffre, the authors of the little French monograph on Kafka, begin the first chapter of their book with a polemic against the kind of criticism which maintains that only the inward knowledge (*connaissance interne*) of a work of art matters and that all other viewpoints must be excluded. And they continue: "Even if inner criticism (*critique interne*) is extremely necessary, it is not sufficient for illuminating Kafka's work . . . Kafka's work cannot be dissociated from his person."[5]

Those were some voices from the other side of the barrier that spans the world. These voices recognize the danger of a dead end, which Kafka research has already come to whenever it let itself be guided by the method of isolating the text—even from the person of the author—or by the method of psychological or philosophical excavations that conceives the author as a self-contained microcosm, from which the work springs to light without the influence of any external factors. On our side of the barrier the opposite fears have been enunciated. One could summarize them most concisely in Ernst Fischer's lapidary sentence: "His [Kafka's] work is incomparably more than the dying cry of a time—it is universal literature."[6] A confrontation of these views challenges us to a synthesis. Allow me to indicate the outlines of such a synthesis, even though I run the risk of

3. Wilhelm Emrich, *Franz Kafka* (Frankfurt am Main, 1960).
4. Jean-Paul Sartre, "Die Abrüstung der Kultur. Rede auf dem Weltfriedenskongress in Moskau," *Sinn und Form*, 14 (1962), No. 5-6, p. 809.
5. R.-M. Albérès and Pierre de Boisdeffre, *Franz Kafka* (Paris, 1960).
6. Ernst Fischer, "Franz Kafka," *Sinn und Form*, 14 (1962), No. 4, p. 497.

being accused of discovering continents which have already been discovered. We know that even the most comprehensive compilation of biographical and historic-social data is not sufficient to grasp a creative personality and its work. We were able to get even to this so self-evident perception only after a whole list of errors, after overcoming sociological vulgarities in literary criticism, which frequently led to an editing of the biographical material into the form of a cadre evaluation of the writer to be studied. Works of literary criticism not uncommonly gave the impression that we were not dealing with works of living people with sensitive psyches, with very complicated and in each case different systems of transforming life experiences and ecstasies of thought and feeling into works of art, but with cleverly calculated declarative statements by representatives of individual social classes, groups, strata, and interstrata. The concept of literature as an art was increasingly lost in this kind of view. Poetry, that fragile and unmeasurable ingredient which distinguishes a work of literary art from a philosophical treatise or a news story, disappeared. On the other hand, it must be equally emphasized that we should be careful not to allow our justified objection to vulgar sociologization to plunge us into the illusion that a work of art and its creator can be wholly comprehended without considering, next to the text, the external, personal, social conditions under which the artist lived and worked. It is a principal fact that a work of art is a social phenomenon and that scholarship and criticism must treat it as such, because only in this way can they provide us with the possibility of discovering its heart, listening to its pulse, recognizing its structure and composition, and penetrating into the secret of its life.

I recall Marx's point that the discovery of truth requires, among other things, that the research method adapt itself to the object to be studied, so that the method remain elastic and in keeping with the object, so that it can sensitively grasp the specific nature of the object. That means that even the very best research method can give the researcher only general guidelines, and that it is up to the researcher, through his own work and in intimate association with his object, to manufacture out of these guidelines that key which will open the most complicated and delicate locks which abound on the path to the truth. When we approach the highly complicated organism of Kafka's work, we quickly perceive that we will not get very far if we limit our investigation to the texts, because it will soon turn out that—as

Kafka himself repeatedly emphasized—it is always a matter of occasional literature in Goethe's sense, of crystallization of his personal problems; that all of the major characters in his works—be they named Bendemann, Samsa, Raban, Gracchus, Josef K., or, like the surveyor, simply K.—mean one person: Franz Kafka. That necessarily leads us to the personality of the author, to his psychological constitution, to the circumstances of his life, that is, to the extra-personal factors which formed his life and his psychological behavior. There are many works of world literature which at first sight do not seem to require such an immediate interest in the author as Franz Kafka's work. Let us take as an example a writer whom Kafka thought very highly of: Flaubert. *Madame Bovary* or *Salammbô* do not arouse our interest in the personality of the creator as much as, say, *The Trial* or *The Castle*. Kafka's texts are characterized by their familiar quality of giving no explanation of the concepts, images, and situations which they evoke, but rather of forcing the reader to provide explanation and commentary. That explains the need for bulky commentaries, the ambiguity of the interpretation, and the enormous quantity of Kafka criticism. Each interpretation forces the reader to weigh aspects which actually lie outside the texts, in the world of the emotional reactions and thought processes of the author, in his biography and the character of his time. Kafka is virtually a textbook example of the principle that it is not enough for a researcher who wants to find out the truth to confront the object of his research with an arsenal of general methodological guidelines, but that in his research he must constantly complement them with instruments which are appropriate to the object. Only in this way can he successfully apply general methodological criteria to the object with the hope of fathoming it. The more complicated the object, the more complicated and refined the instruments must be, whether they have been developed by the researcher himself or taken over from his predecessors. All of this applies naturally also to the general guidelines of Marxist methodology. I am convinced that it provides the best approach to the scientific interpretation of the phenomena of the world and of life, but it cannot be more than a *general* approach and must, thanks to the creative work of the researcher, fit the object—so to speak—as if it had been poured on.

  With regard to Kafka research, a large number of such instruments has already been worked out. We have to test each one for its usefulness and may not allow ourselves to be intimidated by any of the taboos which the dogmatism of a (hopefully) past era put in our path.

As an example of such a taboo, I would like to mention psycho-analysis. We know that Kafka was familiar with Freud's teachings, and that he put his individual psychological problems into the form of (primarily) Freudian symbols—and not only when he expressly said so (see the journal entry of November 23, 1912), but in general. Naturally we have to deal with this side of the matter too and attempt to fathom the secret of Kafka's symbolism in accepting, as an aid, Freud's theory of symbols. Let us emphasize: as an aid. As soon as the aid becomes a principle, research *must* miss the mark. I have no intention of trivializing non-Marxist Kafka criticism. But I cannot help but feel that some psychoanalytic interpretations of Kafka's work silently proceed from the assumption that Kafka wrote his texts only as exercises for psychoanalysts.

I am convinced that Marxist-oriented Kafka research, the first results of which justify great hopes—at least when it lets itself be guided by the spirit we have indicated, when it takes as its model that ruthless defiance of prejudice which we admire so much in Marx and Lenin, when it does not insist on elevating the relative and partial truths of the political moment to universal truths—I am convinced that it is destined to deal with Franz Kafka's work in a truly scientific way and to distinguish what is a momentary and ephemeral reflection of his time from what is lasting in Kafka's contribution to the treasure of world literature.

II

The second question to which I would like to direct the attention of our conference concerns the character of the German literature of Prague at Kafka's time and so the literary and social atmosphere in which Kafka lived and worked. [. . .] Prior attempts to ascertain the specific character traits of Prague-German literature at the turn of the century have found their most plausible results in Pavel Eisner's works, in his view that this literature, in the last decades of the Austro-Hungarian monarchy, developed in an unnatural, insular milieu cut off from a healthy collective body [*Volksganze*] and that the writers lived on this German-speaking island as if they were in a threefold ghetto: a German, a German-Jewish, and a bourgeois ghetto. This correct perception requires expansion in the light of new historical information and especially of our new perspective. The question is: How is it that in such a short time such a significant group of writers, who today occupy the attention of the whole world, could have developed from this relatively little island of Prague? When Kafka began to write, in the first years of this century, there were only a little more than 30,000 German-speaking inhabitants in Prague, a city of half a million people. And when we remember that even in the generation of Rilke (from whose appearance we date the "Golden Age" of Prague-German literature) the Prague Germans lived a kind of caste-and-ghetto life, then it is clear that we cannot find in these circumstances the factor which elevated a former provincial literature to the level of world literature. Rather, we will have to look for an acceptable explanation in the changes in social life which caused such a remarkable activity and ferment (which was the motivating force of their thinking and writing) among the last generation of Prague Germans to have grown up in Austria-Hungary. What were those changes? Above all, the clearly visible lag of the Habsburg monarchy behind the stormy development of the capitalist world in the second half of the nineteenth century. And also the strengthening of the struggle for national liberation on the part of the repressed peoples of the Habsburg empire. A look into the past shows us that the Habsburg empire, which had been created on the basis of no-longer-existing conditions and for no-longer-relevant purposes, was beginning to break apart under the storm of capitalism—in other words, that it was undergoing a development completely opposite to that of the bourgeois national states. Whereas capitalism in the latter was strengthening the unity of the state, it created in Austria a stronger growth of the centrifugal forces than of the centripetal and demonstrated that the union of the states was an anachronism and that disbanding was a necessity. The rapid growth of the labor movement, and therefore the increasingly threatening specter of social revolution, further complicated these conditions. But even all these factors together do not in themselves provide a sufficient reason for the remarkable intensification of intellectual activity on the Prague-German island— above all in its Jewish areas. The historical change which obviously goes along with this frenzy of intensive searching is the transition of the upper bourgeoisie to imperialism. The specific character of Prague-German literature is closely connected to the perception, or the suspicion, of the Prague-German writers that the era of bourgeois liberalism was inevitably nearing its end. As we know, the transition to imperialism caused sharp ideological conflicts in the bourgeois camp itself. A significant portion of the bourgeois intelligentsia was not able, or not willing, to toss the humanistic spirit, the most precious heritage of the progressive phase of their class's development, overboard and to replace it with the antihumanistic principles of imperialism. It was therefore virtually a law of the entire bourgeois world of that time, that with the rise of imperialism many bourgeois artists started to defy it and wanted to maintain the humanist tradition. They did that either by going back to the thoughts of the French Revolution of 1789 and—especially in the German cultural area—to the intellectual heritage of classical German literature and philosophy in order to breathe new life into them, or by leaving the sinking ship of bourgeois liberalism in panic in order to rescue the humanistic inheritance from the ravages of the present and save it for a future which must have seemed uncertain to them. Out of this situation developed late bourgeois humanist literature and art and also—under the specific living conditions of the Prague Germans—the great Prague-German literature after Rilke.

The end of the capitalism of free competition and, on the ideological plane, the end of the liberal-bourgeois illusions, had another important consequence, especially for the development of Prague-German literature. The end of liberalism, namely, meant danger for the entire previous life style of the Jews, because from the very beginning German imperialism wore a militantly antisemitic face. The lower and middle Jewish strata of the bourgeoisie must have had the impression that their fate was bound to that of liberalism. Only if we consider this circumstance can we understand completely why Jews played such an active part in late bourgeois German—and especially Prague-German—culture.

This outline of the special development of Austria-Hungary in the late bourgeois period leads us to the roots of the special development of the German-language literature of Austria. There were above all two cities with a literary influence which then attained great significance for the whole of the bourgeois end-period: Vienna and Prague. This is not the place to discuss the differences between Viennese and Prague literature at the end of the Monarchy. But common to both is the fact that they developed in an atmosphere of agony, in a world that, to borrow a phrase of Hegel's, became increasingly irrational because increasingly unreal. The principal difference between them we find in the fact that from the standpoint of the constantly sharpening national struggles, the Imperial City of Vienna was far in the hinterland, whereas Prague, in the front lines, was one of the main scenes of these struggles, whose intensity was felt especially by the Prague Germans. Under the pressure of a new time, their little island began to crumble away. Within twenty years, from 1880 to 1900, the number of Prague Germans sank from 42,000 to 33,800. In the same time, the number of Prague Czechs rose from 228,000 to 415,000 so that the relative proportion of Germans in the population sank from 15.5% to 7.5%. The decisive factor which turned Prague-German literature from a provincial one into an object of universal interest was, then, the fact that the Prague-Germans, for the reasons just given, were the first social group of the bourgeois world whose writers felt their world heading for the abyss and the end. In Prague, especially in its German part, and within this especially in its Jewish majority, the collision of a number of circumstances with the rise of imperialism had created a situation that allowed the German writers—and especially the German-Jewish writers—a more thorough look at the crisis of the times than was possible elsewhere and that enabled them, as the first, to express historical experiences which the rest of the world would not have until later.

I am dealing with the historical and social elements of Kafka's time not at all because I think that our Kafka research should stop at the conclusions derived from them [. . .] but rather in the conviction that all truly scientific Kafka research must consider such circumstances as background to Kafka's life and work, as factors which gave this life and this work its form and its coloration. Without them, one cannot penetrate to the core of Kafka's work. The primary failing of most bourgeois Kafka criticism consists in the fact that it does not consider such factors, that it tears Kafka's work out of its historical context, does not pay attention to its social determinedness, and therefore mystifies it.

I believe that the thorough scientific illumination of that complex of questions which can be subsumed under the heading "Kafka and Prague" plays the decisive role in this context. And in this regard, the decisive word is far from having been spoken, and many tasks still lie ahead for the researcher.

III

In this report I do not want to deal with the mutual relations between Kafka and the Czech world [. . .]. I will touch on them only peripherally in connection with the third question I should like to bring up here, the problem of Kafka's relations to the working class and to socialism. In this area, too, many problems await their resolution through Marxist literary analysis. [. . .] With regard to Kafka's relationship to socialism, Klaus Wagenbach repeatedly maintains that it was thoroughly positive. "The most important escape attempt," Wagenbach writes,

a kind of secret yearning for community, is the decided turn of the sixteen-year-old to socialism, which he never rejected in later life. Before the First World War Kafka took part in the meetings of Czech anarchists, read the works of Herzen, Kropotkin, and Bezruč, and in one of the Octave notebooks from 1918 we find his plan for a program of the "Propertyless Working Class," which has erroneously been called "isolated" in Kafka's work.[7]

Before I comment on Wagenbach's view, I would like to refer briefly to some circumstances that, so far as I know, Kafka research has so far not recognized and which I consider very important.

Although Kafka had to wrestle with essentially the same problems as his bourgeois fellow writers in Prague, he is different from them in that he did not settle for any of the pseudosolutions that satisfied the others. He was incapable, in the long run, of finding satisfaction in a neoromantic, religious, or other similar escape, and he found himself forced to reject all of these as illusory. I believe that this fear of putting his trust in something that could then turn out to be an illusion became apparent in Kafka when, in his longing for human community, he took up the question—as the first bourgeois writer in our part of Europe—of whether he could solve the problems of his life through an approach to the working class. To clarify: surely there were some works in German literature before Kafka that testify to the writer's sympathy with the working class, but we would search in vain for a writer in whose work the thought took on real shape that an approach to the working class might pave the way to a solution for the problem of a bourgeois intellectual in Kafka's social situation. In my opinion, Kafka took this step as early as 1912, when not a single German writer of his format had yet found his way to the working class or had even considered the possibility. We have to regard one of Kafka's

7. Klaus Wagenbach, *Franz Kafka. Eine Biographie seiner Jugend* (Bern, 1958), p. 162ff., and in the afterword to *Franz Kafka: Erzählungen und Skizzen. Eine Auswahl* (Darmstadt, 1959), p. 154f.

works, which has played an important part in Kafka's reception in Bohemia, as an artistic projection of such considerations: the first chapter (written later) of *America*, called "The Stoker."

For me there is no question that Kafka wished to symbolize the working class as he saw it in the figure of the stoker, whom Karl Rossman meets, deep in the ship's hold, in the hour of his greatest need and who leads him out of his Dantean labyrinths. He is "a huge man" whose physical size Kafka constantly emphasizes; he is doomed to a life in a "miserable cabin" which is illuminated only by a faint light filtering down from higher up in the ship and which is furnished with only the most necessary items and hardly provides room to live in; he is mistreated and systematically robbed of what belongs to him, both materially and spiritually. To be sure, Kafka considered the position of the working class—as that of all classes and strata in capitalist society—to be tragic. The stoker is incapable of presenting his valid and justified demands, or of formulating them clearly and concisely; what hinders him is, on the one hand, his all-too-painful feeling of resentment toward the constant humiliations and insults which, as soon as he begins to speak, put the most painful things rather than the most essential into his mouth; and, on the other hand, his insecurity when confronted by the bosses who have power over him, a timidity which comes from his accepting, in his heart of hearts, the status quo as self-evident, because he knows of no other. His physical power is shackled by his knowledge of the superior power of the repressive apparatus of the rulers, so that he cannot be helped even by a direct action. When we consider these and related facts, we come to the conclusion that Kafka's relation to socialism and to the working class in essence reflects the characteristics of what Marx and Engels in *The Communist Manifesto* call "critical-utopian socialism and communism": namely, that for the adherents of this tendency the proletariat "exists only as the most suffering class." I should like to point to a particular trait of Kafka's world, in which his social and individual-psychological isolation is manifest, namely to the circumstance that the distance between him and other people, especially between him and those who belong to other social strata, is unusually great. Kafka considered, say, the world of the workers as a different world from his, which was that of the bourgeoisie and petty bourgeosie, and he did this much more radically than would have been appropriate for the real differences in the society of his time. That lends something anachronistic, other-worldly, and even demonical to Kafka's world. That increases the significance that we must attribute to his attempt to solve his life's problems through an approach to or even contact with the working class. As is well known, the surveyor K. in *The Castle* occupies himself with such thoughts, but it had been done ten years earlier by Karl Rossmann in "The Stoker."

In this as in many other respects there is an analogy to [Heinrich] Kleist, that late-comer of a class abdicating a whole historical age before Kafka. [. . .] It seems to me we must look for the analogy in the fact that both of them, from the viewpoint of the history of their class, were late-comers, that their fates were those of "disinherited sons," to use a phrase Kafka coined to characterize himself. Or in the fact that neither of them belonged anywhere, which always has two sides: this always torments its victims, but gives them a sharp view free of class prejudices and comfortable illusions. The thoughts of the surveyor K. about the advantages and disadvantages of loneliness and community are well known. So is Kafka's journal entry from 1921:

Whoever has persistent difficulties with life needs his one hand to ward off despair at his fate—a very imperfect gesture—but with his other hand he can record what he sees under the rubble, because he sees differently and more than the others; during his life he is dead, and nevertheless he is the one who survives. This presupposes, of course, that he doesn't need both hands—and more than he has—in the fight against desperation.

That is literally true about Kleist also. He too searched—in vain like Kafka—for contact with the class that was "lower" then but working its way up, and in fact with its Rousseauistic-Jacobean wing. In life in France, the home of this movement, he thought he had found what he was looking for, but he came too late, and what he found behind the elevated rhetoric was only a falsified reality. In contrast to Kleist, Kafka came to the "lower" class of *his* time too soon. His tragedy lies in the fact that he could not overcome the final barrier between himself and the working class (no more than he could any other in his life) and that at that time the labor movement in these countries was not yet a force dynamic enough to have torn down this barrier by itself and attracted sincerely humanistic bourgeois artists. When we consider the story of the stoker attentively, we can see that it contains implicitly a penetrating critique of the weaknesses of the socialist movement of that time, a critique of the lack of militant resolution, of the fuzziness of the ideas on the new social order and the way to it, and above all a critique of the national rivalries endemic in the country and which (like the stoker's idea of Schubal's Romanian nationality) constantly gained the upper hand and muddled the most important questions.

This is not the place for a detailed interpretation of "The Stoker"; I have attempted that in another place. Here I would like to say only that we would be hard put to find, in literature before World War I, a work of a non-proletarian author that views with such deep sympathy, and proclaims the rightness of, the proletarian cause, that is more sincerely carried by the wish that the workers defend their rights more militantly and more consistently, than Kafka's. Above all we would hardly find a work in which the feeling is clearer that the author, even though it may go beyond his power, is trying to free himself from the fetters of his heritage and is leaving his heart on the side of the stoker.

We know that it was the shattering experience of the First World War, and then chiefly the consequences of the October Revolution in Russia, which weakened these fetters for bourgeois artists and which enabled those who so wished to find contact with the revolutionary labor movement. But Kafka was then already a deathly ill man. Nevertheless, in March of 1918, he makes an entry in a notebook which contains his philosophical thoughts: a utopian socialist program for the "propertyless working class." Moreover, toward the end of his life the problem of the revolutionary in society was still occupying him so much that it makes up the largest part of his conception of the figure of the surveyor K.

We have spoken of the archaic character of Kafka's work that results from the fact that he sees the individual social strata as closed worlds, separated by great distances from each other. In his attitude toward the working class, Kafka is intellectually on the level of the utopian socialists. His program for the "propertyless working class" is a typical product of utopian-socialist thinking, and it gives the impression that its author has never heard of the capitalist system or of the efforts of his class. It seems to me that this should caution us in regard to reports of Kafka's contact with Czech anarcho-communist intellectuals. As is known, such reports claim that for several years before World War I Kafka took part in meetings of a group of

anarcho-communists, which was composed mainly of leading representatives of the young generation of Czech writers. But to me something does not jibe with some of the details of such claims. For one
thing, not once in Kafka's notebooks is there any mention of contacts
with Czech anarcho-communists. Kafka's most intimate friend, to
whom he related almost all his experiences during these years, had no
idea that Kafka was attending such meetings; he learned of it only
after Kafka's death, from Michal Kácha, a member of the group. All
that could be explained as Kafka's caution in not telling even his
closest friends, to avoid the possibility of police reprisals against the
group and its members. According to another report, of Michal
Mareš, Kafka was introduced into the group through his fellow student Rudolf Illowý. It is certainly difficult to explain the fact that
Kafka did not personally know S. K. Neumann, one of the most obvious personalities in the anarcho-communist circle, whom he would
have had to meet during his contact with the group for several years.
The remark that Kafka was only a silent participant at the meetings
and didn't take up contact with the other members (for that reason
Kácha gave him the nickname "Klidas," "the Silent One," immediately raises the question of whether anarcho-communists, revolution-
aries, would have tolerated for years the presence in their midst of a
man whom they did not even know—especially since they must have
discussed certain things at their meetings which were supposed to be
kept secret from the Austrian police. All of this permits us the assumption that Kafka took part in only a few of the meetings. Michal
Mareš' memoir, which Wagenbach has reprinted and which reports
a years-long contact with anarcho-communists—and even of Kafka's
participation in a meeting of the "Party of moderate progress within
the law," sponsored by Hašek in the spring of 1912—should in my
opinion be relegated to the realm of fiction. But the main reason for
my skepticism toward the legend of Kafka's long and intimate contact with the anarcho-communists is the fact that nowhere in Kafka's
work do we find signs that he was acquainted with their thoughts.
That pertains especially to the thoughts of modern socialism about
the situation of the working class in the present and the future. For,
as indicated, Kafka's attitude toward the working class did not go beyond the position reached by the utopian socialists long before Marx.
For him the workers were the most *suffering class* (we can find the
roots of this position in Kafka's relationship to his father's employees

and later in his relationship to the workers in the "Workers' Social Insurance Office"), and he considered it a moral duty to help them (which assumes artistic form in Karl Rossmann, the stoker's advocate, and can be seen in Kafka's utopian plan for the "propertyless working class"). And he weighed whether or not he could alleviate the overpowering burden of his existence through an approach to the working class, which appeared to him from the very beginning not as the revolutionary class but as the most suffering one. [. . .]

Kafka Conference

ERNST FISCHER

This Kafka Conference is an event that goes far beyond the borders of Czechoslovakia.

The castle in which we are meeting belonged to some legendary Count West-West. But the institution which occupies it today does not intend to represent an unapproachable East-East. In our day the important thing is to achieve an open East-West debate in all areas. Kafka belongs among the themes of such a debate, this great rebellious writer, whom we Marxists have left too long to the bourgeois world. We have to make up for this neglect.

First of all, I would like to counter the assertion that Kafka is now only of historical interest, that his work belongs to the past. Kafka is a writer who concerns us all. The alienation of men, which he portrayed with maximal intensity, reaches horrifying proportions in the capitalist world. But it has certainly not been overcome in the socialist world either. To overcome it step by step in the fight against dogmatism and bureaucracy and for socialist democracy, initiative, and responsibility is a tedious process and a great task. Reading works such as *The Trial* and *The Castle* can contribute to the fulfillment of this task. The socialist reader will recognize characteristics of his own problems in them, and the socialist official will be forced to argue more thoroughly and subtly on many questions. Instead of regarding Kafka as passé or being afraid of him, one should print his books and thereby occasion a discussion on a high plane.

Kafka is a writer of greatest relevance. Is he a realist? Many Marx-

Ernst Fischer, "Kafka-Konferenz," previously published in *Franz Kafka aus Prager Sicht 1963* (Prague, 1965), pp. 157-68. I have inserted the two bracketed passages on pp. 78-85 and 86-88 from Fischer's essay "Franz Kafka," published in his *Von Grillparzer zu Kafka. Sechs Essays* (Vienna: Globus, 1962), pp. 294-300 and 321-23. In the latter, the passage from Erich Auerbach's *Mimesis* is from the translation by Willard Trask (New York: Doubleday, n.d.), p. 9.

ists claim that he isn't. It is not to my taste to force great writers into specific categories. In nominalist terminology, I would say that God created things and the Devil created categories. Only the mediocre fits into categories; the unusual bursts them.

The assertion that Kafka was not a realist and did not represent reality immediately provokes the questions, What is Realism? What is Reality?

If we define realism narrowly and strictly as a method of representing reality that predominated in the bourgeois world of the nineteenth century, then Kafka does not fit—or fits only partly—into this category.

But if we take realism to be every art and literature which struggles to portray and to master reality—if Homer and Aeschylus, Shakespeare and Cervantes, Rabelais and Swift are counted among the great realists—it is ridiculous to exclude Kafka from their company.

Whether recognized as a realist or misunderstood as a mystic, Kafka is one of the great, one of the essential writers of our century. But agreement on an unambiguous terminology is necessary if we are not to speak past one another: do we mean by realism that the writer is striving, with no matter what methods, to represent reality, or do we mean a particular method of this representation?

And when we say "reality"—what do we mean by it? Is it only the outside world, which it is the writer's function to reflect without distortion, or is it also the mirror itself, this living, active mirror which not infrequently changes its point of view? Aren't the various ways in which the outer world becomes a subjective experience an important aspect of reality? Is reality only what people do and what is done to them, or is it not also what they dream, suspect, and feel as not yet existing or existing only invisibly—what their anticipation includes in the here and now? Isn't the fourth dimension of the future, the possible, that which falls as a shimmer or a shadow into the present, sometimes a deeper reality than the so-called facts which we can touch with our hands? Is the order of reality, which the writer constitutes by ignoring what seems to him inessential and by emphasizing what seems essential, unshakable—or does it not change with the given social and individual situation? Can't what seems in one situation to be a peripheral detail become in another a torch which illuminates essential areas of reality?

Reality is what is never finished; it is the incomplete and the wide open, not a fixed condition, but a process. In the passing reality, the new one constitutes itself; and to discover this unknown is the task of every poet and writer who rises above the average. Even in a highly developed industrial society with all its opaque qualities and its confusing proliferation of facts, its enormous tempo of technological and social changes, the poet and writer retain something of the capacity of seer, of prophet. I would not want to characterize this as intuition—the word has been too much abused—but as the ability to perceive with shocking intensity new or previously unnoticed details, to link them up as signs of a reality still concealed, to join them together as the crystal structure of the crystallizing material.

It was exactly his thin skin, his unusual sensitivity, his powerlessness in a robust patriarchal society that enabled Kafka, that genius of weakness, to perceive such details in the extreme, to differentiate them and to decode them as hieroglyphs of a still undiscovered reality.

The exactness with which Kafka sees the previously unnoticed detail and the precision with which he presents it are recognized even by opponents of his work. What these opponents overlook is the powerfully poetic element within the apparent coldness of the style. What they castigate him for is the supposedly unreal character of the whole to which the real detail is related, that is, the de-realization of reality. What he constructs, they say, is only the negative, the powerlessness, the anxiety of man in the late capitalist world, and this world is not represented roundly and objectively, but one-sidedly and subjectively, indefinitely, deformedly and fantastically.

What Kafka in fact presents above all is the negative of his age. He himself wrote:

As far as I know, I have brought with me none of the requirements of life, but only the general human weakness. With this—in this respect it is a gigantic power—I have powerfully absorbed the negative of my time, a time which is very close to me and which I never have to fight but which to represent I have more or less the right. I had no inherited part in the little bit which is positive or in that extreme negative part which starts to tip over into the positive.[1]

[The alienation of the citizen from the state, the reification and dehumanization of social relations through bureaucracy, is only one—if essential—component of a comprehensive process.

1. Franz Kafka, *Hochzeitsvorbereitungen auf dem Lande* (Frankfurt am Main, 1953), pp. 120-21.

After the failure of *Robert Guiskard*, after the aimless wandering through France, heading toward his "view of the infinitely magnificent grave," Kleist worked for a cabinet maker in Mainz. Kafka too suspected that artisanship might contain the possibility of arriving at a unity with the world and with himself. The product of a handicraft is a whole thing; it is not alien to the producer but rather, proceeding in an obvious relationship from draft to finished product, it is surrounded by an aura of warmth and amity. But this is completely different in a one-sided and specialized labor process. Kafka, who always saw a central problem and the origin of decisive conflicts and contradictions in one's profession, in labor, spoke tersely and seemingly only peripherally in *America* about the feeling of alienation that comes over an elevator boy:

Karl was disappointed primarily by the fact that an elevator boy had to deal with the machinery of the elevator only in so far as he put it in motion through the simple pressing of a button; whereas for repairing the mechanism the hotel's machinists were used so exclusively that Giacomo, for example, in spite of his six months' service in the elevator, had never yet seen either the mechanism in the basement or the machinery in the elevator with his own eyes, although, as he expressly stated, he would have been very happy to. . . .

Man's alienation begins with his departure from nature through labor, through production. "Through it, nature appears as his product, his reality," Marx said in the *Economic and Philosophical Manuscripts*. In the labor product, man objectifies himself as a social being [*Gattungswesen*] "by duplicating himself not only intellectually, in his mind, but also really, through work, and thus seeing himself in a world which has been created by himself." This alienation, which is *necessary* to the development of the social being man, requires continual conquest, through which man in the process of his labor becomes conscious of himself and finds himself again in the product of his labor. The artisan is capable of that, but not the wage-laborer in the extensive division of labor in the capitalist mode of production. He cannot oppose the "act of alienation" through the act of a union with his work, with himself. Karl Marx characterized this "act of alienation" as:

1. The relation of the worker to the *product of his work* as an object which is foreign to him and has power over him. This relation is at the

same time his relation to the sensuous external world, to natural objects, as a world which is foreign to him and opposes him hostilely. 2. The relation of the work to the *act of production* within the *work.* This relation is the relation of the worker to his own activity as a foreign activity which does not belong to him, activity as suffering, power as impotence, creation as castration—the experience of the worker's *own* physical and spiritual energy and of his personal life—for what is life other than activity?—as an activity which is turned against him, independent of him and not belonging to him. This is *self-alienation,* like the alienation of the *thing.* . . .

Kafka's feeling for this alienation, his horror at such an antinatural situation, was intense, and his work is an endless variation on the theme of "activity as suffering, power as impotence, creation as castration. . . ." In "The Great Wall of China" it is emphasized how important it is constantly to give the workers laboring on a little part of the immense project a view of the whole thing. One could

not simply let the lower workers, who were intellectually far superior to their apparently minor task . . . cement stone to stone in an uninhabited mountainous region hundreds of miles from their homes for months or even for years; the hopelessness of such diligent labor, which even in the course of a long life could not reach the goal, would have made them despair, and above all, it would have made them more useless for the work. . . .

In a conversation with Janouch about Taylorism, that is, about the careful dissection of the labor process and the complete transformation of the laborer into a part of the machine, Kafka said, "Through that not only creation is sullied and humiliated, but above all man, who is a part of it. Such a Taylorized life is a hideous curse, out of which only hunger and misery can grow, instead of the desired riches and profits. That is progress. . . ." "Toward doom," Janouch continued. Kafka shook his head: "If only one could say that with certainty. But it is not sure. . . . The conveyor belt of life carries one somewhere, but one does not know where. Man is more a thing, an object, than a living being."

The more the division of labor progresses, the more powerful and complicated the technical, economic, and political apparatus of capitalism becomes, the more foreign the labor product and the act of production become to the worker. The social being man becomes not only specialized and fragmented a thousand times over; he becomes not only increasingly fragmentary and one-sided in his job; but he even becomes more and more divided into a "working person" and a "private person," who are usually completely alienated from one another. A job which has shrunk into a narrow "specialty" is usually not satisfying and is felt to lack "content." And usually the "private life," which has been abandoned to itself, also becomes devoid of "content"; it becomes stereotypical and predetermined by the anonymous "They." Participation in social life generally declines since, in the face of the gigantic and unapproachable power apparatus, codetermination and co-decision seem illusory. But since only the social, the collective, and the communal can unite the working person with the private person, desocialization completes alienation and the destruction of the human personality.

The growth of things beyond human dimensions, the petrifaction of the world of people to the world of things, the tendency of the means to become the end—since the victory of capitalism in the age of romanticism, all of this has called forth an ardent *demand for "directness."* To break through the hard crust of the "outer world" and to unite oneself "directly" with reality became a romantic desire. "Everywhere we seek the unconditional [*Unbedingte*]," wrote Novalis, "and we find only things [*Dinge*]." Shelley too: "It is never more desirable to cultivate literature than in times when the egoistic and calculating principle is supreme. Because the things of exterior life pile up, and the accumulation surpasses the ability to include them in the laws of human nature." It was in an aesthetic *"unio mystica,"* in "intuition," in a *"furore"* that the romantics hoped to return from alienation to unity with themselves and the world. The hope for this "other condition" and disappointment at the result become, in Kafka's dream of the angel, a grand vision of proclamation and reification.

In this dream the ceiling starts to fall apart: above it seemed to be hovering things which wanted to break through; one could already catch the outlines of what was going on: an arm reached out, a silver sword hovered up and down. It was intended for me; there was no doubt about that: a vision, intended to liberate me, was preparing itself. I jumped up onto the table to get everything ready, tore out the lamp and its brass tube and threw them onto the floor and pushed the table out of the middle of the room over to the wall. Whatever was going to come could sit right down on the carpet and tell me what it had to tell me. I had hardly gotten finished when the ceiling really broke open. Still from a great height—I had estimated it poorly—slowly in the twilight an angel in bluish violet cloths, wound around with golden cords, descended on huge, white, silkily shining wings, the sword held out horizontally in his raised arm. "So it's an angel!" I thought, "all day he's been flying to me, and I in my disbelief didn't know it. Now he will speak to me." I lowered my eyes. But when I raised them again, the angel was indeed still there, and he was hanging rather low under the ceiling, which had closed itself up again, but it wasn't a living angel, it was only a painted wooden figure from a ship's bow, like the ones that hang from the ceilings in sailor's dives. Nothing else. The pommel of the sword was intended to hold candles and to collect the melting wax. I had torn down the lamp; I didn't want to stay in the dark; there was still a candle available, so I climbed onto a chair, stuck the candle in the sword's pommel, lit it, and then sat late into the night under the pale light of the angel.

That is not only Kafka's characteristic union of intense vision and carefully portrayed detail, the concentrated prose in which one hears the rustling of poetry; it is not only the constantly recurring experience of the "other condition," the supersaturation of inspiration, from which only a dead angel remains as carrier of a poor candle; it is also a pregnant picture of reification, of the transformation of an expected directness into a lifeless means, of petrifaction into an object. The romantics had felt this shudder and given it form in all sorts of automatons, marionettes, and dead figures that gave a semblance of life. But Kafka was the first to perceive this petrifaction in the *everyday*, this dehumanization of the human, his reification. His artistic method resembles this angel with the sword in his hand who is suddenly frozen in flight and hangs motionless in space.

Angels become things, but things become living beings. Kafka reported about "Odradek," who comes from apostasy, rebellious and cut off, a thing-ghost:

At first it looks like a flat and star-shaped spool of thread, and indeed it seems to be covered with thread, but certainly they could only be old, torn off, knotted together but also unravelled pieces of thread of different kinds and colors. But it is not a spool; rather, from the middle of the star projects a little cross piece, and then there is another one attached to this one at a right angle. With the help of this latter piece on one side, and one of the points of the star on the other side, the whole thing can stand upright as if on two legs. . . .

This creature of fable that seems to be in a new way both funny and eerie, this Odradek, seems to be immortal, "but the idea that it should survive even me too is almost painful to me."

This thing that has escaped from man and is carrying on on its own seems in this form to be alarming but nevertheless innocuous. But in Theresa's story of the death of her mother, in *America*, things become murderous, in a murderous social system. The woman, almost unconscious from misery and exhaustion, plunges from the construction scaffolding:

Many bricks rolled after her, and finally, a long while later, somewhere a heavy board became loose and crashed down on her. Theresa's last memory of her mother was of her lying there with spread out legs in her checked skirt which had been left over from Pomerania, of how the unplaned board lying on her almost covered her up. She had recounted it in detail, which was otherwise not her habit; and just at irrelevant passages, such as in the description of the scaffold uprights, which each projected into the sky alone and for itself, she had had to stop with tears in her eyes. . . .

The board on the breast of the dead woman and the scaffold uprights projecting alone into the sky are presented in their death-dealing power within an inhuman society.

Kafka knew that this was the system of capitalism, but he also knew that this system had grown beyond the bounds of the capitalist and that it overcame him through the power of things. He was speaking with Janouch about a drawing by George Grosz and objecting to it for not being the whole truth:

The fat man rules the poor man within the framework of a particular system. But he is not the system itself. He is not even its ruler. On the contrary: the fat man wears chains too. . . . Capitalism is a system of dependencies, which go from inside to outside, from top to bottom and from bottom to top. Everything is dependent, everything is in chains. Capitalism is a condition of the world and the soul. . . .

This condition—Kafka was sure of that (as Rousseau had also been)—could not be reversed through the means of bourgeois democracy. The description of the nighttime election demonstration, which Karl Rossmann observes from a balcony, has not a word of commentary, and it allows us to recognize the purely formal nature of the procedure through the artistic method alone. Everything, in complete alienation, is seen from the outside as an accumulation of placards, spotlights, automobiles, music bands, propaganda, and the shouting of the opposition: "If the noise became too much for the leading men down below, then the drummers and trumpeters got the signal to intervene, and their crashing, endless flourish, executed with the utmost strength, covered up all the human voices right to the roofs of the houses." The ghostly realism of this portrayal consists in the very fact that in the battle of the huge American party apparatuses the content is lost and the drums and trumpets suppress the human voice. The content of the capitalist world is indicated—seemingly unintentionally, but therefore all the more effectively—on two balconies high above the election uproar: Karl Rossmann is the prisoner of two vagabonds who threaten him with the police, and on the neighboring balcony is the student, who has to work as a salesman all day long in order to be able to study at night—and their situation is not going to change no matter who is elected down below.

Milena, the only woman whom Kafka passionately loved, said: "For him life is something completely different from what it is for all other people; above all, money, the stock market, the currency exchange, a typewriter are completely mystical things for him and they are so in fact, but not for others. . . ." Mystical things? Are we here catching the mystic in the act? Long ago another had spoken about "sensory-extrasensory things," about their "mystic," their "arcane" character; and even the most hard-boiled has never dared to palm him off as a mystic—it was Karl Marx when he analyzed the "fetish character of commodities." In a commodity-producing society the labor product turns "into a social hieroglyph. Later, people seek to decipher the meaning of the hieroglyph, to get behind the secret of their own social product." Kafka had a sense of the meaning of the hieroglyph, but for him, the writer, it was decisive that he was able to *experience* the ghostly reality of the "sensory-extrasensory" things.

Kafka experienced the power of things over people in *Angst* and terror, the fragmentation of being into a reified, alienated "exterior world" and an ego abandoned to itself. The outer and the inner clock, he wrote in January 1932, no longer agree:

. . . the outer one ticks along at its usual pace. What else can happen but that the two different worlds separate, and they separate, or at least pull apart, in a terrible way. The ferocity of the inner movement may have different reasons; the most apparent is self-observation, which doesn't let any idea come to rest and flushes each one out, in order then, as an idea itself, to be flushed out by a new self-observation. . . .

As early as 1910 Kafka spoke about this relentless self-observation as "the way people now turn their telescopes toward the comet." In such self-observation, the ego can hardly find itself; it gets lost to itself. Kafka expressed this alienation of man from himself also by allowing his heroes to escape from their names: In *America* the hero is still called Karl Rossmann; in *The Trial* he is only Joseph K., and in *The Castle* all that is left is a K., the anonymous, the no man and the everyman. One letter to Milena he signed: "Yours (and now I am losing the name too; it has constantly gotten shorter, and now it is just: Yours).")

No other writer has expressed this negative, the total alienation of men, with a similar intensity. This intensity, it seems to me, this exactness of the terror, is very closely related to the superabundance of the negative, to one-sidedness and subjectivity. There are social situations in which it is not possible totally to grasp the new reality in literature; and if it were indeed possible, then the rounded picture would lose in its alarming intensity. Poetry is often ahead of prose in such situations—and how much underground poetry resounds through Kafka's prose! Much that is criticized as weakness in Kafka is on the contrary a component of his poetic power. *Buddenbrooks* did not penetrate so deeply into the darkness of the late capitalist world as the fragmentary novel *The Trial*. Thomas Mann reports on bourgeois development retrospectively (without understanding for the working class); Kafka looks ahead and discovers in today's detail the inferno of tomorrow; he heightens reality to an anticipatory nightmare, to the possibility which has not yet ripened in it. Let us take one such detail: the two men in *The Trial*, who come early one morning to arrest Joseph K., and those other two who accompany him to the stone quarry at the edge of the city to *liquidate* him there. Even then, when Kafka drafted these scenes, there was the knock on the door, the twin pair of police officers; but since it was mostly only criminals whom they arrested, the event seemed trivial. Kafka was no longer alive when these men, like the horsemen of the apocalypse, ranged through the world—and unfortunately not only through the capitalist world. To anticipate the most extreme possibilities in a detail, to have a presentiment of the growing independence of systems of power—only a writer of the most extreme sensitivity was capable of that, someone who saw behind the everyday the monstrous shadow of things to come.

With Walter Scott and other writers of the romantic period, the detail had the function of evoking the milieu with all its appurtenances, of acquainting the reader with customs and costumes, of dispensing cultural history in the work of art. But Kafka's preferred form of the parable, like Brecht's, precludes such broad-ranging description. Terseness, tautness, abstraction are aimed at. Attention is concentrated on details which point up essential parts of the problems. But even where the allegory is most visible, these details are not at all timeless, but recognizable as details of the time—indeed, even as details of the decaying Habsburg monarchy. The dreamlike world into which we are transported is not, as many interpreters have claimed, an impalpable and immutable "Being," or "eternal essence," a cosmic "universal" behind the reality; but rather, stretched between the poles of concrete details, it is recognizable as the social reality of our time.

[Kafka's fantastic satire parallels this reality. It would be a simplification of his polyvalent work if one wanted to grasp it *only* as satire. But since Kafka so far has been either celebrated as a mystic or damned as an irrealist who deforms reality, it seems appropriate to emphasize this satirical character of his work. He who is oppressed by the outside world—to the very point where it seems to be breaking in upon him—always saves himself by fleeing into the distance, from where the horrible presents itself as the comical, and fear of the grimace turns into satirical aggression. Günther Anders speaks of a "monstrously ironic adventure" and adds that Kafka was not up to this adventure. Apparently it was the vagueness, the indeterminacy of the standpoint, satiric objectification and trembling being-right-in-the-middle-of-it and the resulting confluence of opposite styles, that moved Anders to this judgment.

In his book *Mimesis*, Erich Auerbach points to the opposition in epics that existed in past millennia, and he juxtaposes Homer and the Bible:

On the one hand, externalized, uniformly illuminated phenomena, at a definite time and in a definite place, connected together without lacunae in a perpetual foreground; thoughts and feeling completely expressed; events taking place in leisurely fashion and with very little of suspense. On the other hand, the externalization of only so much of the phenomena as is necessary for the purpose of the narrative, all else left in obscurity; the decisive points of the narrative alone are emphasized, what lies between is nonexistent; time and place are undefined and call for interpretation; thoughts and feeling remain unexpressed, are only suggested by the silence and the fragmentary speeches; the whole, permeated with the most unrelieved suspense and directed toward a single goal (and to that extent far more of a unity), remains mysterious and "fraught with background."

The European novel learned from Homer as well as from the Bible, but Homer predominated. In his careful study of Kafka, *Beschreibung einer Form*, Martin Walser juxtaposes Kafka's epic principle to that of the Homeric epos. In the latter, the order of the world is "a continuum, in which everything has its place." The "extensive totality" of this continuum has lost its meaning in Kafka. In its place has stepped the "intensive totality" of man, whose existence "is threatened no longer in his actions, but in his simple *Dasein*." The empirical totality has disappeared through the "solipsistic reduction" which Kafka has accomplished. In *America* there are still references to an empirical world, but:

In *The Trial* and *The Castle* Kafka no longer refers to an available world. Through the development of his autonomous form-capacity, he has already overcome his subjectivity in advance of the work. What he now writes achieves an independent, objective being which, in its pure createdness, does not have to strive for any totality of empirical objects, but which in place of that achieves a totality of the forces which are decisive in human existence.

Walser's thesis that Kafka's works are closer to the epos than to the novel, which results from precise analyses of form, is worthy of serious consideration. The "intensive totality" of his works, their enclosed and independent reality, is undebatable. But I think it is untrue that in *The Trial* and *The Castle* Kafka no longer refers to an available world, that he has accomplished a "solipsistic reduction." One can come to such a conclusion only if one overlooks the eminently satirical character of these works. In fact, Kafka refers hundreds of times to the available (even if incredible) world of the Habsburg monarchy as a model of a world going to ruin. The world which

Swift created in *Gulliver's Travels* is also an enclosed and independent fantastic reality, but nevertheless it refers satirically to the England of its time. The new thing in Kafka's satire is its enormous subjectivity, the complete absorption of external reality into an inner one, whereby the "I" reproduces its counter-world in itself. But the "solipsism" is only apparent, for the intensive "counter-world" is parallel to an extensive, given, and feared reality which is recognized in satirical aggression, in "interpretomania," and in self-humiliation—just as the crushing powers in the unapproachable background parallel in their essence a still available father and parallel in their form the bureaucratic hierarchy of the Habsburg state.

Elements of the Bible and of Homer combine peculiarly in Kafka's work, but the Bible predominates. The basic element in this mixture of styles comes from the dark and not from the light, in other words, from that which is still in need of interpretation, not from that which has already been interpreted. Nevertheless, the concrete and characteristic detail of the external world has been worked out most carefully: that which is seen stands in bright light and in sharp contours before us; and it is only in going further that we lose sight of it in the indeterminate and ambiguous. But precisely this contradiction between precise detail and obscure connection parallels the social situation in which Kafka found himself, and this situation (not his experience in it) is portrayed with the objectivity of the fantastic satire.]

It is the method of the fantastic satire, this conscious deformation to the point of absurdity, which Kafka uses. Through the absurdity of the exaggeration the shocked reader perceives the world in which he lives not as a harmonious and acceptable one, but as deformed. The terrifying thing about this satire, the thing that reaches far beyond it, is the fact that the person experiencing the world does not confront it, like Gulliver, but rather sees himself infected by it, as a party to its guilt. And so no purifying laughter is reached. The comical, which is very present, remains stuck in black terror. Only a weak laughter cuts through the thick gloom. The satirist Kafka does not rise above the troubling world; he is right in the thick of it. But it is just from this involvement, this inability to master the world through angry laughter, that the penetrating power of the narration comes. So here is a writer who does not pretend to be omniscient or a god leading everything to the best, who does not suggest a happy end behind the downfall of his hero or a resurrection behind the crucifixion—but rather one who stumbles on, not knowing where it will end. This sense of being overwhelmed by a catastrophic reality, of being frozen in an eternally recurring experience—the world as a reflection from the mirror of the self—finds an artistic form which unites opposites: an extremely lyrical subjectivism with sober reporting. It is the final step in synthesizing the prose of Kleist and Stendhal, of passionate occupation with the self and of a cold, scientific style.

Kafka's hero, always the same, like Byron's or Stendhal's, is not a romantic hero, but a desperate petty bourgeois in the world of late capitalism. He would like to conform to society and applaud its everyday phenomena such as family, marriage and job—but it doesn't work. The breach is unbridgeable: business success and private happiness, social career and humane personality have become irreconcilable. Whoever keeps on striving in the vicious circle of professional success, awareness of duty, the wish for self-realization through withdrawing from society—he cannot be rescued unless he can jump over his own shadow. In Kafka's writing, the petty bourgeois protest is divested of all romanticism. The moralist who condemns not only his environment, but himself as well, rejects the pleasant but deceptive appearance. What is required is responsibility in irresponsible circumstances, dispensing with all romantic utopias.

In contrast to most writers of his generation, Kafka constantly dealt with the problem of work and profession, that is, with the great problems of the mechanized, industrialized, commercialized world. Horrified by the specialization, Taylorization, and fragmentation of work, Kafka senses the growing divergence between occupation and personality. This conscientious writer, who was not up to the double life of profession and literature, success in work and the desire for happiness, causes many of his heroes to fail because of this division: they are not satisfied with an occupation they feel to be senseless; they are alienated by it and by the relations between things, by their fellow human beings; they are overwhelmed by the vanity of their efforts.

In such stories as "The Metamorphosis" and "A Country Doctor," this motif is heightened into a nightmare, to aggression turned inward in which the defect in society is experienced as a personal failure, as an undefined guilt. The industrial worker, through solidarity, can fight against the unfulfilling nature of the work which is distintegrating his personality. But the still living, still thinking petty bourgeois who has not yet sunk into mental dullness is helpless in the face of this vacuum. He is a victim of society and has a bad conscience. To try to be a decent human being in a social pigpen causes guilt. The country doctor, by nature an isolated person, is vulnerable to the tragicomic contradiction between the idea of being the helper in a wide area and the poverty of his means. He clings to the idea of being a helper, wards off resignation, is ready to sacrifice his private life for his professional ethics, and is forced in the most cruel way to recognize the vanity of his efforts. It would be pedantic to demand of each of Kafka's dream pictures that it justify itself in black and white and do without its vacillating ambivalence. Nevertheless one can recognize in the "unearthly horses" which emerge from the pigpen a fantastic and melancholy satire on ideals which have become ghosts, which are no longer appropriate to social conditions: the categorical imperative, the bourgeois sense of duty, unconditional obedience when the signal sounds. Everything begins with a "false ringing of the night bell." Such an untested false ringing, the country doctor reckons, compels the member of a society which is not prepared to help the helper, in which the decent person's horse has died and in which only phantoms emerging from a pigsty are available as substitutes. We are dealing here with the nightmare of a writer, not with the recipe of a sociologist. Not one word says: "Defend yourself, country doctor! You need a living horse, not ideological ghosts!" But when the ghost horses, who carried him off so quickly, so unwillingly drag themselves through the infinite snow after the death of the patient, we hear the lament, the protest:

Naked, prey to the frost of this most unfortunate age, I, an old man, am driven around with an earthly coach and unearthly horses. My fur coat is hanging in the back of the coach; I can't reach it, and not one of the active churls among the patients lifts his finger. Deceived! Deceived![2]

It is the lament, the protest of him who has been cheated out of the dignity of his occupation; the sense of his life, the echo of a false alarm from the very beginning—not a call to revolution, but also not a recognition of the historically determined as an eternal *condition humaine;* rather, a rebellion against the coldness, the frost of "this most unfortunate age."

I do not presume to interpret in a few sentences the story "A Country Doctor," which is considered difficult. I merely wanted to point

2. "Ein Landarzt" in: Franz Kafka, *Erzählungen* (Frankfurt am Main, n.d.), p. 153.

to that circle of problems which is essential to Kafka and to which it belongs, and to his characteristic position between protest and guilt feelings. In his own crush between profession, private life, and self-realization, in that area of problems characteristic of a man who takes everything that he does seriously, problems which press for self-destruction, Kafka portrayed a central problem of this "most unfortunate age," this late bourgeois world, which pressed on him from all sides. But it is a characteristic of the great writer that his fundamental experiences are representative of basic problems of an age, that out of a fulness of details he is able to grasp those which are essential to a still undiscovered and still fragmentary new reality.

I spoke about that feeling of being equally guilty, the bad conscience of a man who cannot agree with the insanity of late bourgeois society but who is also not in a position rebelliously to transgress the limits of the law. The obscure, exciting parable "Before the Law" seems to me to reflect just this problem. The law is no longer a living being, but a petrified institution, no longer timely, only still intimidating. The guard repels the only one who as an individual requests entry, who is looking for his human rights as an individual. He threatens with his power, with the hierarchy of power: "I am powerful. And I am only the lowest guard. But from room to room there are guards. One more powerful than the other."[3] The searcher allows himself to be intimidated. The energetic individualism of the romantic age, the position of Byron, Shelley, Stendhal, is gone, the position of a post-revolutionary generation which to be sure did not wish to turn society around, but which was determined to challenge it. The feeling of the depleted petty bourgeois, who feels impotent in the face of the towers of power, is obedience, false obedience, the passive game of question and answer, and finally the attempt to bribe the guard instead of pushing him aside and entering through the door which is reserved for the individual ego. Individualism, once Promethean, has become impotent. Kafka portrays this critically. He does not condone the behavior of the one who capitulates in front of the guard. One cannot take everything the guard says as true. No, the priest answers in the great debate, "It is not necessary to accept everything as true, one must only accept it as necessary" (p. 160). But Joseph K. rebels against this attempt of the powerful and their ide-

3. Franz Kafka, *Der Prozess* (Frankfurt am Main, 1963), p. 155.

ologies to justify the *status quo*, even if it is no longer true, as necessary. "Melancholy opinion," says K., "the lie is turned into the world
order." But K. was "too tired to watch over all the consequences of
the story" (p. 161). The reader, however, is challenged to such consequences, to a different if not specific behavior. From such parables
as "The Chinese Wall" and "Josephine, the Singer" it is evident that
Kafka was not counting on individualism, but on a new community
to lead men back to themselves, to a law of life no longer alienated
from them. The essence of this community remained uncertain, but it
was not hope in the otherworldly—rather the vaguely felt possibility
that this world can become different.

In the fragmentary novel *The Trial* it is also a question of a worldly
reality. If the harp player in Goethe complains to the "heavenly powers": "You make the poor man guilty, and then you leave him to his
pain,"[4] Kafka answers in this novel: they are not heavenly, but earthly
powers which make him guilty. But it is no more as it was in the romantic world of the harp player, of Mignon, the hypertensing of feelings, the challenge to the law that becomes guilt, but rather the ero-
sion of feeling, subordination to the law of the ambitious bourgeois
world with its high evaluation of business success. The dirty, corrupt,
deformed power system that calls Joseph K. to its accounts, this
ragged justice worn to the bone that presumes to represent an ethical
world order, is constructed as a terrifying caricature by means of
fantastic satire. But this rotten outside is only the reflection of Joseph's withered personality, and Joseph K. is only a product of this
outside; and since society and petty bourgeois egoism mesh in such a
spectral reality, the one who at the beginning defended himself is
defenseless against the powers; when the black gentlemen pick the
condemned up it is clearly said: "K. walked rigidly between them, the
three of them were interlocked in a unity which would have brought
all three down together had one of them been knocked over. It was
a unity such as can hardly be formed except by lifeless matter."[5] For
Kafka sees the bourgeois world as a lifeless, practically extinct world,
and also those who are caught in it, who protest only individually,
but who are not building a new community.

In our circles one frequently hears the question: What do we need

4. J. W. Goethe, *Wilhelm Meisters Lehrjahre* in *Poetische Werke* (Berliner
Ausgabe) (Berlin, 1962), p. 141.
5. Franz Kafka, *Der Prozess*, p. 162.

Kafka for? Is he good for us? Although such bold utilitarianism—as if it were a function of literature to spur us on to work and to evoke cheery-faced optimism—should be fundamentally rejected, I should like to maintain that we do need Kafka. We need him not only because he is a great writer and because the socialist world should not ignore any writer of his stature, but also because he stimulates us to passionate thought about the problems of modern reality. Even the intellectual preoccupation with Kafka's work is meaningful and forces us to a deeper and more refined argumentation.

We should no longer refuse a visa to this writer, who more originally and more shockingly than many others portrayed alienation, reification, and dehumanization in the late capitalist world. To be sure: it was not with optimism that he participated in the burial of a catastrophic world, but with fear and desperation. But were fear and desperation so completely inappropriate to a time whose greatest event was the October revolution? Weren't there in this revolutionary age two terrible world wars, counterrevolution, concentration camps, mass torture, gas chambers, cannibalism applied with the highest technical perfection? Did it contradict the ideas of humanism to see this society mocking such ideas in the pale light of the inferno and to damn it as antihuman and ghostly without tacking on the hope that everything would work out in the end anyway?

The writer is not obligated to suggest solutions. His question marks are often richer in content than frequent and too boldly printed exclamation marks. *Hamlet* too still owes us the solution—or is Fortinbras supposed to be the solution, the sword as opposed to the mind? And what solutions does Stendhal have to offer, the greatest writer of the romantic period? Or Thomas Mann, who is so often called onto the field against Kafka? Through his total negation, through his implacable "This cannot go on!" Kafka challenges us to the negation of the negation. The solitary person who only as an individual defends himself against the powers is always the guilty one, the one condemned by the invisible court. He is neither capable of defending himself effectively, or averting his fate in impotent self-defense, nor can he sneak into the castle of the rulers to earn their recognition by recognizing their evil, antihuman counterworld. Whoever is nothing but empty individuality, whoever rebels from the shadows of social conditions against them, is powerless and doomed. His Being-Alone in every decisive moment is not only fate but also fault. This is the way that Kafka felt it and portrayed it. Despite the lonely person's tendency to absolutize what is socially determined, he did not transpose social reality to a mystical being. It is we as Marxists who should liberate the work of a great writer from such false interpretations. For the prejudice against Kafka comes not so much from the text as from the interpretation.

In the final analysis, the objection to Kafka comes down to the fact that he was not a Marxist, that he underestimated the power of the working class and the effectiveness of socialist revolution. But one could make the same objection to Thomas Mann and other contemporaries of Kafka, and it would be just as inappropriate in appreciating the quality of their achievements. In a world in which such diverse contradictions are interacting, not only is a variety of artistic methods necessary, but different social and individual standpoints are unavoidable. There is a good reason why the works of such problematic writers as Kleist and Dostoevsky are again being published in the socialist world. It seems to me ridiculous to deny to Kafka what one grants to the others. I hope this conference will contribute decisively to rescuing Kafka from the arena of the cold war, to no longer reserving him to the commentators, but to turning him over to the socialist reader.

I appeal to the socialist world: Bring Kafka's work back from its involuntary exile! Give it a permanent visa!

Comments on the Marxist Interpretation of Franz Kafka

ALEXEJ KUSÁK

In my contribution I wish to concern myself with the problem of the Marxist interpretation of Franz Kafka's work, that is, I want to evaluate the views of some Marxists who have occupied themselves with Kafka, and to indicate my own ideas.

To me Kafka seems a huge, monumental realist of the twentieth century who understood better than many so-called realists how to grasp and to typify not only characters and situations, but also human relations, the demonic in the world, dehumanization—and also the counter movement, the protest, the cry, the angry pain.

The way Kafka expressed the world, how suggestively he revealed the truth about people, how he discovered the movement of reality in its general tendencies and particular phenomena—for me that is the fundamental criterion of his whole work. As a Marxist, I am not the least bit interested—at least not for the purpose of a basic judgment—in what Kafka himself thought about his work, in what he directed to be destroyed and why he did it. I cannot agree with Paul Reimann, who superfluously makes a problem of this fact, nor with the German scholar Helmut Richter, who even makes Kafka's last will the basic criterion of his work. In fact, Kafka's position in respect to his own work is nothing unusual in the history of art. If we wanted to be consistent, we would have to apply the same criterion to Gogol or Tolstoy, who also condemned their work at the ends of their lives. And if we wanted to be even more consistent, we would have to judge all

Alexej Kusák, "Bemerkungen zur marxistischen Interpretation Franz Kafkas," previously published in *Franz Kafka aus Prager Sicht 1963* (Prague, 1965), pp. 169-80.

95

works according to the evaluation of their creators; we would have to consider equally what they did not want printed and what many prolific writers most certainly did and do want printed. We have already said that one can in no way interpret a work through a last will and testament. Let us expand that: neither can one interpret a work with the aid of the author's statements or his diaries. I do not claim that one cannot use them as illustrations or examples to clarify this or that in Kafka's life, but one cannot make valid conclusions about his work from this or that entry. I consider such a method unscientific, since it leads in any case to the purest idealism. After all, it is the duty of the scientist to reveal every mystification or self-stylization and self-interpretation.

So neither Kafka's will nor his statements help us to explain his work. Where is the key that will unlock the doors of his secret? Is it found perhaps in the fact that Kafka was from Prague? Here we have arrived at one of the basic questions around which the discussion has been centered for some time. It has to do with Eduard Goldstücker's view that "one can say something meaningful about a number of Kafka problems only from the standpoint of Prague." Certainly Goldstücker did not mean that this can be done only from Prague because there happen to be particularly brilliant Germanists and literary scholars living here. He has something different in mind with these frequently repeated statements: he is of the opinion that Kafka must be "located," that one must study his life and work in connection with all the historical and social factors. Well, we would understand that to be the self-evident presupposition of all scientific work—to begin by studying the material, by knowing everything about the environment and the time. But we wouldn't waste time talking about it, and even a scholar living in Greenland, for example, can do that if he just collects the relevant literature and studies the historical material for a while at the place. But how does that square with Goldstücker's view that one can see Kafka validly only from Prague? Is Prague perhaps blessed with a particular ether which only Praguers can recognize? Can one unlock Kafka's secret only with the key to Prague's Primator?

If we chose to calculate according to the formula "Kafka equals a reflection of Prague at the beginning of the century," then a knowledge of the sociology of Prague would have to be enough to understand his work, and then everything else would be superfluous—every further interpretation, examining Kafka's typology, his artistic methods, etc. And then for the reader who does not know the Prague milieu, there would be nothing behind Kafka's fables but the fables themselves, and whoever wanted to see something more general in them should hold his tongue, for here we are on guard, we, the old inhabitants, countrymen and eyewitnesses, and we, as Kafka's only friends, will jealously defend the suggestive power of the local color and the secret of the Austrian empire against all uninitiated compilers of perverse interpretations.

But with that we have arrived at the end of any scientific investigation, and it is to this point that making a fetish of Kafka's local roots leads us. A vulgar study of the genesis of Kafka's work is incapable of answering the principal question of Kafka research: How is it that this reflection of Prague in the early twentieth century is so interesting to readers today who do not know that Prague and who are not even at all interested in Prague between 1910 and 1920? What is the difference between Kafka's work and the genre scenes of Ewer, Strobl, Meyrink, and a host of other writers who used Kafka's Prague as their theme? To absolutize the sociology of Prague in Kafka's work is equivalent to reducing that work to the level of genre scenes of the Prague milieu. We must proceed from the genesis to an examination of the structure of his work, and thereby to an understanding of his significance and influence. Otherwise we will land in Taine's positivism and at most learn something interesting about the cultural history of Prague. But such a perspective would prevent us from seeing the essence of Kafka's art, the secret of his appeal, his present and future effect.

In his book *Brief against Misunderstood Realism*, the important Hungarian Marxist aesthetician Georg Lukács works with a similar method of interpreting, but he combines it in a very interesting way with views on the form of Kafka's work. In a prominent place in his study of Kafka, Lukács writes:

The diabolical character of the world of modern capitalism, and man's impotence in the face of it, is the real subject matter of Kafka's writings. His simplicity and sincerity are, of course, the product of complex and contradictory forces. Let us consider only one aspect. Kafka wrote at a time when capitalist society, the object of his *Angst*, was still far from the high mark of its historical development. What he described and "demonized" was not the truly demonic world of Fascism, but the world of the Hapsburg Monarchy. *Angst*, haunting and indefinable, is perfectly reflected in this vague, ahistorical, timeless world, steeped in the atmosphere of Prague. Kafka profited from his historical position in two ways. On the one hand, narrative detail gains from being rooted in the Austrian society of that period. On the other hand, the essential unreality of human existence, which it is his aim to convey, can be related to a corresponding sense of unreality and foreboding in the society he knew. The identification with the *condition humaine* is far more convincing than in later visions of a diabolical, *angst*-inspiring world, where so much has to be eliminated or obscured by formal experimentation to achieve the desired ahistorical, timeless image of the human condition. But this, though the reason for the astonishing impact and lasting power of Kafka's work, cannot disguise its basically allegorical character. The wonderfully suggestive descriptive detail points to a transcendent reality, to the anticipated reality—stylized into timelessness—of fully developed imperialism. Kafka's details are not, as in realism, the nodal points of individual or social life; they are cryptic symbols of an unfathomable transcendence. The stronger their evocative power, the deeper is the abyss, the more evident the allegorical gap between meaning and existence.[1]

Lukács is touching on several questions here. He views Kafka from the standpoint of social psychology—of a strong but deformed artistic ego that creates the world in its own image. The *Angst* of the petty bourgeois—that is, according to Lukács, the basic element in Kafka's personality. It is clear that this idea of Kafka is only a somewhat differently conceived sociological view—for Lukács this *Angst* is the expression of the social situation of the writer, only another finding in the examination of an art work from the point of view of social determination.

But other ideas of Lukács' are more stimulating: especially the problems of Kafka's so-called "prophecies" and of his form, which are also in other Marxist works on Kafka.

The two problems are intimately related, but differently from the way Lukács represents it. I must say right away that every interpretation that has to do with Kafka's premonitions and prophecies, that sees one of Kafka's merits in his ability to predict that the ticking clock leads to the exploding bomb, that—to say it frankly—he intuited the coming of Hitler and the horrors of fascism—all these interpreta-

---

1. Georg Lukács, *Wider den Missverstandenen Realismus* (Hamburg, 1958). The English quotation here is cited from Georg Lukács, *Realism in Our Time: Literature and the Class Struggle*, tr. John and Necke Mander (New York, 1964), p. 77f.

tions seem inexact and incorrect to me, because they ascribe intentions and abilities to Kafka that he did not possess. In my opinion, the matter is very simple. Kafka did not need to prophesy any horrors; he lived right in the middle of them; he was only more sharply aware than others of the murderous dullness of bureaucratic society. The horrors of fascism are essentially nothing more than the concentrated and more clearly appearing horrors of ordinary life in the peaceful bourgeois world. Things are destroyed, lives are destroyed in the one as in the other; the forms are different, but the essence remains the same. But the mutilation of life in the midst of bureaucratic society is largely concealed and it offers less opportunity to direct rebellion and struggle than the much more open and undisguised violence of fascism.

The violence of capitalism, which consists in its turning authentic life into an alienated existence in the shadows, cannot, then, be so easily revealed; if it could, then the fight against capitalism today would be only a chapter in the textbook of history. Kafka's merit does not consist in his having *predicted* some future horrors, but rather in having concretely *seen* the horrors of his own time. And now it is the task of Kafka researchers to determine the means which helped him to concretize this vision. Kafka used a particular kind of parable, and a majority of the Marxists who try to explain him view that as a fault, a transgression against realism. But I am of the contrary opinion: that Kafka worked with this form because he wanted to grasp more reality, because he was a greater realist than those who castigate him. For Kafka this form was a means of typifying, concentrating, demystifying events which he experienced and observed. Literary historians can document for us that the literary form of the parable has a venerable tradition both before and after Kafka: the Bible, Swift, Cervantes, Brecht, and Hemingway—I am taking only some of the best-known works and authors at random. In his study of Kafka, Ernst Fischer[2] indicated that the use of this form has to do with a certain crisis situation of society. (Kafka was well aware of the crisis of his society. In a letter to Milena he writes: "My world collapses; my world rises. . . . How will we go on living?"[3] In such a crisis situation, great phenomena of alienation arise. How should art react to them? In his *The Dialectics of the Concrete*, Karel Kosík wrote:

2. Ernst Fischer, *Von Grillparzer zu Kafka* (Vienna, 1963). [See here, pp. 78-85 and 86-88. *Ed.*]
3. Franz Kafka, *Briefe an Milena* (Frankfurt am Main, 1960), p. 71.

The everyday world that we know is not the known and recognized world. So that it can be *presented* in its reality, it must be stripped of its intimately fetishized familiarity and revealed in its alienated brutality. . . . For man to see the truth of his alienated everyday life, he must gain distance from it and divest it of its quality of seeming known; he must do "violence" to it. In what sort of society, and in what kind of world must men "become" lice, dogs, and apes so that their true character can be adequately expressed? In what "violent" metaphors and allegories must man and his world be *presented*, so that they *see* their own faces and *recognize* their own world? It seems to us that one of the major principles of modern film, art, literature, and theater is the "violence" done to the everyday, the destruction of the pseudo–concrete.[4]

That, I believe, is an accurate description of Kafka's creative procedure. In a similar way, Brecht justifies the so-called artistic alienation as an aggressive answer to social alienation. From this point of view, Lukács' conclusions about Kafka's form seem hardly valid to me. Lukács measures Kafka with the yardstick of critical realism. For example, he investigates the use of the detail in Kafka, compares Kafka's details with the details of the critical realists, and he concludes: the more expressive Kafka's details are, in other words the more realistic Kafka is according to the method of critical realism, the farther he is from reality, the more he tends toward the nihilistic abyss. This whole business is exemplary proof of how dangerous it is to apply the criteria of one literary type and era to those of another. Lukács did not understand that Kafka's work is a great literary model, that it is an achievement which approaches reality more deeply and more effectively than many works which grasp reality in the manner of critical realism. Just as modern physics and chemistry must make use of formulas and models when they press on to a reality which can no longer be grasped by the senses, modern art and literature are also forced to approach certain realities through the aid of models. That is not a quirk of the authors, not simply a desire to be different, but a simple necessity if an essential piece of concealed reality is to be revealed.

Instead of understanding that this was something new in art—which is the precondition of a valid partisan position based on the correct epistemological function of art—some Marxists regard this work with

4. Karel Kosík, *Dialektika Konkrétního, Studie O Problematice Člověka a Světa* (Prague, 1963), p. 60.

mistrust and condemn it from various viewpoints. The Polish literary critic Stefan Żółkiewski, in his book *The Perspectives of Literature in the Twentieth Century*,[5] differentiates between a creationistic and a realistic technique of portrayal, counting Kafka, Camus, Dürrenmatt, Beckett, and others among the creationists. He does not reject them wholesale; in fact he even recommends that so-called realists adopt several formal innovations of the creationists, claims that their technique can enrich realism, etc. That is of course paradoxical—Żółkiewski does not see the most important thing: the change in content, which has revolutionary significance for literature. He sees something positive in the technique, the form, which is secondary and only an aid. And he even recommends that it be taken over by the realists who are supposed to continue the tradition of Stendhal and Balzac, who, as he says, represented social situations as faithfully as possible by piling up details from life and customs. And finally he condemns literature which creates symbolic situations and thereby supposedly leads us astray. In order to support his thesis, Żółkiewski quotes the French Catholic critic Pierre de Boisdeffre, who naturally has the same opinion: bourgeois or socialist realism is for him the expression of a society's will to live; symbolism is connected with a society which does not believe in itself.

   M. Pierre de Boisdeffre (whom Goldstücker also values, as we can see from his contribution) has the capacity to see things very precisely and in sharp contours: literature close to the shepherds of God's flock has a wise exponent in him. From Żółkiewski's division of literature into two parts, one which is realistic and one which presents models, it is only a short step to the most vulgar Kafka interpretations like the one which Howard Fast once produced in his book *Literature and Reality*.[6] For Fast, Kafka is a writer who sits near the top of the "cultural dungheap of reaction," one whose models (Fast quotes "The Metamorphosis") diligently evoke fear and disgust, who establishes in his thinking the equation: man and the cockroach are the same. According to Fast, this model is part of that enormous process carried out by the ruling class and which can only be defined as a confusion and inversion of the essence of objective reality. I quote Fast not out of posthumous piety, but because this view has not yet

   5. Stefan Żółkiewski, *Perspektywy Literatury XX Wieku* (Warsawa, 1960).
   6. Howard Fast, *Literature and Reality* (New York, 1950). [See Fast's essay, "The Metamorphosis," reprinted here on pp. 12-14. *Ed.*]

completely died out; it keeps reappearing in various versions—and not only in Kafka's case. It is paradoxical that this interpretation does not proceed from some sociology of Kafka, or from an analysis of his forms, or from placing him in a particular tendency of bourgeois literature, but rather that it correctly aims at evaluating the effect and influence of his works. For this complicated task it is equipped with tools which could have been borrowed from an archeological museum; and in its naive directness (in which it sees something like a propagandistic merit), it runs straight into the quicksand of subjectivism and idealism. In its enthusiasm it forgets, for example, that such an incontrovertibly great literature as the classical tragedy also aroused pity and fear—apart from such literary midgets as the Bible and other works which demonize reality. It forgets also that since Aristotle we have had the concept of the so-called catharsis, which is inseparably connected with the intended effects of such fear-arousing works.

In coming to the end of my interpretation, I should like to present my view of Kafka's work and of the possibility of a truly Marxist interpretation of it. For me, Kafka is a brilliant tragedian of modern reality, who also understood how to use satiric methods for his purpose. One cannot explain his works exclusively through references to Prague and the local milieu. For me, Kafka is the great poet of man's alienation in the modern industrial society. In that lies the secret of his relevance and of his wide validity. But one must not decipher him merely on this general philosophical plane—many of those who are still vulgarizing Kafka today would agree with that: rather, one must explain him in the context of the individual motifs of his works, in the nature of his characters and situations. As Marxists we must see not only how reality affects Kafka, but also how Kafka can help us to sort out reality. We should clarify how Kafka perceives reality, and if we understand how to interpret that in a Marxist way, then we should also not fail to live according to it.

In Kafka's work, the center lies in his creating types of situations in the alienated reality that struggling people get into; in typifying the feeling of the absurdity of human existence, which is the result of what Ernst Fischer called, in Tieck's phrase, the "loss of reality."

We live our lives, and in them something so peculiar happens that we can call it nothing less than a *Kafkaesque situation*. As if behind our backs things had hatched a conspiracy against us—and it is not our ineptitude which is to blame; it is not that things have simply slipped through our clumsy fingers. There is rather more of our cleverness, of our perfect organization, in what brings us into such absurd situations.

So we cannot explain the fact that Kafka reaches over into our time simply by referring to the analogous continued relevance of great art works of the past. In that more general situation, Kafka's particular and specific significance for our day is lost. For the fact that Kafka is also the poet of our absurdities, that Kafkaesque situations are the model for particular situations in socialist countries during the time of the personality cult—all that testifies for Kafka, for his brilliant ability to typify, that is, for his artistic method. With its help he was able to perceive that a certain degree of opacity in social relations and absolutizing institutional power every day gives rise to situations in which innocent people are accused of crimes they haven't committed, in which it is not necessary to accept everything as true, in which we must only accept it as necessary, and in which the lie establishes itself on the throne of authority.

Paul Reimann wrote: "In Kafka we do not see the discoverer of new worlds, but, on the contrary, the shipwrecked explorer."[7] I should like to say here that I do not see the shipwrecked explorer in Kafka, but rather the discoverer of new worlds.

7. Paul Reimann, foreword to the Czech edition of the novel *Amerika* by Franz Kafka (Prague, 1962), pp. 7-23.

Kafka and Modern Art

ROGER GARAUDY

[. . .]

Studying the work of Franz Kafka seems important to me because it illuminates the broader, principal questions of art in our time.

Every real work of art expresses a certain form of the presence of man in the world.

That has two consequences: there is no art which is not realistic, that is, which does not have any relation to external, independent reality; a definition of this realism is extremely complicated because the presence of man in the midst of reality, as its motivating force, cannot be denied.

Baudelaire remarked that poetry is the real-est reality, which only in the Beyond achieves its full truth.

The definition of realism can only proceed from the basis of works, and is never prior to them.

Although the value of scientific perception can be judged only on the basis of already known laws of dialectics, it is not possible to measure the value of artistic productivity on the basis of criteria derived from previously created works.

We can derive the criteria of realism from the works of Stendhal and Balzac, of Courbet and Repin, of Tolstoy and Martin du Gard, of Gorky and Mayakovsky. But what if the works of Saint-John Perse, Kafka, or Picasso do not fulfill these criteria? What should we do then? Should we exclude them from realism, that is, from art? Should we not rather expand the definition of realism, discover in it—in the light of works characteristic of our century—new dimensions which make it possible to include all these new contributions in the heritage of the past?

We have consciously chosen the second way. . . .

Excerpted from Roger Garaudy, "Kafka, die moderne Kunst und wir" in *Franz Kafka aus Prager Sicht 1963* (Prague, 1965), pp. 199-207.

To demand, in the name of realism, that a work of art must reflect reality in its whole breadth, must sketch the historic path of a certain time or a certain people and express its basic tendencies as well as future perspectives: that is a philosophical, and not an aesthetic demand.

A work of art can also provide a very incomplete testimony about the relation of people to the world in a given time; it can even represent a strongly subjective testimony which can nevertheless be authentic and serious.

For example, a writer can feel this or that aspect of alienation, and express it very well without discovering its causes and the ways of overcoming it—and nevertheless still be a great writer.

In Baudelaire and Rimbaud I do not find the whole lawful development of their century—but do they not nevertheless belong among the greatest discoverers of new territory?

One hopes that the philosophical and political thinking of a writer or an artist are on the same niveau as his talent. But if we limit ourselves to this one criterion then we do not judge the writer as a writer, but as an historian, politician, or philosopher.

One hopes that the writer has a clear idea of the future, because then he will be able to give his work a militant mission. But if we limit ourselves to this one criterion, then we risk repeatedly having to pose Baudelaire's question: namely, whether the honorable and virtuous writers are at all capable of awakening a love of virtue. The moral nature of real art does not come from some kind of recipe but rather from the fact that this kind of art awakens the moral sensitivities of people.

Marxism does not disregard the special nature of artistic creation.

The basic thesis of materialism and—in art—of realism is this: it is not consciousness which determines life but life which determines consciousness. . . . Consciousness (*Bewusstsein*) can never be anything other than conscious being (*bewusstes Sein*)—it in no way implies a mechanical determination of the relationship between consciousness and life.

It would be absurd to trace the *Weltanschauung* of a person from his class position. With regard to social class, Marx was a petty bourgeois and Engels a grand bourgeois. Their *Weltanschauung*, however, was not that of their class. That does not mean that any given *Weltanschauung* can just crop up at any time and in any place. As long as a revolutionary reality does not exist, a revolutionary theory is not possible. Marxism could not develop out of previous utopias and liberate itself from them until the working class appeared as an autonomous historical force. Only then did an *understanding of historical development* permit us to understand completely the revolutionary *Weltanschauung* from the point of view of this developing reality.

Does that perhaps mean that it makes no difference that, say, Kafka's writings are the work of the son of a Jewish tradesman in Prague at the time of the Austro-Hungarian monarchy, at the time of the decay of capitalism? Certainly not. Studying the historical prerequisites which are the source of Kafka's thinking is very important, because all the material of his artistic creation is drawn from this lived experience. But this initial perception has more the character of a question than of an answer. A work of art is not simply the sum of various forces. It is the universal answer to a whole complex of questions which are posed to the artist by his time, the atmosphere of family, society, religion, culture, his personal position in life and in work, his love life—in fact by his whole life. This answer is something different from and more than the sum of the circumstances which determined it. To understand Kafka means first to free his own unique initiative, his independent answer, from the sum of all influences. That is, however, an incomplete answer, incapable of dealing with his time and the laws of its development. With regard to his social origin, Kafka was a bourgeois like Marx; but in contrast to Marx, he never got beyond the perspectives of his class (or, rather, beyond the fact that this class had no perspectives). Kafka, contemporary of the Great Socialist October Revolution and of the powerful workers' movements of the postwar period, remained caught in exactly that alienation which he himself pointed to. He was not able to draw revolutionary conclusions from his knowledge of alienation, although he gave extremely moving artistic expression to that knowledge. So it is extremely important to consider that Kafka was a bourgeois, to consider the concrete conditions under which he lived in Prague, in the Jewish community, in the family, and so forth, without, however, forgetting that the requisite study of the conditions of his life is neither an explanation nor a valid judgment.

Marx warns us against the mechanical and undialectical conception of the relationship between base and superstructure and enables us to understand that a work of art created in the epoch of the historical decay of a particular class does not necessarily have to be decadent.

This complicated dialectic of the relationship of a work to reality and to life is the main object of Marxist aesthetics.

The realism of our day is a creator of such myths, an epic, a promethean realism.

A work of art is at every time dependent on work and myth. Work means the real power, technology, knowledge, discipline, social structure—in a word, everything that has already been done or is just now being done. Myth means the concrete and personally colored consciousness of what still remains to be done in the as yet unmastered areas in nature and society.

When he mentions myth as a "mediator" between base and superstructure, Marx emphasizes the role of the presence of man as the most important element in the definition of artistic reality. In doing that, he really precludes every narrow conception of realism—because a reality which includes man is not only everything that it is, but also that which it not yet is, which it still must become, that which springs from the dreams of individuals and from the myths of nations.

Only in the sense of this perspective, it seems to me, does Kafka's work attain its full meaning for the Marxist, its relevant meaning, its meaning for us.

This sense can be grasped only through a simultaneous inner and outer analysis and criticism in which three principal levels of his vision of the world must be distinguished:

1) the experienced world and its conflicts;
2) the inner world and its ambiguity;
3) the constructed world and its contradictions.

[. . .] Kafka experienced this world as conflict. As a Jew among Germans, as a speaker of German among Czechs, as a writer who was up against his businessman father, as an official among bureaucrats for whom he felt only antipathy, and finally as a man who passionately loved life and health and who was ground down by his illness, Kafka found in the world a prolonged experience of division and tragedy.

Kafka was well aware of his division as that of a man split to the very roots of his being. In his journal we find the entry that it was a frightful dual existence for him which apparently could end only in insanity.

The Marxists have demonstrated that this conflict is ultimately a matter of class character. As a consequence of his personal position,

Kafka experienced the class conflicts, and the alienation which they produced, in an amplified form.

A psychoanalytic explanation is powerless here: the conflict with his father is no illustration of psychoanalytic theses, but rather its opposite, because whereas for the psychoanalyst all further conflicts are anticipated in the first conflict with the father, in Kafka's case the conflict with his father is only a summary and a continuation of social tensions.

Let us look at Kafka's inner world. We could define it as the battlefield of his constant fight against alienation—without his ever having been able to free himself from his alienation. From that derives his tragic character and his ambiguity.

Kafka wrote in his journal: "I have powerfully absorbed . . . that which is negative in my time." And it is true that, even at the price of his self-destruction, he pursued this fight ceaselessly, in which he was finally defeated and confronted the dreamless sleep of alienation with his sleepless dreams.

But the dividedness of his inward life rests on the following dilemma: did his refusal come from the position of revolt, or from the position of religion?

The theologians have speculated very diligently with this dividedness.

The Jewish theologians supposed that they had found in Kafka the last prophet of Israel; the Catholics, such as Rochefort in France, speculated that they had discovered in him a *rebellious soul touched by grace*, and they did everything to compel him to be baptized; the Protestant theologians wanted to make him a brother of Kierkegaard or a disciple of Karl Barth; and still others connected his work with the writings of negative theology.

No doubt Kafka's work does have a religious dimension, too. His sentiments and his way of thinking, his whole inner world, had been formed by Judaism and by reading Pascal, Dostoyevsky, Léon Bloy, Kierkegaard, and above all the Bible. His study of Hebrew, of the Talmud and of the Hasidic tradition, his enthusiasm for the Jewish religious theater—they are witness to the powerful attraction exerted on him by the world of faith, as the most tragic and most personally experienced form of the efforts to overcome. But Kafka is not a mystic: he does not put a face on whatver it is that is behind people. God touches human life only through his absence: to Kafka, he is always only that which people do not have, the feelings of the inadequacy of the world, the negation, the opponent, the obverse of all dreams of humanity.

In Kafka we do not find a single existentialist thought, no belief that the tragic is a kind of metaphysical statute of humanity, and an eternal one at that. He experiences the dividedness, but he passionately longs to escape it, even if he is not capable of finding an exit. He defines the writer as one who seeks happiness.

Kafka's inner world, his ambiguity, is made of that kind of thing. He is not an optimist, for he neither sees nor demonstrates any means of changing the world and rooting out the alienation. But he is not a pessimist, either, because he doesn't accept for one moment the absurdity and the damnation of the world. He is not a reconciliationist.

Kafka is not a revolutionary. He awakens in people the consciousness of their alienation; his work, in making it conscious, makes repression all the more intolerable, but he does not call us to battle nor draw any perspective. He raises the curtains on a drama, without seeing its solution. With all his might he hates the apparatus of repression and the deception that says its power is God-given.

If Kafka's message is still so alive today, if so many men and women recognize in him their own problems and the pictures of their own lives, then that is because we are still living in a world of alienation and because the socialist world, too—even though it demonstrates the perspective of the elimination of alienation and the arrival of a perfect human—is still only in the initial stages of its struggle and still has its own contradictions and alienation in it.

Kafka is not a despairing person—he is a witness. I repeat—he is not a revolutionary. He is an awakener of the sense of responsibility.

His work expresses his attitude toward the world; it is neither a resigned copy of the world nor utopian anticipation. He neither wants to explain nor change the world. He points to its inadequacies and poses a challenge to overcome them.

The world which Kafka created, his work, expresses the attempt to overcome the conflict of his life and of the world. Literary creation is for him the technique of overcoming alienation. Writing is the opposite of alienation.

Kafka is completely aware of his responsibility. He feels entrusted with his mission—the mission of seeking the law and of proclaiming. But he is only a negative Messiah, who points to the inward disorderliness of the world without being able to show us the Promised Land. He condemns illusions; he de-mystifies the *status quo*. He awakens in everyone a longing for the true law and the true life. He gives us the feeling that something is *not in order* in our world, that there are paths without a goal and goals without a path.

The major themes of his work are: 1) the animal-theme as the theme of awakening: man is a being that despairs of his own life ("A Report to an Academy," "The Metamorphosis," "The Burrow"); 2) the search-theme: the search for a new and true life (*The Trial, The Castle*); and 3) the theme of the incomplete, in all his works. These themes are objective expressions and in a certain sense projections of his inner life. In his great works Kafka systematically shrinks from a description of his inner life. He only presents objects which evoke his impressions, obstacles which his longing runs up against. He does this with the ruthless precision of the transcript of a trial.

In opposition to the false order of earth and heaven, he awakens a longing for a real law of life and of humanity. In that way Kafka leads us to the limits of alienation. He himself defined his work as an attack at the border. He tirelessly attacks our borders, without succeeding in crossing them. It is not an accident that his three great works (*America, The Trial, The Castle*) remained incomplete. They are the picture of our life, they are the starting positions on the track toward infinity, toward the attainment of truly human dimensions for man, dimensions of the infinitude of his history, whose representation is limitless. Exactly in that does Kafka have something to say to us Communists. [. . .]

Kafka's greatness lies in the fact that he succeeded in creating a mythical world which forms one complete whole with the real world. Reality in art is, namely, a creation that, thanks to the presence of man in it, re-forms everyday reality. Just as—at the same time—the cubist painters discovered, by means of a conscious transposition, the inherent poetry in the most ordinary things, Kafka created a fantastic world out of the building blocks of this world, which he simply arranged according to different laws. Kafka cannot be defined better than by applying his opinion of Picasso to his own work. On the occasion of the first cubist exhibit in Prague, Janouch said of Picasso: "He is a willfull deformer." And Kafka answered: "I don't think so. He simply registers deformities which have not yet penetrated our consciousness. Art is a mirror that runs 'fast' like a clock—sometimes."

Kafka and the Socialist World

JIŘI HÁJEK

[. . .]

Kafka's world is a world of infinite suffering. But neither in a single line in his fiction nor in his letters or diary entries do we find a glorification of suffering as the natural and unalterable destiny of man. Through his whole immeasurably fragile psychophysical constitution and through his position in the small group of the Jewish population of Prague, which was isolated not only socially but also through differences of language and of cultural consciousness, he was predestined to experience in a magnified way all the darkness which threatens man's existence in the world of the early twentieth century. Even when in his early youth he had contact with anarchists and socialists, his individual constitution made him incapable of drawing revolutionary conclusions from his human experience. The task which he chose under these circumstances seems more modest: to analyze, on the plane of his own emotional and ethical experience, the reasons for human suffering. "Kafka's man," as Karel Kosík writes in his study "Hašek and Kafka," "is condemned to live in a world in which the only human dignity is the *interpretation of the world*, because other powers, independent of the individual, decide about the course and alteration of the world."[1] The way in which Kafka's work realizes this analysis of human suffering turns the apparently "modest" task, to which he sacrifices, with the self-consuming intensity of his creative work, all his powers, health, and life, into a great artistic work which has the value of an ethical act. With him, the literary representation of all forms of human suffering is combined not only with a sharp analysis of its causes, but also with an obstinate hatred of pain and weakness.

Excerpted from Jiři Hájek, "Kafka und die sozialistische Welt," *Kürbiskern*, 1967, No. 1, pp. 77-93.
    1. *Plamen*, 6/63, p. 102.

If Kafka had singled out material misery and the material dependency of man on man as the sole cause of suffering—those things which are consequences of the exploitative order—then he would have been one of the socially critical writers of his time. But this level served him only as a point of departure: in *America*, which he started to write in 1912 in Max Brod's presence, we see the social reality of incipient capitalist superproduction and of big city technical supercivilization with all the brutality of its social differences. Whoever, like Rossmann's American uncle, owns a fortune, has also absolute power over all those who have nothing but their labor power. The stoker, this naive, ingenuous giant, who does not even know how to fight for his most primitive rights, is unaware of his power; in front of the captain, who himself is only the instrument of a foreign and anonymous power, he turns into a poor stuttering devil who gets uselessly worked up. The only possibility of a certain wildcat, individualistic defense is the obvious brutalization, artfulness, and deception of the *déclassé* Delamarche and Robinson, whom Kafka's hero later meets in his search for work. To be sure, there is some support in simple human sympathy and solidarity. But not even the friendly interest and the help of the chief cook, and even less the benevolence of her secretary Theresa, can prevent Karl's downfall as soon as he innocently and accidentally comes into conflict with the representative of a social institution: with the head waiter, who provides for order and discipline among the employees of the huge Hotel Occidental.

But above this plane in *America* there is a second, more general level of analysis of the fundamental conditions of human existence, which is of course causally connected with the first. It is expressed in the fate of the immigrant Karl Rossmann, who looks for work in vain and always remains a foreigner in his American surroundings. Whatever job he takes is always decided by a web of coincidences. As soon as a combination of circumstances makes him lose the patronage of his uncle and he is left to his own devices, his abilities, plans, and will no longer decide anything, but instead irrational circumstances, false accusations, presumed guilt, and the interplay of omnipotent institutions (head waiter and police). He is blown through the absurd, incomprehensible labyrinth of the modern big city like a piece of dust. In order not to perish, he is forced to accept asylum in the strange residence of the unexpectedly elevated Delamarche and to put up with the animalization of his existence at the level of a pet dog.

I agree with Paul Reimann (see his foreword to the 1962 Czech translation of *America*) when he argues with Western European Kafkalogists (L. Bergel) who consider *America* only the first of Kafka's attempts at the novel—not too successful in comparison with the other two—one that preserves the traditional novel form and that does not, like the later works, view reality through the medium of "dream distortions." But I do not believe that we should place *America* higher than the rest of Kafka's work simply because of its supposedly greater social and documentary content. The break between *America* and the other two novels is, by the way, not nearly so abrupt: even in *America*, in such scenes as the visit to Mr. Pollunder's villa, the hotel dormitory and the flight and balcony in the "Asylum" chapter, the description of reality already has the intensity of a frightening dream and evokes the same loathsome fascination as the fantastic motifs in *The Trial* and *The Castle*. And in *America* Kafka already poses himself some of the basic questions of his later work, above all the questions of loneliness and impotence as the first cause of all human suffering.

But in *The Trial* it is not a question of the loneliness and powerlessness that arise from material necessity and declassification. On the contrary, the central figure of *The Trial*, Joseph K., is a boundlessly successful young man in a more than secure position who, through his abilities, has worked himself up to be the Chief Clerk of a large bank and who has a good chance to become the Deputy Director. Not without good reason was Stendhal's Julien Sorel mentioned some time ago in connection with this external façade of Joseph K.'s existence. But in contrast to Sorel, the Chief Clerk Joseph K. is not prevented in his rise by any external hindrances, not even, that is, by the jealousy and intrigues of his rival the Deputy Director. On this realistic and even almost drily portrayed level of the action, Joseph K. is a completely conventional hero of his time. He is capable and appropriately ambitious. His relations to his closest relatives, his mother and his uncle, to his landlady and his co-workers, are very proper. And since at some point one will necessarily have to crown such a successful career with appropriate marital bliss, he also has a girl friend, with whom his relationship is also most proper. Who could demand anything more from such a highly placed and successful young man? From the standpoint of all the moral norms of the society of which he is a part, he is indeed completely guiltless.

A naive sociological interpretation would see in the motif of the "trial" and the "court," which suddenly intervenes in Joseph K.'s orderly and peaceful existence and through which his downfall occurs on a fantastic-symbolic level, only a grotesquely satirical and critical portrait of the omnipotence of the bureaucratic Austrian state machinery and of its judicial instruments. Then the downfall of Joseph K. would be only one of the many cases of innocent victims of the bureaucratic apparatus, which is to some extent externally decorated with fantastic dream deformations which lend it a particularly awful coloring. Certainly, such elements are also contained in the motif of the "trial"; Ernst Fischer apparently had them in mind when he spoke of Kafka's "fantastic satire." But the motif of the "trial" has at the same time another level of meaning: this trial, which is being conducted against Joseph K. by unknown judges because of an unknown transgression, in which the defendant in vain attempts to defend and finally gives up his life to the deputies of the unknown court, but in which the sentence is not passed—in reality Joseph K. is conducting this trial above all against himself. The instruments of justice in the novel are only the fantastic portrait of the institutional "blasphemous parody" of the real moral law which could fill human existence with a profound sense and whose absence Joseph K. feels. But this law is "monstrously masked by the organization of the society, state, and religion."[2] To the very end, Joseph K. never exactly understands what his guilt consists in. He finally ceases his frantic attempts at defense, at winning over the lower instruments of justice (because no one has access to the higher ones and no one knows them), because he increasingly feels that his trial is lost and that his existence cannot be justified. Joseph K.'s guilt cannot be defined with any law of petty bourgeois society. He is guilty "only" through the complete superfluity and senselessness of his life, which is based only on apparent values. He is guilty of the indifference which hides behind the cold propriety of all his human relationships, but which is characteristic of his behavior toward the whole social system. He is guilty for finally taking his attorney's advice, in so far as it has to do with the most appropriate behavior at court as well as with his fundamental attitude toward the world:

2. Roger Garaudy, *D'un réalisme sans rivages* (Paris: Plon, 1963), p. 190f.

The only correct thing is to come to terms with the existing conditions. Even if it were possible to correct details—but that is a silly superstition—at the best one would only have gained something for future cases; but one would have damaged oneself immeasurably in having aroused the attention of the bureaucracy, which is always vengeful. *Just don't arouse any attention!* [my italics—*J. H.*] Be calm, no matter how much that may go against your grain. Try to see that this huge judicial organism is in some way always on the move and that, if one independently changes something in one's place and takes the ground out from under one's feet, one may fall, while the huge organism can easily compensate for the petty annoyance at some other place—everything is connected—and remains unchanged.[3]

Isn't this, including the careful, urbanely cool formulation, a magnificent analysis of petty bourgeois social psychology, the "Magna Charta" of moral non-committedness, of passivity and conformism to whatever system and power happens to exist? That is the main reason for the emptiness and flatness of the Chief Clerk Joseph K.'s quite successful bourgeois existence. That is his cardinal sin. Of all the literature on *The Trial* which I know, Josef Strelka in his book *Kafka-Musil-Broch* aims most accurately at the nucleus of the problem: ". . . Joseph K. is guilty . . . because he believes in the impenetrable web of determination and forced dependency." But does that mean that the representatives of the judicial instruments are for one moment right? Not at all; according to Strelka they represent only blind social terror, which they consider to be a necessary natural phenomenon, and they are therefore convinced of their own infallibility.

"The Metamorphosis" demonstrates, with the devastating force of Kafka's fantastic symbolism, another aspect of alienated human relations and the devaluation of the real values of life. In this story Kafka does not at all "attempt to show" that man "is by nature predestined to loneliness."[4] Loneliness is, to be sure, one of the leitmotifs in Kafka's work and is common not only to the three novel fragments, but also to many of his stories. But never and nowhere does he show that man is naturally and unalterably predestined to loneliness; rather, he perceives loneliness as the greatest evil against which man vainly

---

3. Franz Kafka, *Der Prozess*, Ges. Werke, ed. Max Brod (Frankfurt am Main: Fischer), p. 146.
4. D. Zatonsky, *The Twentieth Century* [Czech], p. 189.

struggles. The "isolation" of Gregor Samsa, who one morning awakes in his bed transformed into a shining, round insect, has a completely concrete meaning: although he saw the sense of his life in keeping his father's bankrupt family above water, he is gradually written off by all the family members as soon as, by virtue of his metamorphosis, he loses his use-value and becomes an unpleasant and heavy burden to them. Even in the condition of an insect, Gregor Samsa remained himself. His relations with the family members didn't change. Nor did his human characteristics: but in a world of absolute reification of human relations these characteristics are overshadowed and concealed by the use-value of a man, his adaptability to earning power.

The surveyor K., the central figure of Kafka's last novel, *The Castle*, seeks an escape from the labyrinth of the reified, alienated world, into which Joseph K., Gregor Samsa, and the majority of Kafka's "heroes" have been exiled. He seeks an escape by trying to join the collective of the Castle's subjects, in order to serve them with his work. Eduard Goldstücker called attention to the difference between the surveyor and all of Kafka's previous heroes: he takes up the struggle to change his fate not from compulsion, but through his own decision.[5] Probably he is indeed the only hero full of activity and the longing for socially useful deeds. But he happens upon a world where there are not yet any "laws for his action,"[6] where no one needs him, where even his activity arouses suspicion. The head of the village, where he is stuck and where he vainly looks for the Castle which is supposed to grant him the basis for his occupation, says to him: ". . . we don't need a surveyor. The boundaries of our little farms are laid out, and everything has been properly registered. A conveyance hardly ever occurs, and we take care of little boundary disputes ourselves. So what do we need a surveyor for?"[7]

In a world in which all the property is divided and all human possibilities are laid out from the very beginning, there is no place for any human activity from which a change in possession or in human relations might result. In this world the surveyor K. is predestined to failure, isolation, and exclusion, all the more so the harder he tries to get

---

5. "Franz Kafka und Prager Perspektiven" in *Sammelband Franz Kafka* (Prague, 1963), p. 37.

6. R. M. Albérès, *L'aventure intellectuelle du XX siècle*, p. 231.

7. Franz Kafka, *Das Schloss* (Frankfurt am Main: Fischer), p. 62.

through the labyrinth consisting of the deception and indifference of the authorities and of the enmity of the simple villagers toward the anonymous sovereign and, thereby, also toward the realization of his mission.

The Trial took place on the sober level of everyday petty bourgeois reality and simultaneously on the level of the terrifying, fantastic, and yet real dream, but *The Castle* from the very beginning has only this second level. This fantastic deformation lends to the most everyday occurrences the dimensions of a nightmare full of naked, raw ugliness and absurdity. Perhaps it is the contrast between the active, stubbornly fighting—if also completely exhausted—hero (who falls asleep at a time when there is some hope that he might get a little bit farther toward the mystery of the Castle), and the brutality and baseness of the Castle officials that makes the atmosphere of *The Castle* the most disconsolate in all of Kafka's works. This world is totally uninhabitable for humans. Above the relentlessly tragic *Trial* there flickered a certain moderating, humanizing light of comedy. But the world of *The Castle* is thoroughly ominous and dark. Is the *The Castle* (perhaps along with the "Penal Colony") Kafka's most nihilistic book? Not at all: it is the book of the most absolute moral judgment. In his monograph on Kafka, Wilhelm Emrich remarks very accurately: "The less realizable, the more utopian freedom appears (that is, in Kafka's individual prose pieces), the more our consciousness wakes up to the fact that it is impossible to go on living this way."

Kafka's entire work has no other purpose than to awaken and stimulate this consciousness. Although his vision is darkly negative, it is nevertheless etched with the values which man inevitably needs in order to live and breathe, in order not to feel himself a stranger in the world. "A truly human existence is possible only outside the boundaries of alienation, against which Kafka's entire work struggles."[8] The fundamental supports of this possibility are determined precisely by what comes into the foreground as the main cause of human suffering in his negative picture: in order for human life to have any sense in the world in which Kafka's heroes live, that factor which robs human relations of their authenticity, directness, and fullness must be changed: the causes of the reification of human relations,

8. Garaudy, p. 206.

which Marx analyzed, must be eliminated, so that people can rein-
stitute the normal hierarchy of values of human life and can separate
the conventional, fictional values from the real values. This is the precondition of man's escape from his loneliness, for his joining a particular social organism to which he can be useful. The feeling of loneliness
and the feeling of uselessness are the greatest torments of Kafka's
heroes. In order to have a feeling of usefulness, people in a time of the
progressive division of labor must have a living, concrete idea of the
social interconnectedness of this labor, of its sense and of their own
place in it. Without this living, concrete consciousness of the whole,
the laborers working simultaneously on different sections of the Chinese wall (see the story "The Chinese Wall") would resemble merely
fantastic ants senselessly exhausting their strength. In this story one
finds the most numerous indications of a positive formulation of
Kafka's "collectivist" hopes: the human masses building the Chinese
wall are above all attempting to unite themselves in the name of a
common goal; each strives to fulfill his little task within the context
of the whole, but precisely because of that each longs to know exactly what his position is, what his work is, and what the intentions
are of the Grand Council, which is directing the whole construction.

The individual needs the collective as a home base, a protection, a
community of labor, a limitation of his self. He does not need it in
order to stop being an individual and to become a number; but rather
so that he may realize himself as an individual. But with its power
apparatus and its anonymous, omnipotent institutions, the state ma-
nipulates the individual as an indifferent unit, an object, an official
document. The whole world is closed for the individual, and it is unalterable through the immobility of the social relations, which are
founded on the power of possession. And in addition to this, all
spheres of human life are divided up under the domination of different, mutually unconnected institutions. People are either only objects
of their manipulation or automatic levers and cogs of the power machinery. They turn into abstract signs; they are robbed of their authentic existence and thus become tools and objects of the activity of
institutions. But even the individual spheres of life and the activities
of individuals separate and become irreconcilable with one another;
the one may lose its sense in face of the other: during Rossmann's
service in the Hotel Occidental, working for his living liquidates his
whole so-called private life. Fischer's interpretation of the story "A

Country Doctor" is interesting in this connection.[9] The country doctor sacrifices his home and private sphere and abandons his young servant Rosa to a cynical voluptuary, in order to fulfill his doctorly duties; it turns out that all his efforts are in vain and that he too, with the "unearthly horses" which his strange guest has lent him, is only tragically laughable and impotent.

It is not hard to read the positive message out of this negative: in order for man to be happy, reality may not be the battlefield of irrational powers that chase him about at will. He must be in his own power; he must have the right of fundamental human self-determination. A place among humans can be found only through love and work. Only in that way can the disparate spheres of human life be joined and become mutually sensible.

In fact, this definition of the basic conditions of a human existence is free of religious metaphysics. It is very simple and earthly. It is simply, as Kafka wrote at one place in his diary, that it is possible for man to become acquainted with the joy of feeling himself in complete harmony with the new day. There is no sense in enlisting his biography and referring to the time in which he was interested in Kierkegaard, Léon Bloy, or Hasidism. In what he wrote, he is neither an atheist nor a mystic; as Garaudy remarked, "God . . . in Kafka is never more than what man is lacking, the feeling of the inadequacy of the world, of the negation, of the enemy."[10] He wages his battle for human happiness—let us call it that—not in the name of religion, but in the name of man. In 1918 he wrote in the Octave Notebooks: "I have brought nothing with me other than general human weakness. . . . I was not brought into life by the already heavily sinking hand of Christianity, like Kierkegaard, and I have not grabbed the last tip of the fleeing Jewish prayer shawl like the Zionists. I am an end or a beginning."

Kafka's work is really an end and a beginning. It is only the absolute negation of the world he lived in, and in which the majority of people still live, and the consequences and influences of which even that part of the world in which socialism is being constructed cannot escape in the initial historical transitional stage. But Kafka's work is not the negation of human existence altogether. It is not a call to desperation, but to resistance. However, it is not a manual for action.

9. *Sammelband Franz Kafka*, p. 156.
10. Garaudy, p. 212.

Nowhere, neither in Kafka's notes nor in his correspondence, do we find any indication that Kafka had any idea of what would have to be done to turn that terrible blasphemy of human law which he experienced into a true law, or that he was aware of the social force that could realize this tendency. He reveals genuine, if sceptical, sympathy for Lenin and the October Revolution.[11] But that is all. If under just these circumstances he follows his analysis of human existence to the most negative conclusions with such a stubborn will to truth, it is as if he is cutting off the very branch on which he is sitting. His act has all the more moral value. Exactly through this absolute consistency of judgment and condemnation Kafka's work is not only an end, but also a beginning. It is not an act of hopelessness, but of hopefulness:

And even if my fund is so miserable . . . even the most miserable on earth, I must, in my own sense, try to achieve the best with it, and it is empty sophistry to say that one could achieve only one thing with it and that this one thing is therefore the best, and it is despair.[12]

Kafka's primary means of expression is the parable. But it is that not because of the author's incapacity for direct representation or from an unwillingness to express himself "intelligibly" or to take a clear stand, as some Marxist critics have interpreted it. It is that above all because the parable allows Kafka space for the widest generalization of his view of the world and man and at the same time makes possible the most radical "destruction"—to use Kosík's word—of the pseudo–concrete. There is no way to maintain seriously that this form only superfluously "encodes," that one can speak without chiffres, that it inevitably diminishes the portrait of reality, or that it is "decadent" and unrealistic in itself, as Kurella for example believes. I have no room here for further theoretical digressions, but it would be possible to prove, starting with the "realistic" nucleus of Czech national classicism, that the fairy-tale symbol (in Tyl) became an authentic and militant expression of social reality. But let us not go too far. However, the parable form is the most basic posture in the most important part of Bertolt Brecht's dramatic work, the realistic credentials of which not even the most hardened dogmatists have doubted. And in its way it is also the fundamental position in the dramatic

11. Gustav Janouch, *Prager Begegnungen.*

12. Diary entry of October 12, 1921; Franz Kafka, *Tagebücher 1910-1923*, Ges. Werke, ed. Max Brod (Frankfurt am Main: Fischer), p. 543.

satires of Mayakovsky and in Evgeny Schwarz's "fairy-tale plays," and so forth, and so forth. Even these arbitrary examples cast doubt on Stefan Żółkiewski's conception in *Perspectives of Twentieth-Century Literature;* he reckons only, for example, Kafka, Camus, Dürrenmatt, and Beckett among the adherents of the "model" representation of reality (or the so-called "creationists") and—even if he does not discount that their technique can somehow enrich the realist tradition—considers their procedure the opposite of the realist method. The parable is surely a form just as old as literature itself, and it is capable of expressing the most various relations to reality. That Brecht, for example, expressed himself through the parable like Kafka does not in itself mean very much. Brecht's parable discloses the recognition of the changeability of the world. Kafka's parable discloses only the recognition of the uninhabitability of the world by man. The symbolic expressions for the situation of man which Kafka found at the beginning of our century show such viability that they are also capable of comprehending many new phenomena of changing historical reality. That is primarily because they comprehend the broadest totality of human relations to the world and because through the intensity of their poetic construction they attain universal validity. Some epigones of Kafka, who attempt a similar universal validity through the literary parable, frequently achieve only the effect that their symbolic expressions can mean either everything or nothing. But Kafka's parable is so infinitely saturated with reality and reveals such a precise illumination from a central point of view that at any time, in proportion to its original absorption of reality, it can take on new (and in the author's intention probably also unexpected) meanings. And is it not the peculiarity of every great work of art [. . .] that it resembles a crystal with a thousand fine facets that is constantly illuminated anew by the new historical experience of mankind? The reasons for that particular combination of concrete specificity and ambiguity Georg Lukács has illuminated in *Wider den missverstandenen Realismus:*

On the one hand, the concrete details, as a result of their being directly rooted in old Austrian society, gain a sensuous "here and now quality," a semblance of social reality; on the other hand, the indeterminacy of the intended objectivity is constructed with the genuine naiveté of mere suspicion, of factual ignorance; and it can therefore more organically grow into an "eternal" *condition humaine* than later reflections of the diabolical,

anxiety-producing social reality, from which the already concretely existing social determinants had to be artistically eliminated or cleverly camou-
flaged by formalistic means of expression.

The strange fate of Kafka's work in the past twenty years can be
explained by these admirable qualities of Kafka's symbolic expression.
For us today Kafka is not only the world of the old Austrian monarchy, in which man is the plaything of the impersonal and inhuman
power of the bureaucratic machinery. Kafka is also the absurd, fantastic vision of the murderous Nazi system, which we have experienced as a historical reality. Kafka is also a picture of the postwar
situation of the capitalist world, whose whole essence is incapable of
freeing man from the grip of those forces that alienate him from himself, that rob him of the possibility of being the master of his own fate,
and that expose him to existential anxiety, insecurity, and anguish.

But Kafka also presents some essential characteristics of the reality
of a socialist society in the throes of formation. Kafka condemns
everything that stands in direct contradiction to the humanistic historical mission of socialism, everything that the Stalinist deformation
brought into our order and all of its consequences that still survive
among us and in us. He warns us against everything that would expose human fate to the effect of mystic forces that appear to be beyond the control of reason and human perception.

There are people who cannot occupy themselves with any artistic
phenomenon without finding a specific pigeonhole for it. I am not
interested in pigeonholes. But for all that we should not hesitate to put
Kafka into a category: he belongs among the great humanists of our
century. This is the only useful and realistic point of departure for
any further discussion of Kafka.

The interest in Kafka must be only a fashion for many among us
too. And the various fetishists are starting to hum around him, the
profoundly orthodox, the pseudointellectual young ladies, and other
suspicious persons. But all that is only foam on the surface. What is
decisive is that the will to a complete and truthful confrontation with
Kafka in the socialist world is becoming synonymous with a commitment to truth and completeness in socialist life ideals, a will to a total,
unself-deceived and unpharisaical recognition of the situation of man
in the socialist world, a will to overcome everything that is contrary
to humanity.

THE SOVIET REACTION

Franz Kafka

BORIS SUCHKOV

Kafka's work has had a strange fate. A writer who died more than forty years ago, the author of three unfinished novels and a few dozen stories and parables, who did not enjoy great renown during his life (although he was noticed by the major literary figures of his time), in our day is regarded abroad as a leading figure of the *contemporary* literary process. His work is widely published and is the subject of animated commentary in numerous articles and essays in which, as a rule, exaggeration and an enthusiastic tone reign.

In such works, Kafka, this interesting and difficult writer who occupies, by the way, a very specific (and not the highest) position in the literary development of our century, grows into a unique prophet who all but sees into the entire fate of contemporary humanity and into those misfortunes which have come upon man in the course of history. In numerous interpretations and critical essays, Kafka appears as a teacher of life, as a great moralist, as an unmasker of capitalism, as a religious thinker, as a rejuvenator of art (especially of realist art), and as a precursor of existentialism.

His work is seen as a kind of "code book" of human relations, as some sort of "model" of life constructed of polyvalent symbols and valid for all forms and kinds of social existence; and he himself is seen as a "poet of alienation," a mythmaker forever affirming in the creations of his imagination the eternal traits of our world.

Naturally, the interest in Kafka's legacy is not uniform, and it has been aroused for extremely complicated reasons. But at the bottom of it lies the attempt to find, in the spiritual culture of the recent past, a tradition upon which it would be possible to base those difficult attitudes which go into the composition of the *Weltanschauung* of the

From "Frants Kafka" in Boris Suchkov, *Liki Vremeni* [Images of the Age] (Moscow: Izdat. Khudozh. Lit., 1969), pp. 3-81.

foreign art of our day and which have developed into the conditions of a revolutionary reorganization of the contemporary world and a sharp exacerbation of social conflicts occurring under the ominous shadow of the atomic and hydrogen bombs.

The unusually deepening contradictions of our century breed in contemporary foreign art different views on the relationship of man and history, man and society. Alongside faith in the future and in human nature, there arises a deeply sceptical and pessimistic attitude toward the world and toward human activity. The well-known English writer, author of quite dismal world-parables and world-allegories, William Golding, for example, said in his speech at the Leningrad symposium in 1963, referring to the novel:

. . . for fifty years already there has been growing in me a certain conviction; I am obliged to think that humanity is struck with a sickness. I look for this sickness and find it in what is for me the most accessible place—in myself. I recognize the very part of our general human nature which we must understand if it is not to run out of control.[1]

Wishing to find the source of what at first appears to be a sickness of humanity but what is really a sickness of society, many artists abroad turn to the experience of Kafka, to the questions raised in his works about the relation of man to history, and to society, and, as it seems to them, correctly raised. That is one of the sources of the present interest in his work. Another is connected with the aesthetic particularity of his creative manner, with that method of representing life which defined the originality of Kafka the artist. Peculiar to his works, which disregard external verisimilitude, is a great emotional and impressive force: the unsteady, alarming atmosphere of his stories and novels, filled with anxiety, has a stupifying effect. However, the sphere of influence of his work has its own boundaries, which are always clearly delineated by the unambivalent nature [*odnoznachnost'*] of the moods and emotions which Kafka expresses. But the nature of the aesthetic influence of a work of art is not at all unambivalent in meaning [*odnoznachna*]. Constituting that nature are both the strictly aesthetic properties of the artistic work and the richness of content [*soderzhatel'nost'*] and the capacity of the generalizations included in them.

1. *Inostrannaya literatura*, 1963, No. 1, p. 225.

That is in order, for art is not an exalted and purposeless "game" to which one abandons oneself in leisure hours; nor is it a source of pure aesthetic delight removed from life. Its role in the life of people and society is incomparably higher and more meaningful for, in satisfying the aesthetic needs of man, art is a special instrument of cognition by means of which man comprehends himself, his spiritual and emotional-sensuous world, his possibilities and richness, and even his own activity, or, in a word, history.

Cognition, just like beauty, is part of the organic peculiarity of art. Both of these fundamental and primary elements are fused in the act of creation, which at the same time is an act of cognition, of understanding things that are usually hidden from view and the peculiarities of life that by means other than aesthetic cannot be understood or revealed. For that reason richness of content, being an aesthetic quality, is a most important and indispensable element of aesthetic influence.

Richness of content is peculiar to realist art in the highest degree, and it arises in the artistic work when the representation of the moral and spiritual world of man is united with an exploration of man as a social being existing in objective connections with the world, people, and society; when the exploration of man grows and rises to an exploration of society, of the connections and relations existing in it; when the epoch is depicted and understood through man; when the self-propelled movement of human cognition and feeling is examined by the artist in an indissoluble unity with the development and self-propelled movement of history.

But art does not only perceive and reproduce its time. It is also a child of its time and bears its unique stamp.

The complexity and diversity of the creative quest has become a characteristic feature of the art of our century, in which is found a reflection of the complexity of the contemporary historical process and the newness of its conflicts, which arise from the masses' struggle for true freedom, from the decline and ruin of the world of private ownership, and from the establishment of new, socialist relations in society.

Realist art, which at the turn of the century collided with new facts and life processes unknown to the realism of the nineteenth century, transformed—not without some fundamental losses—its representational language and the character of its analytic study of man in the element of his social interrelations. Continuing its development, realist art examined and depicted the leading contradictions of the new age and drew a picture of the life of the sons of the twentieth century, a picture that was authentic, sharply detailed, full-bodied and rich in content.

Generally speaking, only a mentality which did not set itself up in opposition to reality, but which examined the real world, was capable of perceiving, in varying degrees of depth, the historical novelty of the social processes arising in our era. A mentality that scorned the examination of the real world, leaned only on itself and sought only in itself for the solution to the enigmas of contemporary history, was capable only of giving a description of life's phenomena, not of detecting the reasons behind them, and it frequently distorted the countenance of the world. It was defenseless before the spiritual crisis gripping the conscience of capitalist society in the period of its transition into decline. The tendency to enclose thought within its own limits and boundaries was itself a sign of spiritual crisis, the most characteristic peculiarities of which were distrust of reality, contempt for reason, and opposing to reason such things as creative inspiration, instinct, and intuition.[2] Not wishing to take the objective nature of cognition and of the world into account, thought capitulated before the novelty of the facts disclosing themselves to human reason in the areas both of science and social existence.

The destruction of the mechanistic and positivistic conceptions which had dominated in science and the inevitability of recognizing, in the light of new discoveries in physics, the limitations of the old picture of the universe, were interpreted by bourgeois consciousness as the destruction of reason, the defeat of materialism. The failure of mechanistic determinism was taken as a triumph of indeterminism and as evidence of the fallibility of views of causality. The possibility of splitting the atom was appraised as a confirmation of the disappearance of matter and the correctness of idealism, which considers the objective world to be the defeat of the spirit or of human consciousness. The relation of bourgeois consciousness to the reversals in natural scientific conceptions at the beginning of the century is correctly defined by Norbert Wiener when he writes that at that time the opin-

---

2. Here we can recall the interpretation of intuition as a form of extra-rational cognition of the world, found in the works of Bergson and other representatives of the "philosophy of life."

ion arose that ". . . the old, naive realism of physics was relinquishing its place to something with which Bishop Berkeley would readily agree."[3]

The feeling of the impermanence and instability of life and of its forms and social relations, of the changes ripening in its bosom, the contents of which were far from clear, savagely shook the foundations of bourgeois consciousness, and at the beginning of the century the dominating position in that consciousness started to be occupied by neo-Kantian, agnostic, and even irrationalistic theories and studies, anthropological and anthropocentric by their nature, which regarded man as an individual torn away from society.

The loss of contact with reality—the dominant trait of the spiritual life of bourgeois society—was manifested also in art, where there developed schools and tendencies whose religion became the disregard for actuality and reality as the initial materials of artistic creation.

Franz Kafka stands at the source of that contemporary art which forfeits the ability to perceive the essence of the social forces that affect man and that distract him from investigating and depicting the connections which tie him to society. Kafka rightly occupies one of the most important places among those artists of today who reject realism as a creative principle and look for support for their aesthetic quest outside its boundaries.

Every authentic work of art absorbs into itself the private and public experience of the artist, his knowledge of life, the individual peculiarities of his nature, his social sympathies and views. But with realist writers, the peculiarities of their personal perception of the world do not usually obscure the objective picture of the world, for their creative imagination, in giving shape to reality, forges it out of the material of that same reality. For them, personal experience is one of the means of understanding life.

In creating phantasmagorical works which largely scorn external verisimilitude, in bringing a fantastic element into them and universalizing life processes, the romantic artists did not cut the threads that united their creations with the maternal soil of reality. For that reason, the contours of the real world and its authentic conflicts can be divined beyond the fantastic elements in their works.

It is different with Kafka. Of course his works reflected some ob-

3. Norbert Wiener, *Cybernetics and Society* (Moscow: Izdat. Inost. Lit., 1958), p. 34. [In Russian. *Ed.*]

jective sides of life. However, in his work that facet was eroded and
destroyed which, with the artist, always divides the observation of
his particular personality from the realm of art, where the element of
being, including his personal experience, which is felt and generalized
by the artist, becomes objectified. To a significant degree, Kafka's
works were a straight continuation, fictionalization, and record of his
inner states and visions: uneasy, full of contradictions, disturbed by
the stories of chimeras and excruciating fears which possessed his
consciousness and darkened his unhappy life, which transpired in a
bourgeois milieu, behind the desk of a petty clerk, in the hopeless
struggle with illness, in cheap *pensions* for the tubercular.

[. . .]

All these years Kafka lived a double life: the monotonous work
oppressed and tortured him. The daily round arose before him like
a dismal and monotonous desert where he felt tiresome loneliness,
defenselessness in the face of his own misfortunes and those of others,
where petty thrift reigned and where human existence seemed like
indifferent vegetation. The life which had been presenting itself to his
view frightened him and engendered a feeling of hopelessness. Kafka's
refuge from this was art, which could oppose the daily monotony,
and which he loved and prized above everything. In that way, the
sphere of art was separated and removed in Kafka's consciousness
from the sphere of life with its real social conflicts. Life, that vale of
evil and misery, became for him the lowest reality; the highest resided
in the realm of art, which for Kafka possessed an independent and
independently valid meaning.

He looked at life from the side, as it were: with a distrustful keen-
ness approaching sickness he peered into his surroundings, intently
observing the petty and significant deficiencies of his own people and
of the cultural circles with which he came in contact during his brief
travels. At work he clashed with the bureaucratic arrangements of
the decrepit Austro-Hungarian monarchy and the fervent belief in
the power of paper characteristic of its innumerable officials. He collided with the intensified feeling of hierarchy, of the class-determined,
property-based, national inequality of peoples, which had gone into
the very body and blood of the officials and philistines. Every day he
witnessed bureaucratic red tape in dealing with the affairs of the
clients of the institution where he worked, the wearisome pilgrimage

from desk to desk, from official to official, of people who had suffered from their work in little factories, industrial workshops, repair shops, and so forth, of disenfranchised, obscure workers seeking legal assistance and completely dependent on various officials from the head of the "desk" to the heads of chancelleries, sections, and subsections. Kafka's eyes confirmed the apparent power of paper over people, a force which renders them impotent and devoid of rights before the faceless might of the bureaucratic apparatus.

The spectacle of a dull and monotonous life repulsed Kafka and inevitably drew him to art. But even in this refuge it was not easy for him, because, in leaving contemplation of the outside world for the realm of the spirit, of creativity and the imagination, in creating a different world dissimilar to the real one, he was not able to escape from himself, from the feelings of anxiety, longing, and fear which constantly possessed him and which crushed the ironic nature peculiar to him.

He endured with torment the incompatibility of creative interests with everyday occupations, and he wrote in his *Diary:* "For me it is a terrible, dual life, from which, possibly, there is but one exit—insanity."[4] The dramatic character of his moods was aggravated by Kafka's fanatic relationship to his artistic vocation, which completely and exclusively devoured him: "I am reading Flaubert's letters: 'My novel is a rock to which I am chained, and I don't know what is going on in the world.' I too have felt the same thing" (*T*, p. 280). Being devoured by art, however, did not enrich Kafka and did not widen his communication or intercourse with the world. On the contrary, he remained enclosed in his own personality, plunged deeper and deeper into self-contemplation, which prevented him from seeing the multicolored variety of the world, where the colors of hope and joy have not died out and somber tones are by no means the rule. He felt this himself and sought intensely for an explanation of his peculiar disunity with life and people: "Who corroborates for me the truth or accuracy of the fact that only by reason of my literary vocation am I so indifferent to everything and therefore so heartless?" (*T*, p. 263). The ascetic service of the demon of art forced Kafka to renounce many natural human needs.

4. Franz Kafka, *Tagebücher 1910-1923* (Frankfurt am Main: Fischer, 1951), p. 41. [All references to Kafka's diary are to this edition and are cited subsequently as *T* in the text. *Ed.*]

In the days when the family was preparing for his marriage, he elaborately weighed the future and outlined in his diary a "Comparison of everything that speaks for and against my marriage." Here are some of his hurriedly noted "pro's" and "con's": "Inability to tolerate life alone; not the inability to live; on the contrary it is even improbable that I know how to live with someone, but I am incapable of tolerating the exigencies of my own life, the requirements of my own person, the attack of time and of aging, the vague pressure of my joy in writing, sleeplessness, the nearness of insanity—all of this I am incapable of tolerating alone." Further: "I need to be alone a lot. Whatever I have achieved has been a success because of being alone. . . . I hate everything that does not have to do with literature; it bores me. . . . The fear of union, of flowing over. Then I will never again be alone" (*T*, p. 311).

Kafka's engagement fell through. But the loneliness in which he remained was joyless and brutal. Art did not solve the inner conflicts of his personality; creative work did not bring joy; but the act of creation itself passed in a semiecstatic condition, similar to the ecstasy of mystics. "My happiness, my ability and even whatever possibility there is to be something useful lies now in the sphere of literature. And here I experience states . . . very close to states of clairvoyance." In such moments Kafka felt a limitless expansion of his personality, as he said, "to the limits of the human" (*T*, p. 57). With the years, these states, which were frightening to him, became more frequent and more powerful. The diary is sown with notations: "Vision"; "Sleepless night. Third in a row. . . . I think this sleeplessness comes from the fact that I write" (*T*, p. 73f.). "The following night sleep even more difficult. . . . Again the reason—the power of my visions, which, while I am still awake, pierce me so much that I cannot sleep" (*T*, p. 76). And again: "Vision." "I cannot sleep. Only visions, no sleep" (*T*, p. 309). Many of these visions were transformed into the symbolic parables which comprise a significant part of his creative legacy. "This story, 'The Judgment,' I wrote in one sitting in the night of the twenty-second to twenty-third, from ten in the evening to six in the morning. . . . *Only thus* can one write, only in such a context, only with such a complete opening of body and soul" (*T*, p. 293f.).

The strains and states of frenzy inherent in the very act of creation in no way contradict artistic creation, for often merely in straining and overstraining his spiritual powers, can the artist subdue his material and overcome his inertia. But with Kafka it was different. He was not master over his thoughts, moods, and feelings; rather, they gained the upper hand over him, plunging his consciousness into the element of chaos, not yielding to the influence of natural logic. In essence—and this appears to be the dominant characteristic and peculiarity of his poetics—in his works he tried to bring logic into the illogical and strove to put into order that which cannot be ordered, for it was cut off from authentic bonds of life and he disregarded the objective causality based in the very nature of things. The place of causality in Kafka's works was occupied by a fatalistic state of conditioning [*obuslovlennost'*] to what was transpiring, one which resisted explanation and solution. For that reason there is inherent in many of his works an irrationality of situations and circumstances which goes as far as a complete break with living verisimilitude. But how true are the words of Igor Stravinsky: "Art demands of the artist above all fullness of consciousness."[5]

Clairvoyance, which, in Kafka's words, expanded his inner "I" to the "limits of the human," really only uncovered and maximally sharpened his inner feeling, the morbid condition which mastered his body and mind. The diary is replete with self-confessions on that score.

[. . .]

Were there happy and peaceful days in Kafka's life? Yes, there were, during short visits to Italy, Paris, and Germany in 1911-1912. But even when at the end of his life he experienced a great love for the Czech journalist and translator Milena Jesenská, with whom he had become acquainted in 1920 (the monument to this disconsolate love is the *Letters to Milena*), his feelings were clouded by the usual emotional states that break through the jocular tone of the letters, that are imbued with a hearty warmth unusual to Kafka. "For here it is, the explanation I promised yesterday," he wrote Milena. "I am spiritually ill; the pulmonary disease is only a spiritual illness which has broken its banks."[6] "Moreover, I do not love even you, but only my own existence which is given to me through you."[7] Even in love

5. Igor Stravinsky, *Chronicle of My Life* (Leningrad: Gos. Muz. Izdat., 1963), p. 157. [In Russian. *Ed.*]
6. Franz Kafka, *Briefe an Milena* (New York: Schocken, 1952), p. 50.
7. Ibid., p. 101.

Kafka was unable to break out of the solitary confinement of his own "I."

Many reasons prevented him from giving himself up freely and openly to his feeling, both material hardship and illness. "Surely you have noticed that I have not slept for several nights. It is simply 'fear.' There is something really robbing me of my will, something tossing me around according to its whim so that I no longer know what is up or down, right or left."[8] But the days of this love, like Kafka's own days, were numbered: his last letters to Jesenská date from 1923, and in the summer of 1924 Kafka died of tuberculosis.[9] The end of his life was made easier by the selfless love of Dora Dymant, who became acquainted with Kafka not long before his death.

All his works and personal papers he ordered to be burned. But his friend and executor Max Brod did not follow Kafka's will, and almost everything Kafka left behind has been published.

In Kafka's diaries there are, among notes on books he had read by Kierkegaard, Hamsun, Gogol, Dostoevsky, Hauptmann, Dickens, and many other thinkers and artists, some notes accurately characterizing the direction of his own artistic interests. They demonstrate that Kafka unerringly found kindred aesthetic directions in the literature contemporary to him: "All yesterday morning my head was dazed by Werfel's poetry. At one moment I was afraid that the unceasing rapture would lead me to insanity" (*T*, p. 202). And further: "How harrowed and inspired I was after hearing Werfel" (*T*, p. 229).

Other notations reveal those artistic principles which became fundamental to his poetics. "*Everything arises before me as a construction*" (*T*, p. 329; Kafka's emphasis); and "I am on a hunt for constructions" (*T*, p. 331). From his very first creative steps, Kafka decidedly and unconditionally aligned himself with expressionism, one of whose founders was Franz Werfel, and he continued to develop as an expressionist. That was natural and to be expected.

His phantasmagorical and desolate inner world, but equally his sickly condition, undoubtedly contributed much to defining the spiritual tone and particularity of his works. Much, but by no means all. The frame of mind voiced in his novels and parables and even the stylistic peculiarities of his creative manner, with all its deeply indi-

8. Ibid., p. 104.
9. Milena Jesenská died in 1944 in the concentration camp at Ravensbrück.

vidual traits, coincides in its essential characteristics with that social frame of mind which, in the first decade of this century, came to light in expressionism and its poetics.

Appearing as a kind of antagonist and negator of impressionism and symbolism, the art of the expressionists pretended to a fuller expression of the mysterious essence of life and the human soul; however, in place of an artistic analysis of the authentic conflicts of reality, it frequently substituted a purely emotional reaction to the conflicts of life, often taking recourse to symbolic allegory, which lent an abstractness to many works which arose from the bed of this art.

Characterizing expressionism, Thomas Mann remarked in his *Reflections of an Unpolitical Man* that the new tendency in art deeply disregarded reality and withdrew from its obligations toward reality. This formulation truly defined the inner contradictoriness of the expressionist world view, which, more firmly than the whole aesthetic conception, united artists and writers under the banner of the new direction in art. "Expressionism is a collective conception of a complex of feeling and contemplation, but not a program," wrote the prominent expressionist Max Krell, and that corresponds with the reality.[10] The expressionists started from the idea that art does not reflect life but completes it, allowing humanity to recognize in it its eternal countenance raised above the course of history, above transitory human affairs and preoccupations, and turned to higher life, to the cosmos, the universe, and infinity. "The phenomena which expressionism treats never consist of a representation of a specific reality," wrote Max Krell in his article, "On New Prose."[11]

The world begins with man, exclaimed Werfel, defining the point of departure of the expressionist world view. This philosophical principle, fundamental to expressionism, reveals the duality of the expressionist view of life, man, and the interrelationship of art and reality. Behind this philosopheme lies an undisputable and open sympathy with man, the victim of a mechanical civilization which castrates his creative and constructive sources, a victim, according to the expressionists, of incomprehensible metaphysical forces of evil and horror flowing into life and rendering it tragic. But in considering man the beginning of the world, the expressionists removed him from

10. *Expressionism* (Moscow: GIZ, 1923), p. 73. [In Russian. *Ed.*]
11. Ibid., p. 90.

the stream of authentic ties with life and placed him above the world and life and proclaimed the birth of his fantasy and the fruits of his imagination to be the principal value of life.

That same expressionist world view revealed itself to be a mixture of the most disparate elements: antibourgeois sedition, personal willfulness, anarchistic relation to society, pacifism, liberal and starry-eyed faith in abstract goodness—all these combined with a horrible pessimism approaching a cry of despair, with a loss of the capacity to resist the forces of evil. Rationalism and mechanistic thinking combined with a self-satisfied intuitivism which gave way to mysticism. That which considered itself and was the expressionist "complex of feelings and contemplation" could not remain isolated for very long. At the beginning of the twenties, expressionism disintegrated into the hooting of the dadaists and the mockery of the surrealists, who erected upon its ruins the edifice of their own ephemeral aesthetics.

But for the expression of the moods, feelings, and thoughts which possessed them, the expressionists found an appropriate poetic language: "The contemporary poet no longer doubts that what appears in the aspect of external reality is not genuine," Oskar Walzel wrote of the expressionists:

He demands, rather, that reality be made by us. For him the picture of the world is contained only in ourselves. . . . For expressionism the moment is devalued; it seeks the eternal. It takes man away from the humdrum routine of his condition. It frees him from his social bonds, from family, obligations, ethics. Man can be simply man; he ceases to be a citizen, but he is not simply a citizen of the universe. . . . The examination of the human soul and of the various conditions into which it falls, setting itself off against the world, proves purposeless. Henceforth the purpose is the expression not of the varied moods of the soul, but of the one great feeling. This feeling is revealed only in ecstasy.[12]

Ecstasy, as the ruling temper in expressionism, demanded the representation of exclusive, unusual situations, but the negative relationship of the expressionists to the details and particularities of life led their art into a unilinearity in characters, in the psychology and relationships of the characters, turning them into what Kafka very accurately termed *constructions*. To the eyes of the expressionists the world revealed itself as the focal point of human suffering, as a collection of

12. Oskar Walzel, "Impressionism and Expressionism in Contemporary Germany," *Academia* (Petersburg), 1922, p. 88. [In Russian. *Ed.*]

symbols and signs beyond which lay some incomprehensible thing called life. At the same time, the world arose in their works as a scheme consisting of constructions extremely remote from the full-bodied, concrete, weighty, and earthy purposefulness of life. Naturally, the tendency toward the use of symbols united expressionism with symbolism, its predecessor, but the tendency toward abstraction from reality, from concrete living and historical conditions and circumstances, made it the precursor of dadaism, surrealism, and abstractionism, which were rooted in expressionist aesthetics.

[. . .]

But like every major artist and original talent, Kafka was wider in scope than the school to which he belonged and broader than its aesthetic canons. He was linked to expressionism not only in poetics, but also through the conception of man contained in his works, which constitutes the main singularity of his work. Like the expressionists, Kafka regarded man as some kind of *construction* bereft of a fullness of ties, of weight, of the many qualities inherent in human nature, a construction that narrows the emotional, spiritual, and intellectual world of the personality in comparison to the world of real man engaged in activity, struggle, and suffering, experiencing both defeat and triumph in an authentic life.

As with many other expressionists, Kafka's conception of man tied his work to European decadence at the turn of the century, in so far as decadence was not only an aesthetic phenomenon. Decadence is an expression of a particular stage in the development of bourgeois consciousness, marked by a completely clear view of man and his interrelations with the world and society. The characteristic and fundamental sign and peculiarity of the decadent world view is the feeling that *man is not free*. Truly, man in the conditions of capitalism is deprived of genuine freedom, and the decadent artists discerned and reflected the objective reality of the world. But their relation to this objective fact is different from that of the artists who did not fall under the influence of decadence.

For them, man is known to be subordinate and subject to certain irrational forces which exist outside of man himself. In the decadent world view, the nature of these forces remains unknown or, in any case, extremely unclear. Regarding a man as a separate individual standing in opposition to society, as an extrasocial person, decadent art scorns examination of man's social ties and renounces the analysis of his interaction with his surroundings and with history. It does not admit the idea of development and negates the mutability of history, not recognizing the reality of historical time. The decadent consciousness rejects man's material, substantial, and genuine ties to society, concentrating on the depiction of the experiences of the individual excluded from the temporal and historical stream, hyperbolizing and inflating his internal world to a universal standard and not seldom apologizing for the self-willfulness of the person who neglects the commonly accepted norms of morality. Relating sceptically to reason, the decadent consciousness leans on irrationalism as the foundation of thought and makes intuition the tool of cognition.

The feeling of destruction of capitalist society which runs through the decadent world view lends it pessimism, a disbelief in the creative possibilities of man, in his ability to break the fetters of slavery, to free himself from the powers that subjugate him. Apocalyptical moods gain possession of the decadent consciousness because it regards the decline and ruin of the proprietary society and order as the destruction of all human culture and the whole human race. Appearing as an expression of the most profound spiritual crisis of capitalist society, decadent art and the decadent world view reflected the process of the alienation of man in the twentieth century, which has been so pregnant with and abundant in social shocks.

Alienation is a completely real, objective process organically tied to the very nature of proprietary capitalist social relations. Its economic foundation is the alienation of the products of labor from the producer, which transforms the producer from the master of things and the products of labor into their slave, and that introduces fragmentation into the relations between people. But the process of alienation also has unmistakable spiritual and ideological consequences: appearing in the sphere of consciousness and deforming it, it prevents consciousness from penetrating to the essence of social relations between people and from recognizing, behind illusory notions of reality, its authentic and real contours.

Characterizing the most substantive aspects of alienation and examining the concrete forms of its appearance, Marx wrote:

Capital reveals itself more and more to be a social force, the functionary of which is capitalism; it does not yet exist in any correspondence to what the labor of the individual person could create. Capital turns out to be an alienated, isolated social force which stands opposite to society as a thing and as the force of the capitalist through the medium of this thing.[13]

Bourgeois and, especially, decadent consciousness, discusses only that side of the process of alienation which subjects men, because upon immediate view it is that which comes to the foreground: ". . . the object produced by labor, its product, stands opposed to labor like some *strange being*, like a *force not dependent* on the producer," Marx remarked, revealing the "mystery" which surrounds the process of alienation and which is incomprehensible to bourgeois consciousness.[14] "If the product of labor is alien to me, if it stands opposed to me in the quality of a foreign force, then to whom in this case does it belong? If my own activity does not belong to me but is a foreign activity, obligated of me, then to whom in this case does it belong?"[15] Marx asked, and pointed out that the master of the alienated activity of man in the condition of capitalism can be only another man.

In other words, the possibility of alienating from man his productive, creative powers is a consequence of social injustice. And if bourgeois ideology considers such a situation natural, then Marx underlined that the most important and inevitable condition for the liquidation of alienation must be the revolutionary restructuring of society:

From the relationship of labor and private property it follows . . . that the emancipation of society from private property, and so forth, from bondage, takes on the *political* form of the *emancipation of the workers*, in so far as it is not a matter only of *their* emancipation; for their emancipation includes general human emancipation. And this is because all bondage of humanity is contained in the relationship of the worker to production and all servile relationships are in essence only mutations and consequences of this relationship.[16]

In not seeing this real, determined, historically conditioned perspective and possibility of social development, bourgeois consciousness and decadent art was unable to overcome the spiritual consequences of alienation and provide an objective characterization of the contemporary era, whose sense and countenance are specified by the

13. Karl Marx and Friedrich Engels, *Works,* XXV, Part I, 290. [In Russian. *Ed.*]
14. Marx and Engels, *Selections* (Moscow: Gospolitizdat, 1956), p. 560. [In Russian. *Ed.*]
15. Ibid., p. 567.   16. Ibid., p. 570.

decline of capitalist social relations and the affirmation of new socialist ones.

With strongly graphic and impressive precision Kafka mirrored in
his work the ideological side of alienation which enslaves and oppresses man, but he completely excluded from his field of vision the
possibilities of overcoming it which have been opened in the course
of history and in our century by the great socialist revolution and the
radical dismantling of the bases of proprietary society. In the treatment of those themes fundamental to his work that are concerned
with the representation of various consequences of alienation, we
notice Kafka's usual attraction to the construction and the scheme
that lead to the view of man as a passive, suffering being who feels
on himself the pressure of unavoidable, huge forces of evil, who exists
in a condition of horror or pain, seized by the feeling of the frailty
and doom of life.

[. . .]

In his works Kafka was undoubtedly repelled by actual real-life
conflicts, but he portrayed them unrealistically, lending them traits of
timelessness and eternity, and he consciously, in the spirit of his poetics, deprived them of their historical concreteness and, at the same
time, of their living authenticity. Such an approach to the object of
alienation appeared in Kafka from his very first artistic step and continued throughout his creative career. In this regard, his artistic manner is distinguished by an exclusive constancy unchanging through
the years, and his early attempts differ from the later ones only in
stylistic purity.

Even his first works—the incomplete novella "Description of a
Struggle," the parables collected in *Reflection*—bore the seeds of unchanging representation of the alarming and harrowing themes that
were important and dear to him and that, in the works of the mature
part of his life, he merely varied, maintaining a constant adherence
to the creative problematics emphasized early on. Kafka's first stories
and parables clearly reveal his attempt to give unlikely situations an
external probability, to clothe a paradoxical content in an intentionally
prosaic and common form, so that an event or observation, not yielding to a realistic foundation, may appear more authentic and probable
than the genuine truth of life.

For Kafka art in general and, in the first place, his own art seemed

more true than empirical reality, which he drew on only for an indirect confirmation of his own thought or mood. Reality was never
for him a high judge or measure of the content of his fantasy, which
created an independent superimposed world where unusual principles
of thought were operative and where the logic of human relations
developed in accordance with the law of paradox. He soon found an
artistic form appropriate to him: the parable, sometimes resulting in a
moral sentence, sometimes turning into an extended metaphor. In
essence even his stories were constructed like expanded, branching
symbols, the sense of which often flew away from the soil of reality
and became abstract, and sometimes inexplicable.

The initial premise of his parables and novels, as a rule, has the
semblance of authenticity, of everyday simplicity and unobtrusive-
ness. However, as it develops and is elaborated with shades and details
it changes—at first not very noticeably, gradually but stubbornly and
persistently leading the initial rational premise into something contradictory not only to common sense but also to reason, from the point
of view of the laws of the objective world.

The paradoxical nature of the situations and of the logical constructions which lie at the base of Kafka's parables and stories was intended
to emphasize and did emphasize the alogicality of the world itself,
the instability and unsteadiness of human existence, the enslavement
of unknown forces which determine its fate and life.

For him man is not at all a master of nature proudly asserting himself in life. Man for Kafka is a stepson of being, dust, a lump of clay,
an unprotected, weak, and powerless creature who with every fiber
feels his isolation from life, his unconnectedness to it and its powerful
stream which washes him but does not penetrate to that secret, mysterious, and hidden region which constitutes the heart of human nature.

Regarding man as a suffering creature who bears in himself constant
spiritual torment, Kafka arrived early at the thought that the sources
of torment and suffering lie in man himself, in his nature. In 1903 he
wrote to his friend Oskar Pollack:

We are abandoned like children who have lost their way in the woods.
When you stand before me and look at me, what do you know of my
sufferings, and what do I know of yours? And if I threw myself at your
feet and cried and spoke to you, what more would you know about me
than about hell, if someone told you that it is terrible and hot there?
Should we humans then, because of that, not hold to one another rever-

ently, as thoughtfully and as lovingly as if we stood before the gates of hell?[17]

But if the mysterious essence of man is unknowable and alike to hell, then it is completely natural that man's very life and the world he lives in cannot be anything but horrible, since the first cause of the horrible is located in man himself.

Kafka rejects the general point of view that man is a part of the world, a part of humanity. He regards that truth as false, for something else is true for him: the separation of man from life. Man's connection with the world Kafka considers only a semblance, a delusion, proposing that, if one merely looks intently at the world, then the justice of that observation is revealed, and all of life appears to the inner gaze of man as something shaky, incomprehensible, uncertain (the parable "The Trees").

Human nature is not only isolated from life, closed in itself, but it is also unchangeable and eternal. Time cannot change it and only leaves scars on it—some deep, others more shallow. It stamps the human soul with signs of good and evil, but it cannot change its inner constitution. A man can discard the past in him, the way one treats old-fashioned, worn-out clothes, but he is not in a condition to change his old-fashioned, worn-out face, which is the soul's mirror. To it man is united strongly and forever, like the convict chained to the heavy wheelbarrow which he is doomed constantly to push before him (the parable "Clothes"). But although human souls are hidden from view and bear in themselves the principle of good and evil, they cannot expose themselves or give any information about themselves, revealing the fundamental foundation of human thoughts and deeds.

Since Kafka was completely convinced of the strong, ubiquitous force of evil and of the limitlessness of its power over life and human nature, he was not at all confident of the possibilities of good. For that reason the shadowy, wicked, and horrible side of human nature inevitably bursts open, in spite of all efforts and pretences to conceal its cold, corroding, insensible force. In Kafka it arouses hatred—this power lying in wait until it is time to ambush its victim in the dark nighttime streets and alleys of big cities, at crowded crossings, in the homes of people, in houses where wealth serves as a protection against

17. *Le Figaro littéraire*, Sept. 30-Oct. 6, 1965.

catastrophe; this force filling life, lurking everywhere where evil may hide itself, gradually entwining the human soul, embracing it, striving to capture and strangle man, to draw his conscience into a dirty deal (the parable "Exposure of a Scoundrel").

The all-pervading force of evil disunites and disconnects people, turns them into mutually repelling monads. It disarms man, eats away at his feelings of compassion and love for his fellow man and even the desire to help him, to approach him. It makes man a passive contemplator of life, one who does not wish to penetrate into its sense and content so as not to overburden himself and not to take onto his shoulders the extra burden of goodness and love of mankind. This powerful force makes the man strolling at night through the lifeless city flooded in moonlight stop at the sound of steps and watch how people run one after another, sucking air into themselves with whistling noises, with faces distorted by intensity, and makes him stand by the side ruminating about what is hiding behind this strange event, about what, after all, flashed before his eyes. Or a chase to the death where victims run from assassins; or two people united by one passion—possibly hatred—pursue a third; or simple ordinary residents hurry home after their difficult and heavy day to their habitual burrows, their cheerless beds and dreary homes. Nothing is clear; not one of the actions of the people can be understood and explained— and it is better to stand to the side of the action and to contemplate it, not meddling in anything, for it is possible to become an accomplice in a crime or its innocent victim; it is possible unexpectedly to carry the responsibility for something unknown to you, at the same time that you are chained and crushed by fatigue and the time of life has robbed you of the will to struggle and resist, and you are only up to watching what is happening, what is pouring into your wide open eyes. This philosophy of life, so characteristic of Kafka and expressed most clearly in the parable "The Passers-by," the key to his world view, also predetermined his relationship to social conflict and to the movements of his time.

Kafka's unrealistic perception of real-life contradictions is explained not only by the peculiarities of his creative nature, by the capacities and peculiarities of his mind; it results also from Kafka's social views— he regarded any aspect of social conflict as senseless and incapable of changing the course of things, the existing order, of checking and correcting the world's evils.

Kafka was a contemplator in social questions as well. Once, after his usual conversations with his friend, the well-known Zionist Max Brod, who was trying to interest Kafka in his ideas, Kafka made an extremely important entry in his diary: "What do I have in common with the Jews? I hardly have anything in common with myself; I can only be quietly joyful that I am breathing, hidden in a corner" (*T*, p. 350). Kafka dared say this not only of his kinsmen, whose fate was not indifferent to him, for the Jewish question in Austria-Hungary was very difficult, but of others as well. The energetically proceeding process of assimilation, which had seized Kafka too, nevertheless did not resolve the nationalist contradictions and conflicts which characterized the decrepit monarchy. It was something that he could say also of the partisans of social movement—the anarchists, with whom he was acquainted from Prague, or the socialists, whose teaching and ideas he knew and which at one time interested him but which he gave up as he considered them unrealizable in practice.

The difficult situation of the working class aroused Kafka's sympathy. Writing in his diary his impressions from visiting factories, he very accurately described the slavish condition and the stupifying and exhausting labor of the girls, whose outward appearance aroused his sorrow. But at the same time he unequivocally expressed doubt at the ability of the workers, reduced to the condition of semiautomatons, to see their situation, not to speak of attempting to change it. One time he told Brod that he was surprised at the behavior of the workers who, instead of destroying the insurance office where he worked, pleaded for help. No—in the masses he never saw the moving force of history, the active principle of progress, and he did not think that oppressed and enslaved people could change and restructure the world. Such a hope seemed to Kafka impossible and just as senseless as life itself, which human adversity colored in the sombre tones of the humdrum and commonplace and deprived of passion, the heroic principle, and the impulse toward struggle and great feats. These words and concepts don't even exist in Kafka's vocabulary. Life appeared to him as a flat plain, boring in its prosaic nature and monotonous in its convulsive sufferings, unchangeable and eternal like fate itself. And that is also the way he portrayed it—as obscure, dull, barren, provisional.

[. . .]

The mood reflected in Kafka's parables could have been an impetus to investigate life, to a search for the answer to the question of what makes life the way it is, why it is hostile to man and why man, living a short span and existing in an abyss between two gaps marked by his birth and death, cannot enjoy his days, but passes them in suffering and spiritual anguish. In order to answer these cursed questions, Kafka would have had to turn to reality and try to recognize it and uncover the true reasons for human suffering.

But that was a task that went beyond his power and the power of his art. Undoubtedly, Kafka represented certain peculiarities of life as peculiarities of life in capitalist society. For example, the young merchant whose story is told in the little story "The Neighbor" very accurately states the feelings of a participant in the competitive struggle: from the day when, alongside his little but prosperous office, someone else has settled—also a merchant, by the name of Harras, about whom, however, nothing is known, and who has opened his own office—he has no peace; day and night he is poisoned by suspicion, for Harras, possibly, is eavesdropping through the narrow partition which separates their offices, listening to business conversations on the telephone, and, being sure of his neighbor, he slips, noiselessly, like a mouse's tail, out of the house and pokes about in the city, intercepting clientele and doing a little dirty business behind his back. Possibly it is so, and possibly not, for the story, written in the form of a confession, an intimate acknowledgement, does not admit of the truth, insofar as the confession is built up on the narrator's guesses and conjectures, which are themselves in need of confirmation.

[. . .]

Kafka carefully removes from his narration the principle of the conditioning of human behavior and in its place puts the unexpected, inexplicable, and unforeseen which is born of many motives, not one of which, in Kafka's sense, can be regarded as necessary; for, in his opinion, man's tie to reality, where cause and effect are intertwined, is questionable and relative, as even the interaction of cause and effect itself is relative.

It is possible to suggest that Georg Bendemann, the hero of "The Judgment," perishes as the victim of his own egoism. For, instead of going to the aid of his friend who has gone to Petersburg and become ill there and suffered business losses, he writes him empty letters, not failing to mention his own success and even his imminent advantageous marriage. Georg's father was right to accuse him of lying, throwing into his face the charge that he has no such friend in Petersburg, for one does not deal with friends like him. Yes, carried away by business and by the establishment of his own happiness, Georg has stopped looking after his father, who without his son's affection and attention has begun to decline, feeling the secret hatred of his son. Egoism may serve as the reason for Georg's censure; but that is hypothetical, for the furious father, administering to his son justice and retribution, starting the whole domestic trial over Georg, has been turned by Kafka into an embodiment of fate, into its avenging hand, and the story becomes a depiction of the collision of man with fate, in which man suffers an inevitable and irreparable defeat. Sentenced by his father to death by drowning, Georg, seized by an unknown force, runs headlong from his father's house and hurries onto the bridge where, waiting for the approaching bus to cover the sound of his fall, and with words of love for his parents, he throws himself into the water.

Apart from the tragic definitiveness of the ending, the content of the story is devoid of definitiveness, for the real motives behind the actions of its heroes are unclear. They are unclear to Kafka too, but totally apparent to him was the irreconcilable dissociation and isolation of people, both in the family and in society, the alienation of man from life. That thought, having become the dominant one in his works, preordained the uncompromising nature of the conflict between father and son in "The Judgment." Kafka confirms it not so much through the psychology of the characters—for the characters of his heroes are always distinguished by psychological poverty—as through the whole situation in which they find themselves. Even sharper is the similar situation in the story "The Metamorphosis" (1914), the hero of which, the minor traveling salesman Gregor Samsa, is suddenly turned into a repulsive insect and ends his days in that disastrous state.

Most probably the chimerical picture of extreme human loneliness depicted in "The Metamorphosis" was born in Kafka's brain during his nocturnal visions when, crumpled by fear, he felt himself completely cast out of life. But that does not exclude the fact that some of its shades were culled from reading Dostoevsky, one of his favorite writers:

. . . it is brown and has a hard shell, a crawling reptile, about seven inches long, at the head about two fingers thick but gradually becoming narrower towards the tail, so that the very end of the tail is not wider than a tenth of an inch. About two inches from the head, at an angle of forty-five degrees, two feet emerge from the trunk, one on either side, four inches long, so that the whole animal, if viewed from above, looks like a trident. I did not scrutinize the head, but I saw two antennae, not long, resembling two strong needles, also brown. Also two feelers at the end of the tail and at the end of each of the feet, which made altogether eight feelers. The animal ran around in the room very quickly, supported by its feet and tail, and when it ran, both the trunk and the feet coiled up like a snake, with unusual speed, and in spite of the shell—and it was very disgusting to watch that.[18]

One could think that this is a description of Gregor Samsa's appearance after his ill-fated metamorphosis. However, it is Ippolit's vision in *The Idiot*.

Samsa, after he became accustomed to it, loved to climb on the walls and ceiling, leaving sticky, slimy tracks behind him—and the "animal" which appears to Ippolit also secretes a white juice resembling the juice of a crushed cockroach. In Dostoevsky the disgusting insect embodies the loathsomeness of the horror of death; but in Kafka Samsa's metamorphosis was a reification of his feelings about humanity and society. Moreover, none of the many pessimists in world literature who in various ways have expressed disbelief in man and contempt for him, even in their darkest meditations on the nothingness and imperfection of human nature, have reduced him to such a pitiful situation as Kafka has done.

The idea of the prostrate condition, the powerlessness of man, is deep-seated and fundamental in the decadent world view. It also dominates in Kafka's work. But one cannot call him a misanthrope. Kafka, for all the egocentricity of his nature and his constant involvement with the world of his own suffering, was open to understanding the sufferings of others also. Moreover, he believed that torment is

18. F. M. Dostoevsky, *Collected Works*, VI (Moscow: Goslitizdat, 1957), 441f. [In Russian. *Ed.*]

not a part, but the essence of life, and that therefore every person inevitably bears its burden and feels its onerous weight.

Kafka sympathizes with Samsa, who lived the miserable, limited life of a petty Philistine and died of hunger in his room, where the family had tried to hide him from the importunate eyes of strangers. But with even greater energy and inward conviction Kafka affirms with his story the idea of the impossibility of changing the condition and situation in which man finds himself. The insect Samsa can do nothing to break the power of fate that has deprived him of his human face and of those modest possibilities which his position as a minor employee allows him. He does not even inwardly protest against the unhappiness which overtakes him—and that is very characteristic of Kafka's world view, which considers the struggle against the forces which oppress man to be senseless.

Nor can the Samsa family do anything, upon whom, since his metamorphosis into a hideous insect, has fallen an inhuman ordeal; and the sigh of relief which escapes from his relatives upon his death is completely natural. For that reason it is hard to see in Kafka's story a critique of the bourgeois family. Even thematically it does not move in the direction of Jules Renard in *Poil de Carotte*, Roger Martin du Gard in *The Thibaults*, Johannes R. Becker in *Farewell*, or of François Mauriac in his cycle of family novels—those artistic realists who ascend from a critique of the relationships dominating in the bourgeois family to a critique of proprietary bourgeois society. It is possible only to pity the Samsas, those limited little people, for the monstrous calamity which befalls them. To be sure, "The Metamorphosis" reflects the subjective feelings of Kafka, who felt himself a stranger in his own family, but the content of the story goes beyond the representation of a private, intrafamilial conflict.

It is Kafka's attempt to mirror the character of man's relation to life. It was not only to amplify the aesthetic effect of the horrible that Kafka placed the drama of the Samsas in the element of the everyday. By saturating the narration with tiny prosaic details, he strives to show that the horrible and monstrous is hidden and lurks in the bosom of normal, everyday life and simply waits there for its chance to ambush man. Life in its constancy and invariability is unchanging and hostile to man, who has no means or possibilities of influencing it. Collision with it ends for him in catastrophe. The grotesque figures of the participants in the Samsa drama are invoked to demonstrate this

final thought of the story, to affirm the ordinariness of the extraordinary, the naturalness of the unnatural, the logicalness of the illogical.
Kafka described not so much the psychological reaction of a man to
something exceptional—the psychology of the characters in the story
does not much interest him, and he does not peer into the souls of the
participants in the strange occurrences in the Samsa family—he depicted the tragically unsolvable and fatal situation which throws
Samsa out of the company of men and dooms him to eternal isolation.
Important for Kafka is the eventful side of the action, the unresolvability of the conflict embedded in it, that, in his opinion, reflected the
unresolvability of man's conflict with the world.

   None of the participants of the Samsa drama even reflect on the
cause of such an improbable occurrence as the transformation of a
man into an insect and, taking what happens as something that does
not fit in with life's norms, they reconcile themselves to it, trusting
to patience, for the power of evil is limitless and man's strength is
modest. That conclusion was logical to Kafka too, for, considering life
horrible and unchangeable, he surmised that to overcome human unfreedom was impossible. This thought runs through another of his
central works too, the story "In the Penal Colony," where the same
set of ideas is developed as in "The Metamorphosis."

   Going beyond the limits of a private and exceptional case, this story
also preserves traces of Kafka's attentive reading of Dostoevsky, who
deeply influenced all the expressionists. "German youth adopted and
chose Dostoevsky as their herald and prophet," as Karl Otten correctly observed in his study of expressionist art,[19] and Kafka was not
excluded from that influence.

   The reflections on good and evil and on their conflict, which comprise the heart of Dostoevsky's works, deeply occupied and disturbed
Kafka. For Dostoevsky the power of evil was limitless not only over
the soul of the individual man, but on a universal scale. Condemning
social injustice, he sought the way to social harmony and was prepared
to accept the results of revolution accomplished in the name of social
justice, but he did not accept the methods of revolutionary struggle.
For Kafka the power of evil was absolute; but in his opinion the attempt to establish social justice and harmony inevitably turns out to
be an evil more terrible than the evil that is, so to speak, natural and

19. *Ahnung und Aufbruch* (Darmstadt: Luchterhand, 1957), p. 16.

normal, for it is undertaken in the name of the good. This thesis he developed in the story "In the Penal Colony" (1914, published in 1919), in which he unequivocally reflected his conviction of the enormity of universal evil.

Recounting the story and the prosaic explanation of the officer who operates the monstrous punishment machine that has been constructed on some island penal colony, Kafka underlined that it was invented by the old commandant not for the sake of sadistic enjoyment of the torment of its victims, but for their own good; it is an instrument of justice, considered good just as the rack and garrot, the fire of the *auto-da-fé*, the guillotine or electric chair were also considered instruments of good by those who through these means tried to embed in life their understanding of justice and the good. "Be just"—that is the testament of the old commandant, and the officer operating the machine fanatically follows this testament to the very end. He himself willingly becomes its victim when he is convinced that the world order which ended with the death of the old commandant is no longer valid. With him the machine too perishes, but the vague prophecy remaining after the death of the old commandant foretells his return, and with him the return of the order he established in the colony. Not counting what the officer considers minor details, such as the constant executions to which people are subjected on the machine, the order that the old commandant founded was excellent, for all the inhabitants of the colony were happy and joyfully observed, during the grave ceremonies, how the victim's brow beamed with the understanding of justice imparted to him by means of the torture machine. And apparently the victim was satisfied too, licking up the dark rice mush put before his mouth during the execution. No one tried to oppose the punishment meted out, for it was taken to be inevitable.

It seems such an inevitability also to the ignorant and crude people—to the *Okhranka* [1] soldier and the condemned who at first take part in the execution and then become witnesses to the officer's self-punishment, for in their heads there is no room for thoughts of insubordination to the existing order of things. Although after the death of the old commandant the mood in the colony softens and the new commandant disapproves of the activity of the officer operating the

[1. The *Okhranka* was the Secret Police in tsarist Russia. It is naturally Suchkov, not Kafka, who makes this analogy. *Ed.*]

machine, it continues to work as before, and everyone—both executed and executioners—consider its existence to be tolerable and punishment to be inevitable. Only chance removes it from the order.

A powerful shadow is cast on the figure of the old commandant by the figure of the Grand Inquisitor from the legend which Ivan Karamazov tells his brother Alyosha, who, according to Dostoevsky's design, had to leave his monastic novitiate for the revolution.

But Ivan understood and knew that that well-regulated world constructed by the father inquisitors, with the help of *autos-da-fé* and torture, is not and cannot be the only reign of harmony and human happiness, for in it there is no room for mercy and true love of man. For Kafka the order established by the old commandant, this prototype of the world that could arise if the dreams of social utopians were realized in practice, is the only possible one, for the only possible path to the establishment of justice—through bloody horror—leads to it. Absolutizing the idea of good and evil, divesting them of concrete historical meaning and content, abstracting from the real conditions of life, mechanically juxtaposing good and justice—for him these concepts do not coincide—Kafka deprives the concept of justice of sense, makes it relative, doubtful, ambiguous, and debatable. Only evil appears undebatable and unquestionable, dissolving and swallowing up justice in itself, impregnating it and assuming its countenance.

The relativity of good and evil, as of other moral values, is extremely characteristic of the decadent world view. It is peculiar to Kafka too, who considered that justice inevitably turns into evil and for that reason every struggle for justice is senseless, for it leads to the victory of injustice. Kafka considered the achievement of social harmony impossible, as its cornerstone principle, justice, degenerates into evil. But if reflection on the false paths to the genuine well-being of all men gave birth in the great Russian novelist to profound philosophical generalization breathing with inspiration and poetry, then from Kafka's pen runs a unilinear allegory containing a quite naturalistic description of torture and an instrument of torture.

Kafka made great efforts to understand and examine the concrete causes which turn life into something hostile to man. He tried to undertake such an investigation in the novel *Lost Without a Trace* (begun in 1913), which Max Brod called *America* for publication. However, the loss of contact with reality greatly weakens and reduces to nothing the cognitive capacity of Kafka's art; and equally the disdain for the analytic side of art, which was so typical of the expressionists, prevents Kafka from comprehending and representing the contradictions and conflicts in life as contradictions of the capitalist system of social relations. For this reason his novel does not reveal the historically concrete causes which make man's existence onerous, difficult, and tortured.

As a novelist Kafka moved in the narrative tradition of the nineteenth century and constructed his first novel—as he did both of his others, *The Trial* and *The Castle*—on the collision of the individual with society. This classic conflict allowed realist writers to depict broad social manners and to provide a many-sided analysis of social life. They usually placed their hero at the crossroads of social antagonisms and contradictions, and for that reason his personal fate assumed a general significance and his character acquired richness of content.

Kafka did not utilize the possibilities inherent in this conflict, although the external background of the narration in *Lost Without a Trace* is much broader than in his other works, and the events of the action are more clearly outlined than in *The Trial*, not to speak of in *The Castle*.

The subject of *Lost Without a Trace* is the adventures of Karl Rossmann, a modest, naive, and simple-hearted boy who is banished from his parents' home in Prague because the maid has seduced him.

But the unexpected reversals of fate which follow on many adventures do not help in understanding the world and the society he finds himself in. The reason for that is not the novel's mixture of two kinds of narration: a realistic one distinguished by verisimilitude and exactness in the observation of life; and a fantastic one which displaces authentic living relations, leaves unexplained the motives of human actions, and transforms the face of the world in which Karl Rossmann acts. The reason is that Kafka removes the fantastic from its nourishing soil of reality.

And if the realistically described scenes in the novel give some idea of the American form of life and of the exploitation which in that country oppresses the poor people, the fantastic episodes, for all their entertaining qualities and inventive brightness, lead the narration away from examining the difficult social causes of the hostile relation of man and society in the capitalist world.

As always, in Kafka's novel the fantastic arises from the prosaic and the everyday and assumes the traits of the usual. But in *Lost Without a Trace*, the fantastic also exists simply as the inexplicable and improbable, and for that reason it only weakly influences Karl Rossmann's fate and does not explain the characteristics and peculiarities of the world in which he finds himself and which he must understand in order to survive in it. To a significant extent his fate is predetermined by chance and external circumstances which to him are incomprehensible, fateful, and not subject to change.

[. . .]

The whole development of the theme shows that the novel's content deals only in certain episodes with the theme of the real conflicts and contradictions in American life which made up the tragic background of the "muckrakers," for example of the early Sinclair of *The Jungle* and *The Metropolis*, of Dreiser's novels, or of London's antimonopolistic utopia, *The Iron Heel*. It seems that Kafka, who himself had never been in America and who knew it only from books, travelers' notes, and the stories of eyewitnesses who had been in the United States, was able to give only the outward coloration of American being and way of life: the sparkling skyscrapers, the stream of automobiles, the noisy election campaigns, the crowds of strikers, the unemployed—all this he knew from secondhand. But in one very important episode of the novel, the story of Karl Rossmann's service in the Hotel Occidental, there is authentic depiction, in horribly true detail, of the monstrous exploitation of child labor, the exhausting work of young people, their lack of rights and dependence on the administration, the inhuman conditions of their lives. The description of their dormitories reminds one in its grimness and gloominess of Dickens' descriptions of schools and children's homes resembling prisons, where the spirits of the charges incarcerated there languish and their bodies suffer, enslaved by pitiless inspectors and ignorant tutors.

Kafka read Dickens carefully; the grotesque manner of writing, the tendency toward condensation of the figures, the hyperbolization of life's phenomena impressed him. Although the Dickensian element is clearly present in *Lost Without a Trace* in some of the scenes spiced with bitter humor, Kafka's relationship to the English realist was two-sided. Kafka's diaries contain unambiguous testimonies to his complex and many-sided reception of the Dickensian legacy.

Dickens' *David Copperfield* ("The Stoker" is a direct imitation of Dickens, and the conception of the novel is so to an even greater extent), Kafka notes in 1917, is the story of the trunk, of cheering and enticing, of love for names and dirty houses, and so forth, but it is above all a method:

As I now see it, my intention was to write a Dickens novel, but enriched with brighter lights taken from the times and duller ones taken from my own self. Dickens' richness and unconcerned, powerful flowing—but because of that passages of terrible impotence, where he only exhaustedly plays with what has already been done. Barbarous the impression of the senseless whole . . . Heartlessness behind the manner freighted with emotion. These wedges of rough characterization that are artificially driven into each character, but without which Dickens would not be capable even once of quickly climbing up his story. (*T*, p. 535)

This assessment—subjective like all assessments from Kafka's pen—resembles least of all a respectful appreciation of the legacy of the great artist. It is inspired by a spirit of distaste for the full-bodied living Dickensian prose, which seems to Kafka to be excessively coarse, barbarian, excessively *objective*. And it is no accident that he took the dark tones of his novel not from life, as Dickens did in his works, but drew them from his own soul, subordinating the objective depiction of events to interpretation and illumination through the subjectivist limits of his personal experience.

It is not paradoxical that Kafka further charges Dickens with the abstractness of his metaphor. In fact, he himself shuns metaphoric style as a narrator. His prose is bare and exact, dryish, businesslike, somewhat ceremonious and, it seems, neatly cleansed of floridness and ornamentation. His comparisons are strict, solidly and rather unilinearly united with what they are supposed to explain. Kafka does not misuse associations; he tries to adhere to a straight narration which seems designed for the trustworthy transmission of authentic events and for the description of clear and simple spiritual conditions.

But the peculiarity of his artistic manner, hidden and confirmed in the constant inward contrast between the method of exposition and the content of the depiction, is completely opposed to truth and clarity; it is alogical, phantasmagoric, monstrous; it cuts all real connections between events and factually appears as an unfolded metaphor, a symbolic allegory in which abstractness is inherent from the very beginning and is present in it just as organically as salt in sea water.

In essence, almost all the major episodes in the novel *Lost Without a Trace* are marked by the abstraction from reality and life's concreteness that are characteristic of Kafka. But into the depiction of child labor in the Hotel Occidental Kafka put his own ample observations which he made during his work in the insurance office. He simply transferred facts known to him onto American soil, recording in that way some traits of capitalist society. However, in stating the stunning and depressing facts, he was not able to connect them with the peculiarities of the American system of enterprise and described it as if it were not at all different from the bureaucratized state system of Austria-Hungary. In his mind, the same kind of hierarchy that dominated in the civil service apparatus of the Austro-Hungarian monarchy also reigned in bourgeois-democratic America.

An unclear understanding of the social relations existing in a mature capitalist society gave birth in Kafka to fantastic conceptions of its structure. The administration of the Occidental sits somewhere on the upper floors of the hotel; it is almost faceless, anonymous, and fatefully omnipotent over its great numbers of employees. Its power is realized through numerous senior waiters and their substitutes, the simple waiters, senior cooks, porters, junior porters, and so on. Describing the fantastically overgrown management of the hotel, which symbolizes the power that enslaves man, who forever finds himself somewhere at the foot of a gigantic hierarchical pyramid, Kafka did not discern the particularity of new forms of exploitation and enslavement of man peculiar to a mature capitalism with its flexible and disguised methods of subjugation. Therefore, the truth of the private observations in his novel comes into conflict with the content of the artistic generalization, which acquired an abstraction that hinders understanding and perception of reality. The fantastic line of the novel became just as abstract, for Karl Rossmann's painful wandering through the endless dark corridors of the country estate to which he was invited by an acquaintance of his uncle, or the description of the strange life of the singer Brunelda, a woman of excessive and inhuman obesity who is capable of screaming for hours at the slightest noise and of arranging her nightly bed out of everything that is located in her room—these have purely ornamental character and are devoid of all the higher content which makes the fantastic and grotesque a tool for the investigation of the real world.

In describing the situation in which his hero finds himself, Kafka disregards an investigation of his inner world, a depiction of the reactions of Karl Rossmann's inner "ego" to the strange and unusual events of the outer world. Kafka is also little concerned with the psychology of the other characters in his novel. In a similar way, the unwillingness or inability to look into the souls of others appears to be a characteristic trait of his work.

In the novel, Karl Rossmann's conflict with the society he is in lost its historical and living concreteness, its grounding in reality, and became one of the possible variations on the collision of man with life, with people; it serves as a confirmation of Kafka's cherished belief in the constant disharmony of human existence. The sources of this disharmony he saw in the dissociation of people, in their inability to overcome the mutual estrangement which seems to be stronger than everything—stronger than the ties of kinship, than feelings of love, than friendship, and so forth.

The vast separation between people—a phenomenon characteristic of bourgeois society and born in it—acquired in Kafka's eyes the significance of a universal law dominating the forms of interpersonal relationships. Similarly, absolutizing a historically concrete phenomenon removed from its socially conditioned soil led Kafka to a false view of both human nature and the place of man in the world and society. In his view the separation of people and their disconnection grow into the distrust of one person for another. Distrust quite naturally engenders suspicion, and suspicion, in its turn, rouses conviction in possible human guilt, the thought that man has some fault hidden in his soul. On this basis, even without being guilty of anything, he can be subjected to blame, punishment, and penalty. Therefore, the officer-executioner in the story "In the Penal Colony" can declare with military definitiveness that "guilt is never in doubt." In general, Kafka shares this point of view which is directly expressed by his hero, agreeing that in the eyes of society and of other people, a man either is always guilty or can be considered guilty. Therefore the operative and possible form of illuminating the truth, that is, of penetrating into a man's inner thoughts, is for Kafka the court of law, a legal trial in which the accused, without himself knowing or perceiving his guilt—for *he appears guilty only to outside observers*—is already condemned. In such a trial no one can be, and no one is, acquitted.

In "The Judgment" Kafka puts the father and son into the relationship of judge and accused. The father, having no possibility of penetrating into his son's soul by way of an impartial interrogation, sentences him to death. The whole legal process breaks out over poor Karl Rossmann, who had left his post at the elevator in order to help a drunken vagrant. True, having hung their court and mock justice over him, the administrators of the Hotel Occidental have no power to sentence Karl to death, but in throwing him out onto the street and depriving him of work, they direct him onto the path leading to ruin.

There is no basis for believing that any theological or religious point of view is reflected in Kafka's conception of the constant guilt of man, or that his thought is founded on the idea of original sin or the idea of redemption and retribution for sins committed. Kafka's religiosity, which his biographer Max Brod insists on, is very problematical, for Kafka was essentially an unreligious person who maintained neutrality in religious questions, as he did in other social questions as well. His conception of human guilt was not a distorted, perverted, or deformed unrealistic reflection of a real social phenomenon—the social disconnectedness of people—the nature of which he was in no position to understand; and therefore he mystified it, turned it into an abstraction, a universal, which he did not attempt to corroborate and found on concrete, authentic facts of life. That is why the living background is so abstract in his novel *The Trial* (begun in 1914), in which Kafka with great thoroughness and precision mirrored the conviction, fundamental to his world view, of man's helplessness in the face of the omnipotent and unknown forces over him, and his cherished thought of man's fateful guilt.

In its artistic merit and the intensity of the mood expressed in it, *The Trial* stands considerably higher than *Lost Without a Trace*. *The Trial* is marked by great inner drama; the action moves energetically; its fragmentary character and the fact that it is unfinished are barely noticeable; and the ending breathes icy tragedy.

Kafka's poetics, calculated and suited for the communication of the illogical, improbable, and horrifying, wins the day in this novel, saturating the narration with an atmosphere of unspecified omnipotent fear, which seems to have been poured into the humdrum of daily life and which, slowly penetrating the soul of the hero, gradually seizes his whole nature and finally breaks his will and neatly robs him of his ability to oppose the unknown exterior forces dooming him to ruin.

As in Kafka's other works, the main thing in *The Trial* is the portrayal of the situation in which the hero of the novel unexpectedly finds himself one morning: the bank officer Joseph K. is arrested by unknown authorities and remains free until the end of his trial. The theme of the novel made Kafka establish his thought about human guilt, and the narration contains not a small portion of philosophical sophistry, sometimes very refined, sometimes running to allegory, allusion, and symbolic parable. The fantastic element in the novel is organically interwoven with the solidly prosaic reflection of the ordinary, so that the whole narration, and within it the story of the misfortunes and downfall of Joseph K., takes on an unreal, vacillating, and polyvalent character. But in the end this polyvalence promises more than it delivers, for the content of the allegories, allusions, and symbols is marked by abstractness. Only the main theme is certain—the fate of Joseph K., about which Kafka speaks with inner emotion, plunging the narration into an atmosphere of fear which is all the more impressive for growing out of extremely prosaic details of life.

Apart from the novel's philosophizing and complicatedness, Kafka arranges the relations between his characters as a construction which is not enriched by living details. He omits important links in their doings and intentionally does not adequately motivate their actions. The poetics of the novel does not contradict the spirit of expressionist aesthetics, which is also furthered by Kafka's attempt to clean and free his hero of real ties with life; and for this reason the hero appears in the novel not so much as a typical figure as a human essence abstracted from reality, as man in general, man as such, alone in the world and life.

Kafka's departure from the principle of typifying his heroes reveals the unrealistic nature of his work, for typifying is an indispensable sign and characteristic of realist art, by virtue of which it rests on social analysis and is able to investigate, recognize, generalize, and therefore also to typify phenomena of life.

Kafka creates characters who are for the most part very schematic, but not types; therefore his hero is characterized by abstractness and conventionality. Very imperceptibly, almost in passing as it were, Kafka communicates only minimal information about him, for the social genesis of the hero is not important to Kafka. In essence, Joseph K. is a "man without qualities," as Robert Musil well called the hero of his novel, the figures of which, like Kafka's, were mainly masks, personifications of ideas and moods of their creator. Kafka's novel does not provide distinct indications that would allow us to understand and find objective reasons for Joseph K.'s strange arrest, either in his past, about which almost nothing is known, or in his present, about which a bit more is known, but not enough to locate the grounds for the beginning of the trial. Joseph K.'s life is quite ordinary. Most of his time he spends at work, where he has even made a career for himself; the evenings he whiles away with his colleagues in some cafe or another; Sundays he spends with his girlfriend, who receives her visitors in bed, or goes to visit superiors who are benevolently inclined toward him. An impersonal existence, bare of any individual particularities. And Joseph K.'s principle place of residence is the bank, which is portrayed in the novel just as cursorily and non-concretely. A bit more distinct is the depiction of Frau Grubach's boardinghouse, where Joseph K. stays and to which the lowly servants of the court come to arrest him and to inform him that henceforth he is deprived of his freedom and figures among the accused who are required to answer before the court.

Nor are there in the novel any allusions to exterior reasons which might explain Joseph K.'s guilt and the grounds for the persecution he is subjected to, reasons which lie beyond the limits of his private life, as they lie beyond the limits of the life of the accused Block and of a majority of the other people who spend hours and days in the evil-smelling chancelleries and waiting rooms of the court, beneath the red-hot roofs of the attics where this strange administration is located, in the impossibly small rooms of the lawyers, defending themselves against the unknown but ubiquitous and omnipotent power of the court and its hierarchical apparatus.

Neither exterior nor inner reasons allow us to explain the sources of Joseph K.'s guilt, if it in fact exists, nor the aims of the massive persecution of the citizens of a "lawful government." Only one thing is sure, and that is Joseph K.'s innocence; although after protracted pacing up and down in the court chancelleries, where he is stupified by the improbably stifling air and stunned by the looks of the accused who are crushed by their fate so much that they have lost any concept of human dignity and rights, and after worrisome talks with the lawyer initiating him into the secrets of the legal proceedings and the dispositions of the court officials, Joseph K. begins to doubt his own innocence and passionately begins to search for faults in his own life that could explain why and of what he is guilty.

Kafka casts off all possibilities of a real foundation for what has happened and places his hero in opposition to some anonymous force endowed with judicial status and the right to punish people. With great artfulness Kafka portrays the situation of victimization into which his hero gradually falls. Having overcome the initial confusion at the unexpected news of his arrest and having recognized that he is truly under judicial examination, although temporarily remaining in his former condition, with his former life style and occupations, Joseph K. begins to feel searching and observing looks directed at him from all quarters. Unexpected coincidences and, it seems, unimportant facts—the inopportune appearance of a boy at the door of the home where Joseph K. lives, the arrival of a relative of his landlady, a sudden knock heard during an important conversation—everything acquires a horrible meaning for Joseph K., for everything that happens can at the same time be both accidental and not accidental. All the more so as Joseph K. gradually begins to see how extensive the legal system is which is opposing him, how deeply it has seeped into the pores of the society in which he had lived without cares and not without pleasure.

Among the court functionaries who visited him on that fateful morning when he was informed that he was arrested and that the trial against him had begun, Joseph K. sees his co-workers from the bank, and later on he is even present at the punishment of the guards, which takes place in a storeroom of the bank, where an energetic flogger whips them for having shown unnecessary greed during Joseph K.'s arrest, for hankering after his underwear and eating up his breakfast. A direct relation to the court is also maintained by the children in the house of the artist Titorelli, who with their noisy and insolent thronging around Joseph K. and with their eavesdropping and spying interrupt his serious and important conversation with the painter about the judicial system. In this and many other episodes of the novel one can feel a clear connection with those scenes in Dostoevsky's works in which the Russian novelist's magical power of depiction lends a fantastic coloration to events of external life, tinting them an unreal, spectral color, allowing us to look beneath the masks of things and appearances and to see behind them the mysterious abyss of life. The cloudburst and rain which accompanied the dying Svidrigailov on his nocturnal wanderings about Petersburg also accompany Joseph K. on his last walk to the cathedral, where he hears his fate from the mouth of the prison chaplain. And here it is not a question of external, coincidental agreement, but of deep connections in the coloration of both episodes, of their inner artistic resonance. The scene with the children in Kafka's novel has a ring of the scene of Svidrigailov's delirium, especially in the episodes where Svidrigailov is horrified at the devilish transformation of a poor freezing girl into a defiantly insolent camellia. Having suddenly escaped from behind the child's face, evil appears in Kafka's novel too from behind the faces of the children who follow Joseph K. on his visit to the painter Titorelli, and it especially horrifies Joseph K. when he suddenly sees beneath the external gentleness of the hunchback girl a monstrous primeval perversion. The concept of the metaphysical force of evil makes these scenes in the novels of Kafka and Dostoevsky akin. And even Titorelli reveals himself to be the hereditary court artist, painting portraits of judges and magistrates according to petrified rules established in the past, dishonestly embellishing their prosaic exteriors. That the court exists and that a serious trial has been begun against Joseph K. is known to many, and no one is surprised at this news. It is seen as a sad but usual fact of normal life.

In portraying the ubiquity of the judicial system, Kafka strove to underline the inescapability of the situation in which its victim finds himself, who cannot escape from the jaws of the accusation; and if some one did succeed in winning the trial, then that was equivalent to a miracle.

Through the novel runs the notion of the uselessness and impossibility of resisting those strange and ominous forces which rule over man's life. Joseph K.'s fate illustrates this most important idea of the novel, organic to all of Kafka's work. At first, apprized that misfortune has befallen him, Joseph K. cannot believe that what is happening to him is not a bad joke, a nasty prank. But very soon he begins to feel that some invisible trait is isolating him, separating him from other people, and, although he is still in society, he is already alienated and cut off from society. The court inspector did not want to shake his hand, for it is really not pleasant to shake the hand of an accused person who is deprived of rights. And Frau Grubach, the landlady of his boarding house, who thinks highly of him, also avoids shaking his hand, as if distracted or forgetful.

It is natural that Joseph K.'s first impulse is directed toward escaping from the absurd situation he is in. He starts to look for help—

naively, awkwardly, and aimlessly. Joseph K.'s attempts to defend himself are portrayed by Kafka in a grotesque, ironic manner, which emphasizes all the more the inescapability of the situation of the novel's hero. He shares his plans with his neighbor Fräulein Bürstner, a lowly typist who does not shun evening meetings with cavaliers to earn a little on the side. Joseph K. counts on her help, even though this reckoning is ridiculous. For a while he yields to the hope that Leni, his lawyer Huld's nurse, will be able to help him. She enters into an affair with Joseph K., as she does with other clients of her employer. At the beginning of the inquest, going to the court chancellery for interrogation, he gives an audacious speech which demonstratively expresses his contempt for both the court and the accusations brought against him by the court. For a while he even tries to live free of cares, as if nothing had happened, not denying himself love's passion, which Kafka describes so straightforwardly. The schematic depiction of Joseph K.'s emotional life in the novel is partly explained by the fact that the art of psychological analysis, the ability to penetrate into the consciousness and emotional world of others as well as his own, is foreign to Kafka—for as a writer Kafka is a great egocentric. The reason for it is in the schematism of his artistic thought, in the tendency toward simplified, constructivist reproduction of life and human relationships, which was also characteristic of expressionist poetics.

But in time a powerful weariness and hopelessness inexorably subjugates Joseph K. and paralyzes his will to resist. He begins to feel that the ordeal which has befallen him is beyond his strength. The condition of persecution and subjugation overwhelms him. The thought of the purposelessness of struggle becomes natural to him and crowds out all other thoughts. He decides to give up the fight, and the decision ripens in him during his conversation with the prison chaplain in the cathedral, in that scene written in dusky and grave tones which appears to be most important for elucidating the design of the novel. Therefore the prostrate and defeated Joseph K. is not taken by surprise by the two men with the shabby and baggy faces of opera tenors who appear at his home late one evening, take him by the hand with the grip of death, and go with him through the city streets flooded with the cold and deadened light of the moon to the abandoned quarry, where one of them thrusts a narrow butcher's knife into his heart. Joseph K. was waiting for them; he had anticipated their arrival. Killed like a dog, he died alone, useless to all. No one interceded for him or protected him from that mortal danger, the horrible and merciless court.

But what is this monstrous legal machine which trampled Joseph K. underfoot and ground him between its stones? Much is said about it in the novel, but in the end nothing is said. Kafka describes its chancelleries in detail, the dispositions of the judges and magistrates, who are capricious, like children, and just as trusting; and he also describes the bar, which entwines the powerful trunk of the court organization, whose officials, despite the fact that they stand in guard of the law, are greedy and excessively ambitious. But, despite the detailed and ample description of the court, which occupies many pages in the novel, its nature, provenience, and assignment remain unclarified. It is unknown whose power it expresses and what kind of order it defends, although, essentially, the court in Kafka's novel is a mystified representation of the system of bourgeois law and order, upon which is founded the order of capitalist society.

The court appears in the novel as some kind of abstraction. And here it is not a question of Kafka's having fantastically exaggerated the omnipresence of the court system or of having had recourse to the grotesque in the depiction of the court offices. Dickens described the "Ministry of Circumlocution," a gigantic bureaucratic machine running on empty. Another great artist, Sukhovo-Kobylin, himself a victim of a years-long legal trial, in breaking down the mechanism of the bureaucratic judicial system, divided it into quite abstract categories: "Authorities," "Powers," "Subordinations," "Nothings or private people"—and he even brought a completely unexpected unit into the hierarchy: "Non-People." In legal concepts there is generally a certain quantity of abstractness, for they rest on laws which formulate certain general rules of human interaction and behavior. But laws are not empty abstractions, for they generalize and make norms of the rules of communal life, which are worked out in real life, through the concrete experience of people. One may not tear laws out of the soil which gives birth to them.

Of course, Dickens and Sukhovo-Kobylin and Saltykov-Shchedrin, those realist artists who portrayed and critized the bureaucratic and governmental apparatus of proprietary society, always filled the abstract categories of the law or the bureaucratic system with extremely clear social content. The grotesque and exaggerated, the provisional and fantastic were to them instruments of social analysis, that is, means to a realistic comprehension and representation of life.

Behind the picture of the court in Kafka's novel stands an incomprehensible reality. Apart from the fact that the judicial system described in *The Trial* reflects characteristic traits of the state apparatus of the Austro-Hungarian monarchy, one cannot consider the picture which Kafka has created as anything but a fetishized representation of the governmental-bureaucratic political machine. The figure of the court in Kafka is also a personification of unknown forces of evil inherent in life and hostile to man, a mystified and therefore abstracted reflection of them in the consciousness of man, who feels the oppression of the capitalist system and cannot understand the sources of the oppression, against which, according to Kafka, it is impossible to struggle. He repeatedly emphasizes in the novel that it is no ordinary court which is judging Joseph K., but some anonymous power.

It is indeed difficult, and hardly possible, to struggle with an unknown evil and, to the person who comes in conflict with it, the strength of evil seems incomparably greater than it actually is. Starting out from his own weakness, Kafka exaggerates the strength of world evil and in the parable of the Law, which the prison chaplain tells to Joseph K., he absolutizes it into something indestructible and invincible. This very parable seems a model of sophistic casuistry with the aim of demonstrating the indisputable uselessness of man's struggle with evil in the name of justice, which is what the Law embodies.

The peasant who dies in the arms of the doorkeeper at the entrance to the Law, since he has not made the decision to go through the entrance, was apparently not able to do anything else but follow the doorkeeper's denial, that is, realize what was inevitable and designed beforehand. Only just before his death did he learn that the entrance was designated for him alone and that no other could go through. But he can do nothing with this truth, for now it is more than useless to him—it clouds the last moment of his life and makes his whole previous existence meaningless. The interpretations of the parable in the chaplain's speech, however, do not clarify, but intentionally obscure, its meaning and the true situation of the things reflected in the parable. In the end, it is not so important who is subordinate to whom— the doorkeeper to the peasant or *vice-versa;* or whether the doorkeeper knows what is hidden behind the door to the Law or not; or whether after the peasant's death he is or is not supposed to shut the opening to the Law forever. What is important is that a man who has come to know and find Justice is left with nothing, and that the Law, for which he has thirsted, is inaccessible to him.

If one follows that sense of the parable which the chaplain very cleverly forces on Joseph K., then it is possible to surmise that the man who was thirsting for justice became a victim of circumstances which are stronger than he and that it is only because of that that the Law is inaccessible and unattainable to him. But the pessimistic conclusion of the parable is deeper and more hopeless. The man *himself* did not want to enter the door to the Law; he took fright at the doorkeeper's words and voluntarily sat down at the side on the stool the doorkeeper put there, and did not once disobey his order and try to enter the place he had to go to, even though nothing in the parable says that he cannot do that.

That order or disorder of the world, which is imbued with evil and coercion and which reigns in life, is unalterable not only because it rests on power and might, but also because people themselves willingly bow to the order, and because any thought of the possibility of changing it is foreign and inaccessible to them. This conclusion of the novel received philosophical completion in the parable of the Law and became an added confirmation of Kafka's deep disbelief in man and his constructive possibilities.

But the whole conception of the Law has an ambiguous meaning for Kafka. For the peasant the bosom of the Law radiates an alluring glow; there he tries to find liberation from all his troubles; there his lips, which have been parched in the desert of life, cling to the eternal fountain of Justice. But this hope of the peasant is empty and deceptive, for the path to justice is cruel, thorny, and terrible, and in its absolute, perfect meaning, justice is inhuman. To the Law its design, principles and execution are important; but not the welfare of the man. They judge Joseph K. according to some predetermined law, but what did this law court turn into? It concluded by stabbing a knife into its victim's heart in an old stone quarry, for such is the Law.

Joseph K.'s relation to society runs over into the legal process. To Kafka it was evident that the condition of dissociation among people, which in his mind breeds suspicion and the conviction of human guiltiness, inevitably leads to pernicious consequences. Therefore the search for a possible solution to the conflict and antagonism between man and life constantly occupied and disturbed his imagination. And he regarded his own isolation and separation from life and people as a misfortune. Toward the end of his life, in 1922, he wrote in his diary that he saw a higher happiness in nearness to people. But that happiness remained unattainable to him. All of Kafka's attempts to establish an effective inner contact with the world and reality ended in failure, and the conviction of the impossibility of the union of people, of the impossibility of overcoming the reasons for their disunion, incessantly gripped his mind. This conviction pervades his third novel, *The Castle* (begun in 1914, continued 1921-1922) as much as it does both of the preceding unfinished ones.

If the living background of the drama of Joseph K. is provisional and unrealistic, then in *The Castle* the process of abstraction, of Kafka's departure from reality, has greatly increased. It does not allow us to get to the bottom of the novel's symbolism and adequately understand the meaning of many of its figures and scenes, especially the central image of the novel, the castle itself, which it is possible to interpret variously as an embodiment of power, or of the world order, or of the law. And the reason for that is not the novel's fragmentary nature and incompleteness, but something else. Kafka's creative development was extremely paradoxical: with the years his hand became firmer and his style acquired transparency and austerity, but the content of his works lost clarity. It is as if content has slipped out of the creations of his imagination and only remotely resembles real life.

The Castle is not an exception. It may be compared to a strange jellyfish taken out of the depths of the sea and placed under the hot rays of the sun. Shimmering in iridescent mother-of-pearl colors, its body evaporates and opens to our view a fragile calcine skeleton consisting of the finest threads joined in a complicated and strange pattern. But from the pattern it is difficult to restore the natural beauty of the creature of nature which pleased our eyes with the play of its colors. The real and living content only barely shows through the plot of *The Castle* and the complicated relationships of its hero: it is elusive and vague. The events depicted in the novel draw the narration into the character of the fantastic, which destroys and erases the ties connecting the novel's content with the authentic conflicts and contradictions of life.

Joseph K. in *The Trial* had already represented an abstract human individual connected with real life only by some aspects of his worldly customs and appearance. The hero of *The Castle*, the land surveyor

K., is completely deprived of individuality, very much in the spirit of expressionist poetics, the canons of which demanded less an authentic person than his abstraction and reduced the variety of human characteristics to the naked social essence of man, dislodging his individual qualities. For this reason the heroes of expressionist works are named with unquestionable simplicity: "The Capitalist," "The Merchant," "Engineer," "Unemployed Worker," and so forth.

It is almost impossible to find out anything about the surveyor K.'s past; his figure is so abstracted that even his exterior appearance remains unknown. However, disregarding a description of the exterior details of his hero's life, Kafka underlines with painful constancy K.'s consuming inner aspiration to penetrate the castle at any price. The castle reigns over the village, and K. arrives there one cold winter day, hoping to obtain from the authorities the right or permission to become not only one of the village inhabitants, but an equal member of the human community composed of the castle and its village, which has become a temporary and unstable refuge for K. The inner aspiration of the surveyor K. to overcome, cast off, and destroy his isolation from human society is the moving spring of the novel's action, its fundamental motive, which specifies all its hero's thoughts and actions.

It is not known what in K.'s past separated him from people, what caused his disagreement with the world. Having no realistic foundation, K.'s conflict with life also had to be resolved unrealistically. Therefore the fantastic element in *The Castle* acquires a self-sufficient meaning and, losing objective content, it frequently degenerates into the inexplicable. Walking along the snow-covered streets of the village and looking into the home of one of its inhabitants, the surveyor K. sees how, in a steam-filled room, some men with long beards are bathing in an unprecedentedly enormous tub; and in an armchair a weak and sickly woman is reclining, holding a sucking infant in her arms, while two other children play beside her. The room acquires gigantic dimensions, losing itself in clouds of steam and deep darkness. Such fantastic and strange scenes occur throughout the whole novel.

After the surveyor K. has succeeded in establishing an extremely tenuous connection with the castle—tenuous because it is based on ambiguous instructions which cannot be interpreted clearly—he gets two helpers from the authorities: medium-sized, dark-faced youths with long pointed beards, named Arthur and Jeremias, who are dressed in tight coats stretched over their bodies that do not conceal, but rather emphasize, the inhuman nature of these creatures. It is hard for K. to understand who they are: spies or servants. They appear before him at the most unseemly times, including the moment of K.'s intercourse with Frieda, a girl from the castle. Lively and curious like children, they pester the surveyor, who deals very sternly with them, turns them out of the warm room into the frost, thrashes them, and finally refuses their service.

But even more fantastic are the order and disposition of the village, the character of the relationship of the inhabitants to the castle, and the castle itself, to which the surveyor persistently and tenaciously makes his way along the snowy village streets that lead him, against his will and desire, farther and farther away from the goal of his striving. However he strives to approach the castle—to approach it physically—he does not succeed, and the decayed, unsightly buildings of the castle recede from him, as if some invisible force were removing them. He can get into the castle only after having received permission from the castle authorities, but this permission he can get only after having reported in person to one of the responsible bureaucrats in the castle, in particular the steward Klamm, who remains inaccessible and elusive. In addition, Klamm's very appearance and behavior change according to his mood, and it is almost impossible to recognize him.

Like Joseph K. in *The Trial*, the surveyor K. runs up against an unusually extensive and hierarchic bureaucratic organization which operates according to rules and regulations known only to itself and which are incomprehensible to people outside. The bureaucratic apparatus has seized with its tentacles all spheres of the village life and has subjugated almost all its inhabitants, who are constantly aware of their dependence on the power which stands above them. The villagers well know the systems established by the castle's menials and officials, but to the surveyor K. these systems are revealed only gradually, and the more he learns of them, the gloomier and more disconsolate appears the life of the village and its people. It is imbued with severity and sorrow and, most importantly, it lacks that to which all men at all times strive: freedom.

The villagers are not free, and although the castle menials do not mete out punishment, they possess enough power and opportunity indirectly to make rebellion particularly unlikely and daring, and rather than oppress the people, they lead them to complete moral defeat and destruction. The highest happiness for the villagers consists in gaining the benevolence of the castle authorities. The youth Barnabas, to whose family K. becomes close, spends his days in the uncomfortable chancelleries of the castle, in the hope that some official will notice him and give him an errand. Barnabas has no proper right to that, as no one has officially confirmed him in service, but he considers himself an employee of the castle and a holder of the rank of messenger.

The villagers' voluntary service to the castle is a typical phenomenon, and Barnabas, with his confidence in his own belonging to the vast castle authorities, affirms the accuracy of the established view of the relationship between the castle and the village. But that gloomy life which appears to the surveyor K.—and this is characteristic of Kafka's social views—attracts K., and he gets into a fight with the castle authorities, not for the liberation of the villagers from their voluntary servitude, but for his own right to join in the monotonous and colorless life before him, for he does not think he has any other possibility, and he does not know and does not want to know any other life.

He sacrifices much in this struggle: his own integrity, for in allowing him the right to be in the village, the castle authorities give him the lowliest work as janitor in the school. He also sacrifices love, which he found with the village girl Frieda, Klamm's former mistress. The girl courageously and firmly rebels against her fate and is ready to go to the end of the world with the surveyor. As always with Kafka, the hero's love relationships are portrayed extremely directly and without any psychological delicacy. But Frieda's attempt to escape to freedom ends in a terrible failure. Feeling that K. needs her only as a means to the accomplishment of his own goal, a personal meeting with Klamm, she leaves the surveyor and falls into even more humiliating servitude than before in uniting her life with Jeremias, one of the surveyor's former assistants.

All attempts to cast off the burden of the castle's power end just as lamentably for the villagers. The story of Amalia, which K. hears from her sister Olga, serves to underscore that. Having rejected the suit of the important official Sortini, the proud girl ruins her family, for the villagers, feeling the castle's covert ill will toward the disobedient woman even though it never comes out into the open, create around her relatives an atmosphere of mistrust, suspicion, and deadly enmity. Amalia's father, having been ruined and having lost house and home, is forced into the cold to watch over the road in the hope of meeting one of the powerful officials and pleading for himself and his daughters. And Olga becomes the concubine of the castle menials, to whom she turns at the beginning, trying to intercede for her sister, who has fallen into disgrace. Thus the freedom–loving act of one person becomes equal to the defeat of another, and in the end the balance of unfreedom is established in life, because freedom in general is unattainable. This thought informs the whole novel, penetrating all its episodes and authenticating its general frame of mind.

K. also recognizes the inevitability of unfreedom in the life to which he aspires, but he is prepared voluntarily to wear the yoke of subjugation, if only he is not separated, isolated, and torn away from people. In essence, the surveyor K. capitulates before life, accepting its inhumanity and cruelty. He also capitulates before the unknown forces which reign in life and deal with man's fate however they can. But the castle doesn't need his capitulation. The novel was supposed to end with K.'s destruction. And nothing is changed by the other version of the novel's ending communicated by Max Brod, according to which the surveyor achieved the right to live in the village. The right was granted to a man already dying of exhaustion.

The tragic ending of all three of Kafka's novels is not accidental, for the conflict of man and society, man and life is, in his opinion, not resolved, and the isolation of people cannot be overcome. This conclusion very clearly reveals the pessimistic character of Kafka's social views, his conviction of the impossibility of man's changing the conditions of his existence for the better.

The social milieu in which Kafka's heroes act is deformed and conditional. Only a part, and not a large one, of the objective processes which proceed in real life have percolated into his novels. Highly characteristic of them is the uniformity of situations and of the manner of resolving the fundamental conflict, for Kafka chooses only situations in which man is plunged into a state of fear and hopelessness and inevitably goes to his doom. The suppression of a realistic, analytical examination of the social milieu, which essentially remains unrepresented in his novels and is replaced by the description of the conditional living background, led to the impoverishment of the heroes' characters and to the schematization of their relationships with one another and with the surrounding world. Kafka did not want to and could not examine the principal connections of the social phenomena predetermining the tragic end of his heroes' conflict with life, and therefore the conflict he portrayed acquired characteristics of the timeless, the eternal, and the fatalistic. Compared with realist artists of the twentieth century, with Maxim Gorky and Thomas Mann, Romain Rolland and Martin Andersen Nexö, Bernard Shaw and Sean O'Casey, and the younger ones like Sholokhov, Hemingway, Faulkner, Roger Martin du Gard and others, who created the epos of our century, Kafka provided an extremely one-sided picture of the world. And it is not only a matter of his having portrayed life in conditional forms—real art is never a mirrored reflection of life and the world. The reason is that the abstractness of the content of his works does not allow the representation to sharpen the real conflicts of life, to make them clearer and more graphic.

But what did Kafka bring into the art of the novel and art of the twentieth century in general? An extremely poignant feeling of the tragedy of life in bourgeois society, of its instability and hostility toward man. His tragic view grew into blind terror of living.

These moods dominating in his work grew worse with the years. The grandiose historical events which Kafka witnessed not only did not change his outlook on the world and life, on the place of man in life; on the contrary, they strengthened the pessimism of his social views. In the days of the First World War, he was not overcome by chauvinism, as happened with many bourgeois artists, but neither did he take a position against the war, as did the best representatives of the progressive European intelligentsia. He perceived the war as a natural disaster like an earthquake, a flood, an outbreak of world evil, to fight which people have neither the strength nor the possibility.

In life, cut by the world war into two separate parts—the past, which was pregnant with strange calamities, and the present, which in Kafka's opinion promised only new fears—he saw nothing that could give people inner support or inspire them with faith in themselves and allow them to hope for an affirmation of universal human happiness. "In days of peace nothing comes out of you; in days of war you lose blood" (*T*, p. 531), he wrote in his diary in 1917, a year which, in Mayakovsky's words, came to earth "in the thorny wreath of revolution." The very possibility of restructuring capitalist society, of changing the conditions of human existence, seemed unrealistic to Kafka. "Why do the Chukchi not leave their awful country?" he asked. "They would live better anywhere, in comparison with their present life and present wishes." And he answered with the fatalistic formula: "But they cannot do that. Yes, everything possible happens; but only that which happens is possible" (T, p. 349).

Kafka saw, and could not help but see, that the capitalist system of social relations is fertile soil for evil and violence, cruelty and inhumanity, for everything that horrified him and filled his works with gloom and hopelessness. He recognized, and could not help but recognize, that capitalism brings and causes great catastrophes to man and perverts human nature. But the power of capitalism, which he hated, seemed to him none the less limitless and struggle with it purposeless. In his efforts and intentions he was locked within the borders of what already existed, and no other perspective on social being seemed possible to him. Therefore only one thing was left him: to repeat and vary the uniform motifs of his works, to paint the different colors of evil, to which he lent universality, having established his thought of freedom as an unattainable and illusory dream.

The world war, the decline and fall of the Austro-Hungarian monarchy, and the October revolution in Russia shook the world and changed the course of the world historical process; the outbreak of revolution in Hungary and Germany, and also its defeat—all these enormous social cataclysms left a deep trace in Kafka's consciousness. In his diaries there is hardly an entry that has to do with the events of contemporary history. But his fiction, especially the later works, conforms with the general temper, full of inner resonances and meditations on what he has seen and experienced.

If in the prewar years life seemed to Kafka gloomy and joyless, then, in his opinion, the war and the following years of social turmoil plunged human life into the darkest night, where the light of hope could not gleam or illuminate the icy gloom of existence. Thomas Mann, describing the conversation of Adrian Leverkühn and the devil in *Doktor Faustus*, made glacial cold an attribute of hell and of the master of darkness, as required by demonological tradition. But cold which freezes the soul and penetrates everything that exists—Kafka made this an attribute of life.

The surveyor K. wanders along the icy and snow-covered streets, striving to arrive at the castle of Count Westwest, which is inaccessible to him. An unheard-of cold, emanating from the world and the universe, forces the hero of the parable "The Bucket Rider" out from his uncomfortable shelter, and he takes leave in the hope of finding warmth and human sympathy. But his pleas for help and understanding, directed at people who could warm him if they wished, remain unanswered; sitting on his bucket, he is carried off from the world of the living into an icy region where only cold and eternity reign. The thought of the icy indifference to the sufferings of others, which is peculiar to people and which lies at the foundation of this paradoxical parable, grows in Kafka into the thought of the impossibility of showing support for people in trouble, and it turns into the conviction of people's inability to help one another. The short story "A Country Doctor" is imbued with a conviction of that sort; it develops in its own way the basic motif of Gustave Flaubert's *Legend of St. Julien the Hospitaller*.

This "legend," tinged with decadence and aestheticism, was a remarkable landmark denoting the crisis of humanistic ideas not only in the work of Flaubert himself, but also in Western European literature in the second half of the last century, into which drafts of decadence started to blow. In describing and aestheticizing Julien's enforced charity in warming a leper with his body and breath, one who is covered with purulent sores and ulcers, Flaubert followed the spirit and letter of the ascetic hagiographical tradition which demands of man martyrdom and mortification of his own nature. But such a forced sympathy has nothing in common with genuine humanism, for love of people must be as natural as breathing and not forced by such perverse means to verify man's capacity for charity. Julien acts in that way in order to mortify his flesh and to repent for unheard-of sins, and for that action he is taken to heaven.

Kafka's country doctor, living a poor and barren life, does not receive such a reward. Through cold and blowing snow the devilish horses whisk him to the patient, whom he cannot help, just as he cannot help his maid Rosa, who becomes the victim of violence on the part of the groom who turns up from no one knows where and who, in a violent rage, breaks down the door of the doctor's home, where the poor girl has locked herself in. Having appeared at the sickbed, in a stuffy room, through whose windows the diabolic horses stick their heads, and having felt the suspicious looks of the sick boy's relatives, the doctor asserts that he can do nothing to cure the strange and worm-infested sore on the side of the patient, who is praying for life and rescue. Julien himself wanted to ease the pain of the leper; the country doctor is put into the patient's bed, so that he may warm him and alleviate his suffering. But the leper in Flaubert's *Legend* feels gratitude toward Julien, while Kafka's patient, succumbing to his sores, hates the doctor. God took Julien to his bosom; the country doctor is saved by retreating hastily from both patient and charity, while thinking only of his sad and pitiful life. The ending of Kafka's story reveals his profound doubt of the efficacy of humanistic ideas, his conviction of their practical uselessness and impracticability.

Another Kafka parable is dedicated to a demonstration of the impracticability and impossibility of human solidarity. In "The Bridge" he likens man to a bridge that spans the yawning abyss of life, which another man was supposed to cross; he makes the metaphorical bridge crumble, for people are not capable of solidarity, of being a hold and a support for one another. Some characteristic quality slumbers in them and suddenly frees itself, but it is only cruelty, fear, and the will to violence. These characteristics of human nature push people to evil which is inexplicable and therefore all the more horrible, inevitable, and tolerated by indifferent contemplators, as in the story "A Fratricide," in which the motif of punishment for a crime is displaced by the depiction of the lust for murder seething in man's soul and ready every minute and every second to break out at will, opening the path to bloodshed, torture, and malice.

The sceptical view of humanity in Kafka's works became stronger through the years. Characteristic in this respect is the story "The Great Wall of China," in which Kafka proclaimed and sought to prove the idea of the tragic futility of both the private and the collective works of man. A project which seems grandiose, capable of uniting and inspiring the popular masses—the construction of a huge wall intended to protect the inner territories of the country from the fearful, squinting, and hirsute peoples of the north—turns out to be an absurdity, and not because it is not completed, but because any project which aims to unite people—be it the construction of the Tower of Babel or the Great Wall or anything else—is unrealizable. Those who propose the idea of unification—in the story Kafka calls them the authorities—only want people's submission and blind obedience; they know and understand that human nature is unchanging and uncontrollable and that human existence is finally weightless and like dust in the wind, tolerating no ties. If it is not tied to something important and significant, if the aspirations of its intellect are not limited to known borders, then it soon begins to tug furiously at its shackles, to tear both itself and the wall, to which its fetters are attached, apart.

At first glance it might seem that Kafka is criticizing the social teachers of mankind, those who take upon themselves the mission of correcting human nature and who destroy it in the name of their doctrine, or that he is censuring those potentates who, for the sake of retaining their power, subjugate man's external and internal freedom. The profound idea of the story is, however, both broader and more sceptical.

Just as in *The Trial* it was the parable of the Law, in "The Great Wall of China" it is the parable "An Imperial Messenger" which expresses the secret idea of the work. It is just as well known as the parable from the novel. It is not only the external will directed against human nature that is pernicious; there is something else inescapable for man, something directly opposed to the instruction and edification which issues from the mouths of the instructors and authorities, and that is: there is no important or significant news such as man dreams about and impatiently awaits. The messenger, filled with power and sent by the Emperor from his death bed with an extraordinary message for you, man, never gets to you, for he gets lost in the immensity of the court halls and passages, in the infinite throng of courtiers, among the staircases, corridors, and courtyards. You can only wait for the news at your lonely window and imagine it, but even a thousand years are not enough for it to get to you.

The device of artistic paradox, which is characteristic of Kafka's poetics, helps him to make the demonstration of the story's fundamental idea visible. Whatever thing is narrated in the story becomes devoid of meaning, for the huge expanse, in the midst of which the narrator lives, hinders the completion and conclusion of that thing, just as it restricts the establishment of lasting bonds between the narrator's countrymen. Therefore, for example, the events of many centuries past, preserved in legends and finally reaching the inhabitants of distant regions, suddenly appear to them as fresh news and either cause joy or sadness; whereas the events of the very moment, say, the news of a revolt or rebellion, because of the different dialects caused by the great distances separating one region of the country from another, appear as an ancient story of no contemporary relevance or meaning. In developing one motif of the narrative, in this case that of great distance, and in carrying the theme to absurdity, Kafka renders meaningless even the idea against which he comes out in his work. That the system of his argumentation is based on paradox and a notorious improbability of the initial situation and merely makes the demonstration visible, does not trouble Kafka, because for him the main thing is the self-development of the artistic idea, the immanent and, essentially, formal nature of its movement, and not the development of an objective phenomenon of life, which gives birth to or provokes the artistic idea.

Desiring to emphasize more strongly the absurdity of human life and intentions, and in order to outline more clearly the imperfection of man's animal nature, of which he was deeply convinced, Kafka paradoxically changes the character of the narration. And so he produces stories the heroes of which are animals telling about their lives, and who appear as nothing other than aliens in human life or as means and forms for its appraisal.

In their particularly human life they do not reveal anything good, inspiring, or encouraging. In "A Report to an Academy," written by an ape who, after quite tortuous practice and trials, has been able to pass from an animal state into the human state (that is, to grasp human spirituality and, thanks to that, to enter into a form of life peculiar to people), Kafka's ironic scepticism turns into a brutal satire on the human species.

However, what has been decisive in the ape's spiritual development? Above all the loss of freedom, of that happily unthinking self-satisfaction, of cloudless days before the ape's capture, until it wound up in a cage. Observing human life, it comes to the conviction that freedom, about which people debate so much and to which they aspire, is in fact a fiction, an essentially ambiguous and dubious phenomenon. "People very frequently deceive themselves with this word," the ape wrote about freedom in its report. "People count freedom among their most exalted feelings, and therefore the lie of freedom is considered exalted." But what in fact is human freedom?

Before appearing on the *variété*-stage I often used to observe some couple which had been working on the trapeze, right under the cupola. They were swinging, flying up, capering, flying into one another's embrace; one was holding the other in his teeth by the hair. "And people also call that freedom," I thought, "the freedom of movement." What mockery of material nature! If they showed this "freedom" to the apes, the walls of the circus would come crashing down from their Homeric laughter.

Then the step by which the ape ascended to the human state became its uniting with the race of people. An important role in its humanization was also played by the absence of other possibilities of rescue or, as it writes in its report, the absence of a way out, in the literal and figurative sense of the word. Of two evils—becoming as man or finding itself behind bars in the zoo—it chose the lesser, which allowed it to live the life of a famous artist, tired of notoriety and dominated by its impresario.

"A Report to an Academy" is one of Kafka's most gloomy works.[20] Fragments he wrote at the end of his life, "The Investigations of a Dog" and "The Burrow," depict life, in very pessimistic tones, as something burdensome, woven out of unknown dangers, fears, cares, troubles, which fill human life with painful efforts toward security. In the story "The Burrow," a woods animal has constructed a huge burrow with numerous entrances and passages, but it does not for a minute experience the condition of peace, because danger looms before it on all sides, forcing it to change its place in the burrow every minute and to rebuild it. Fear of death constantly dominates it and subordinates it to itself. This frame of mind dominates in the works of the last years of Kafka's life, which crown his creative development.

The scepticism which accompanies the final state of his work led Kafka to imagine the ruination of all spiritual values in the world in which he lived, and to the conviction of the unrealizable nature of all social ideals which had inspired mankind on his long, arduous ascent up the steep slope of history. Even art, which Kafka had for many years considered his sole refuge, his only calling, started to lose in his eyes its objective significance and to appear as a diversion unnecessary to people and society.

The wise and patient mouse who tells the story of the singer Josephine ("Josephine, the Singer, or the Nation of Mice") in her detailed and unhurried story debases the very concept of artistic value

20. There is reason to surmise that "A Report to an Academy" is partly borrowed from Hoffmann's "Letter to Milo, an Educated Ape, to his Friend Pipi in North America," from the second part of the "Kreisleriana." In this letter, a "former ape, now private artist and scholar," shares with his friend his observations on human culture and human stupidity. But how great is the difference between romantic irony and Kafka's sharp despair!

and the artist's vocation. Josephine, who was endowed with somewhat greater ambition than the common mice, convinced her compatriots that her squeak and squeal were more harmonious than the squeak of ordinary mice who live their stark and difficult lives in a world filled with cares and dangers. Her tenure in the role of servant of the muse was possible only because among the mice there existed something like a private convention recognizing Josephine's particular but, in essence, ephemeral right to be their comforter in times of sorrow or to please them with short hours of joy, which rarely fall to the lot of the mice. Josephine's squeak and squeal grip the imagination of the mice, who on the whole are unmusical by nature and who in the depths of their souls prefer quiet to any music, no matter how good it may be.

With bitter irony, Kafka portrayed the scale of relationships between the artist and society: Josephine allows herself to shock her admirers and even the whole mouse nation; she loves to emphasize her independence from public opinion. But she comes to feel both enmity and malevolence; she feels mistrust of her apparently not very humble trade. At a moment of danger which befalls the mice, she is suddenly filled with a prophetic fever and, straining her whole being, strives to communicate the rapture and alarm which have seized her to her compatriots who do not hear, above the usual noise, the sounds of approaching danger. No, despite all her whims, fancies and oddities, it is impossible to consider Josephine a useless member of society. But the mice had only to doubt her unwritten rights for her career as a free artist to come crashing down and for herself to disappear from the horizons of the hard-working mice and for her memory to fade out of mind.

Kafka's doubt of the objective social meaning of art is expressed even more clearly in the story "A Hunger Artist," which tells of the fate of a man who makes an art of his ability to starve for long periods. For some time his astonishing and rare art arouses interest and attracts attention, but it gradually goes out of fashion. Forgotten by all, living in the circus where he can give himself freely to his strange art, the Hunger-Artist, having starved himself to death, at the last second reveals the secret of his trade, of his fantastic devotion to the art of hungering. He dedicated himself to this art only because there was not a food in the world that was to his taste. An ambiguous confession. Art is necessary only to the artist himself, and it leads him to ruin; and it is necessary to him only because no other spiritual values and ideals by which human society lives attracted or inspired him.

Continuing, as in his early years, to consider art a refuge from the boredom of life, an autonomous realm of spiritual activity independent of the real world, Kafka surmised that it cannot participate in the resolution of the burning questions of life, which, however, it is impossible to solve by any means, for nothing can be changed in life. Therefore, in a collision with an ill-fated chain of events, the high ideals and dreams which have moved man to efforts to change the course of life suffer defeat and degeneration. For the artist there remains nothing but to remind us of that and of the imperfection of life, of the evil, dangers, and cruelties in its bosom. For the sake of that he keeps his vigil while others sleep (the parable "At Night").

The thought of the degeneration of social ideals in the contemporary world, which is fundamental in his spiritual development, informs all of the works of Kafka's final years. The figures which have inspired people by their greatness, nobility, and daring, he persistently and constantly demeans and trivializes. Poseidon, the ruler of the sea, appears in the parable of that name as a boring bookkeeper buried in his dreary accounts, who has not time even to look at the sea under his direction. He has only the hope that he will be able to look on the seas and oceans shortly before the end of the world, when he will have a free minute. Don Quixote, the Knight of the Mournful Countenance, champion of the orphaned, insulted, and deprived, is portrayed in the parable "The Truth about Sancho Panza" as a stupid demon tamed by Panza. Alexander of Macedon's war horse, a partner in battles which have shaken the universe and changed the shape of the world, appears in the parable "The New Lawyer" as a modest and shabby employee, Mr. Bucephalus, who is sympathetically accepted by his colleagues in the lawyer's office. Although the ability to kill has not diminished in our age and their own Macedon seems narrow to many, the times of Alexander the Great have passed, and therefore Bucephalus can do only one thing—adapt himself to a monotonous life bereft of any greatness. Even the memory of the daring feat of Prometheus, who stole the heavenly fire, is fading, for it is powerless to overcome the incredible exhaustion of both gods and men, who have convinced themselves of the complete purposelessness of fighting (the parable "Prometheus").

Similarly, Kafka's frame of mind did not spring only from his own decadent view of life which depended on the conception of the omnipotence of evil. He came to very decisive, but one-sided, conclusions from historical events happening before his eyes. The defeat of national movements and revolutions in Europe strengthened the pessimism of his social views. The parable "The Helmsman" very clearly reflects his appraisal of what was happening. The helm of power, the commanding position in life, is seized by decisive people who stop at nothing; and with the complete submission of the masses, they lead the masses to obedience. The workers are not even capable of reflecting on the consequences of their submission; they can only remain silent and obey. In substance, Kafka laid the blame for the defeat of the revolutionary movement on the popular masses, which very clearly reveals his tendency toward simplification of living conflicts and the schematism not only of his artistic thought, but also of his social thought.

Kafka's distrust of the constructive and creative potential of the popular masses increased markedly in the last period of his life. If evil is ineradicable and the conditions of life are unchanging and unchangeable, if high social ideals degenerate and cannot inspire people, and if the popular masses are inert, sluggish, and blind—then what horrors await mankind? Only one, Kafka answers. Like a passenger whose train has been wrecked in an endless tunnel, where the light from either end barely penetrates and where he sees only monsters born of his own confused imagination or an empty play of colors, man must put up patiently with his catastrophic situation and not ask "What should I do?" or "Why should I do that?" for such questions are senseless, like life itself, and there are no answers to them (the parable "Train Passengers"). With this note of the deepest disbelief and despair, Kafka's work is essentially concluded.

But he would be only an ordinary decadent if the sceptical and pessimistic ideas prevailing in his consciousness were the fruit of cold speculation, the result of a cynical and indifferent relation to life. However, one of the most important reasons that Kafka's work did not die along with him is the great impressive power of his visions, visions born of the sincerity of the tragic world view that, without exception, is peculiar to all of his works.

In the parable "The Vulture," describing how the vulture tears at the hero of the parable and finally thrusts his bill into the hero's heart, whose running blood engulfs the vulture and everything else, Kafka painted his own relationship to his work and his creative fate as an artist. Like the hero of the fable, he was defenseless before the onslaught of evil, and he paid just as dearly for having depicted evil and only evil. From nowhere did there appear to him a ray of hope, and therefore he gave his own despair such a general character, believing that hopelessness is an indispensable attribute of life itself. He likened himself to the hunter Gracchus, the hero of the story of the same name—whose name represents the latinized form of Kafka's family name—who, because of an error on the part of the ferryman of the dead, finds himself between the world of the living and the dead and carrying to the world of the living a breath of the icy wind of the nether regions of the realm of the dead. Deeply convinced of the inability of man to free himself from the power of evil reigning over his life, Kafka strove in all of his works to demonstrate the truth of that view, creating a gloomy, sad, and closed picture of the world.

However, this picture, which is impressive in its parts, is lacking in the main thing: exact in the details, it is inexact in the whole; for the true face of living history, with the multifarious tendencies of its development and the multiform forces active in it, its abundant contradictions and social conflicts, escapes from Kafka's art. He did not so much reproduce life in its authentic contours as he created a myth of the world he lived in. He abstracted from the actual existing conditions which determine the movement of history and man's relationship to it, conditions behind which always stand the most complicated interweaving of cause and effect, the struggle of heterogeneous social principles.

The life with which the heroes of his novels and stories and even the lyrical hero of his parables come into conflict appears as an abstraction, as some kind of unanalyzable, incomprehensible element standing above man and subjugating him. In it there exist and rule only forces hostile to man, the origin of which is unknown, for they are inherent in life as its function and nature. Life possesses no other characteristics, and man has only one possibility and prospect: to be defeated in the struggle with evil, which is constant and only changes its appearance. It is natural that such a view of life did not give Kafka the possibility of seeing in it the birth of those social processes which lead to the elimination of evil and to radical change in the conditions of human existence.

And humanity too is just as abstract in Kafka's works. Situated in a theoretical, mythologized environment, man is extremely impoverished, as his spiritual, emotional, and intellectual world is restricted to a few protective reactions; and in his relations with the outside world, the connecting link is fear and the instinct for self-preservation.

This picture of the world that derives from Kafka's works is monotonous and insufficiently rich in content. But Kafka did not strive toward a full communication of life's contradictions and events; his portrayal is limited to the twilight side of life.

Kafka's artistic evolution took a different route, and along with the reduction in the contentual richness of his work went an obvious complexity of exposition, which makes many of his works difficult to understand. These are mutually related phenomena, and the reason for them is rooted in the peculiarities of the imagery in Kafka's works.

The parable "Community" is characteristic in this connection; it contains the fundamental motifs of his novels and of many shorter pieces:

We are five friends. Once we came out of a house behind one another; first one came and stood next to the door, then came the second out of the door—or, rather, he glided as light as a little bead of quicksilver—and positioned himself not far from the first, then the third, then the fourth, then the fifth. Finally we were all standing in a row. People became aware of us, pointed to us and said: Those five came out of this house now. Since then we have been living together. It would be a peaceful life if a sixth didn't keep butting in. He doesn't do anything to us, but he is annoying to us and that is enough; why does he keep forcing himself in where people don't want him. We don't know him and we don't want to accept him. Of course, we five didn't know one another before either and, if you will, we still don't know one another, but what is possible and tolerable to us five is not possible to that sixth and is not tolerated. Besides that, we are five and don't want to be six. And anyway, what sense is this constant living together supposed to have—it doesn't make any sense to us five either, but now we are together and will stay together, and we don't want any new alliance, because of our experiences. But how should one make that clear to the sixth—long explanations would almost mean taking him into our circle; we would rather not explain anything and not take him in. No matter how he curls his lips, we push him away with our elbow, but no matter how hard we push him away, he comes again.[21]

21. Franz Kafka, *Beschreibung eines Kampfes* (New York: Schocken, 1946), p. 140.

What, essentially, is represented in this parable? Some situation, abstract, shorn of living preciseness, the *construction* of some condition, without an explanation of the reasons for its existence. The existence of some sort of community is recognized, a very external and inorganic one, into which a new element strives to enter and become a part. It is possible that this situation implies Karl Rossmann's attempts to find his place in American society or those of the surveyor K. to become an equal member of the village community located at the foot of Count Westwest's castle. But the situation in the parable permits of another interpretation: that the alliance or community which Kafka describes is disinclined to allow any one at all into its midst. Then the parable appears in turn as a praise of the closedness, isolatedness, and disconnectedness of the alliance's members from outside, exterior forces. The polyvalent character of Kafka's symbolism turns out to be a lack of full content [*bessoderzhatel'nost'*] and becomes a purely formal-logical structure based on various assumptions, which are themselves equally insufficiently founded. In examining the development process of Kafka's artistic fantasy, it is impossible not to take into consideration the fact that fantasy, as a most important constituent part of artistic creativity, cannot be restricted to a combinatory art operating with heterogeneous siuations removed by logic from the stream of life's phenomena. Fantasy opens to artistic thought the possibility of penetrating into the essential regions of the processes, connections and events of the objective world that are not subject or subordinate to logicalization, abstraction, or formalization on the part of reason and that possess all the fullness and richness of life. Fantasy is a means of analyzing reality, but this is a special analysis, which includes in itself the rational factor of intuition. The freedom of fantasy from formalization, which inevitably impoverishes phenomena, opens a space for true creativity and understanding of the world. But Kafka was inclined to occupy himself with an art of combining elements and facts of life, striving to unify, universalize, and formalize them. This path to art is connected to eliminating, from the artistic work, the concrete and the individual, which are always richer and fuller in content than the abstract and formalized.

The concrete side of the image, consisting of the totality of all the information contained in it, does not reduce merely to its conceptual side. As Hegel emphasized in his time, it is always greater and broader than the literal, logical sense at the heart of the image, for the image "places before us, instead of the abstract essence, its concrete reality"[22] and therefore is able infinitely to enrich man's consciousness and feeling, awakening in him a chain of associations, reflections, and emotional experiences.

But Kafka removes not only superfluous information from his images—which is necessary for any art which does not want to fall into a naturalistic copying of life. He also removes essential information, strips his works as it were, disorganizing their content and lending them an external complication which in fact leads to obscurity. Contemporary apologists for Kafka see his chief merit in this peculiarity of his imagery. However, the nature of his influence on contemporary—primarily foreign, unrealistic—art is more complicated and is not limited merely to an exploitation of some of the peculiarities of his artistic manner.

[. . .]

Kafka's well-known thought about man's inability to become the master of his own life, to free himself of the irrational forces dominating his individuality, finds resonance not only in existentialistic conceptions of man, in art professing the "philosophy of the absurd," but also in democratically minded artists who draw a one-sided conclusion from the objective difficulties of establishing new social relations and who doubt or do not believe in the coming victory of socialist revolution in that part of the world where capitalist social relations are still extant. They strengthen their doubts through Kafka's experience, through his conception of the relationship of man and history, and his view of man as a tool of fate—and at the same time they regard him as a renewer of art.

In the very passionately written article "Extorted Reconciliation," the prominent West German aesthetician, cultural philosopher, and defender of the avant-garde Theodor Adorno, opposes Georg Lukács' schematic view of nineteenth-century realism with his own not less schematic—as we note—view of contemporary art. He emphasizes as one of the chief merits of Kafka, Joyce, and Beckett that "in their monologues echoes the hour which has sounded for the world; therefore they excite so much more than what communicatively portrays

---

22. Hegel, *Collected Works* (Moscow, 1958), XIV, 194. [In Russian. *Ed.*]

the world."[23] Surely, Kafka's work reflects one of the colors of the social temper of our age. One can say without exaggeration that Kafka was crushed by this temper, which drew a thick curtain across his artistic view, one that he was not in a position to see through.

But for art it is not much to be only the echo of these or those social emotions. Limiting itself merely to that task, it becomes flat and loses its opportunity truly to evaluate the real condition of the world, and the battle of history ceases to be audible to it. Art preserves its ability to evaluate—one of its fundamental genetic characteristics—only when it takes hold of material reality and penetrates to the sense and essence of what the world so communicatively reveals to the human mind.

Art does not stand still; it is in motion, like life itself, whose undeviating course it follows. But its genuine development and enrichment can never be realized if the artist rejects understanding the world or neglects the cognitive capacity of artistic thought. Kafka's dramatic fate confirms once more the correctness of this truth, which is simple, but which also has the character of an aesthetic law.

23. Theodor Adorno, *Noten zur Literatur II* (Frankfurt am Main: Suhrkamp, 1958), p. 173.

Franz Kafka

EVGENIYA KNIPOVICH

[. . .]

Kafka's fame was posthumous. And it grew by leaps and bounds. The first wave rose approximately ten years after his death (Kafka was born in 1883 and died in 1924) and coincided with the triumph of fascism in Germany. The second, and higher, wave rose at the end of the Second World War. I believe it is correct to say that two-thirds of the existing studies of Kafka have been written in the postwar period. The eighty years since the birth of this writer have been marked by a series of studies which have also appeared in the countries in the socialist bloc. These are works of unequal value, for in some of them their Marxism is felt mainly in their terminology. In particular, this was characteristic to some degree or another in several of the papers presented at the conference on Kafka's works held in Prague in May of 1963.

One can read and hear various things about Kafka. That he is a fantastic realist, a visionary; that he gives preeminence to the inner life of man over and above the reality of the world about him; that he is an all-negating nihilist and passionate advocate of the "indestructible" in man; an anarchist; a Zionist; an anti-Zionist—such is the many-voiced choir of the admirers of this deceased writer.

[. . .]

To start with, some historical and literary amplifications. I do not believe that Gogol departs from nineteenth-century realism even when Maj. Kovalyov's nose dons the civil servant's uniform and reels around the chancelleries of Nicholas' Russia. Nor did Shchedrin

From E. Knipovich, "Frants Kafka," *Inostrannaya Literatura*, 1964, No. 1, pp. 195-204. The two passages in brackets (pp. 197f. and 201-04) I have inserted here from the somewhat expanded version of this essay which appeared in Knipovich's book *Sila Pravdy: Literaturnokriticheskie stat'i* [*The Power of Truth: Essays in Literary Criticism*] (Moscow: Sovetskii Pisatel', 1965), pp. 343-45 and 349-54.

186

leave realism, despite all the absurdity of the action of his gourmand-policeman who with his wail "Mamma! Tidbit!" lopped off and gobbled up a good chunk of the stuffed head of his high superiors.

The whole point is that Rabelais, Swift, Gogol, Shchedrin, Maya-kovsky expose the social absurdity of a certain stage in the life of classical society. And so the grotesque does not encode and does not deform actual reality, just as a magnifying glass or a microscope does not deform the object observed. Hašek's book joins this great tradition. Schweik, if one can put it this way, makes the absurd his weapon in his struggle with the absurdity of the Austro-Hungarian monarchy. He carries the orders which his superiors give him to their logical conclusion, thus revealing in a logical way their hidden absurd content.

The Schweikian interpretation of the orders the "authorities" give him is just that "negation of the negation" to the rank of which Ernst Fischer, the author of a series of detailed studies of Kafka, tries to elevate the "total negation" that, in his opinion, is embodied in the work of the author whom he investigates.

Not in the least doubting the personal integrity and human nobility of Franz Kafka, it is nevertheless impossible not to see that, using in his own way the material of the social absurdity of the empire of Franz Josef, he tried to give a picture of the perpetual metaphysical absurdity of the world and of human existence.

Equating Kafka and Hašek is, in essence, the embodiment in concrete material of a certain general tendency peculiar to a number of the papers read in Prague. Both Eduard Goldstücker and František Kautman called for a rejection of the notion of decadent art, maintaining that the demonstration of the deformity and inhumanity of private and public attitudes may be at all times a valuable form of social criticism.

I believe that here too it is a matter of obliterating the border between phenomena of different orders. When an international, or, even more so, a global conflict is in preparation, it is naturally reflected in the life of all classes and social groups, as well as in all the areas of ideology. Along with the criticism of social reality that arose among the democratic and socialist elements in the national culture, the appearance of discontent within the old society is mirrored in literature and art. Thus, neither Andrey Bely, the author of *St. Petersburg*, nor Fyodor Sologub, the author of *Melkii Bes* [*A Petty Demon*], appears in his works as an apologist for the social order in bourgeois-manorial

Russia. But both of them, in deforming the material of actual reality and clothing social evils in metaphysical or mystical garb (as Alexander Blok once said of another author of such works), "instead of decipering difficult things, put simple ones into code."

One who deciphered difficult things was Gorky, the founder of the literature of socialist realism, in whose works all the various sides of life, all the phenomena of social crisis are revealed in the light of Leninist truth, precisely defining the border which separates fundamental processes from side issues and attendant matters.

Decadent literature—this is not just a label, but a precise definition of the work of those artists who "encode reality" and who pass off the "side issues" and the attendant phenomena of social crisis as its basic sense and essence.

That is why it is impossible to admit as objective truth the attempt to locate Kafka's works outside the pale of decadence—that attempt which appeared in the papers of the Prague conference. And even if, as Eduard Goldstücker says, Kafka is used in capitalist countries not only by political reactionaries to understand contemporary reality, it still does not follow that Kafka's work lies outside the realm of decadence.

Not long ago at a meeting of European writers in Leningrad, the West German poet Hans Magnus Enzensberger said that Kafka was indisputably a realist, for he, Enzensberger, had repeatedly fallen into situations which Kafka had described. I think that this is inexact: not the situation itself was Kafkaesque, but the thoughts and emotions, that *understanding* of the situation taught to Enzensberger perhaps not even so much by Kafka as by his foreign interpreters. His experience was put into the context of the scheme given earlier by the artist and his critics. And I do not believe that it was the best context for a real life experience. No, Kafka was not a realist, but he was truly an artist searching, to the best of his capacities, for the truth. And that is why Marxist investigators have a foundation for a somber and serious appraisal of how the "frightful world" of Kafka's work was born and how actual historical reality is reflected in it. In one of his recent works on Kafka (published in the journal *Sinn und Form*), Ernst Fischer says that it is incorrect to give Kafka's work a religious interpretation, as Max Brod does—this, says Fischer, is "an even more crass simplification than the attempt to see in the artist's works only a reflection of the social world, paying no attention to the artist's originality and to the interaction between this originality and the social situation, nor to those aspirations, hopes, and disappointments of humankind which go beyond the borders of the historical moment." We would undoubtedly have to agree with the first part of Ernst Fischer's wishes, if the second part did not turn the whole question on its head.

[. . .]

The differentiation between "eternal" and "historical" aspirations in the history of the human species lets in through the window that religious interpretation of Kafka's works which Fischer himself has just thrown out the door. The eternal and absolute has no other means of incarnating itself in life than through the historical and relative. That is the reason why Kafka's work, if we wish to give it an objective estimate, must be seen in the context of that moment of eternity in which it was born and formed.

[. . .]

The world revealed in Kafka's works is a world of tormented people of all classes and situations. According to the testimony of one of his friends, Kafka said one day while examining a drawing of Georg Grosz's which depicted a capitalist and a worker, that the artist had not captured the real truth: "The fat man rules over the poor man within the limits of the given system. But he himself is not the system. He is not even the master, on the contrary! Even the fat man wears chains. Capitalism is a system of dependencies which go from the outside to the inside, from top to bottom, from bottom to top. Capitalism is a condition of the world and the mind."

Thus, a just feeling for the inhumanity of capitalism led Kafka to the picture of a unified "monolith," an insuperable public order above all classes, oppressing equally the exploited and the exploiters. This conception of a "continuous" capitalism was fatal to the course of Kafka's life and artistry, drying up for him the springs whose moisture nourished the great art of Russia and the West in the first quarter of the century.

Kafka was a contemporary of the October Revolution. The Bavarian Socialist Republic and the Hungarian Commune rose and were drowned in blood literally right next to him, the inhabitant of Prague who moreover sometimes visited Budapest. And in these years he visited Berlin also, where the blood of the murdered Spartacists was still wet on the pavements. And he did not understand that from the trenches of the First World War had arisen people firmly resolved to settle their accounts with the past. Not only Alexander Blok heard the rumbling of the fall of the old order. This rumbling resounds in the work of the elders—Romain Rolland, Bernard Shaw, Thomas Mann. It fills the first works of Bertolt Brecht, Johannes R. Becher, Louis Aragon—those verses and songs of a burning hatred for the old world, a hatred born only of a love of man, of faith in his power and future.

How is it that the personality and work of Franz Kafka evokes a feeling different from the legacy of a number of his modernist contemporaries and from the creative birth pangs of his epigones? For Kafka the universal humility of people in their vail of sorrow, as he imagined the whole world, was the greatest tragedy. He did not trifle with ideas, did not indulge his pessimism, did not play at being the terror of the drawing room or the cheap mystic, as Meyrink and Leo Perutz did, alongside of whom some people occasionally try to place him. He did not laugh at the concept of "historism," did not treat it as a banal and dogmatic invention of the "sociologists" the way that Eugène Ionesco or the leaders of the French "anti-novel" have recently done. He harbored an aversion to the world, to its dreadful immobility, parts of which he felt himself. But just this "inseparability" closed for him all paths to the future. Beyond the borders of our land there were and are philosophers, cultural philosophers and writers of *belles-lettres* who were and are entrenched in their pessimism, so to speak, with all conveniences. They gladly flirt with dividedness and despair in front of their admirers, and especially so if these are women. Reciting about the invincibility of "evil," promoting a conception according to which history unfolds "in circles," repeating themselves endlessly and senselessly, these cultural activists essentially sermonize about the rules of social irresponsibility. No, to Kafka all-powerful evils were not the material for parlor games. It is curious that Kafka, who meticulously kept a diary beginning in 1910, entered nothing in 1918, and almost nothing in the years 1919-1922. The reason for this is not his illness. For these were for him years of intensive creative work and copious correspondence. Perhaps the answer must be sought elsewhere? In the impossibility of believing in what was rising in front of his eyes, in the spectacle of the people and the whole folk, which did not want to live in the old way?

[. . .]

In his essay "In Memory of Count Heyden," Lenin speaks of three aspects of the servile condition of man: "The slave who is conscious of his slavish condition and struggles against it, is a revolutionary. The slave who is not conscious of his slavery and vegetates in his silent, unconscious, and speechless servile life, is simply a slave. The slave whose mouth waters when he self-contentedly describes the charms of the servile life and is delighted with his kind and good master, is a serf and a boor."

The majority of the people in Kafka's novels and novellas are "simply slaves," suffering, humiliated, taking their degradation as the norm. And despite the author's sympathy with their slavish condition, he is nevertheless inclined to think that it is impossible to find an escape from it. Occasionally some of Kafka's heroes vaguely doubt that the reality in which they live is reasonable. Other heroes, on the contrary, gradually give birth to traits of servitude. Of all Kafka's works, in my opinion, it is in the novel *The Castle* that the straightforward serfs and boors, who disgusted him, arise in full force—the self-satisfied and mercenary myrmidons of their oppressors.

And the chief heroes of the novels and novellas: Samsa ("The Metamorphosis"), Georg ("The Judgment"), Karl Rossmann (*America*), Joseph K. (*The Trial*), the surveyor K. (*The Castle*)? Who are they, these people, his inner kinship with whom the author does not hide? Well, in *The Castle's* initial variants the narration was in the first person. There was no surveyor K.; there was an "I." Not without reason Kafka thought for a long time that the fundamental problem of his life would have to be the creation of his autobiography.

I think that in the personality, character, and fate of these chief heroes is embodied the effort to encode, to translate into a metaphysical plan, the perception of their servile state, in order in that way to recognize beforehand the fatal impossibility of struggle. Kafka says, as it were: yes, capitalism is a frightful "condition of the world and of the mind"; but to the extent that it is universal, every attempt to fight it only disturbs the humiliating equilibrium—which is at least an equilibrium—and only makes more difficult and more excruciating the situation of someone who is seeking justice or of those whom he wishes to help. "Justice"—this is a word which to Kafka, as also to Arnold Zweig and Lion Feuchtwanger, sounds "as if old Bach had sat down at the organ." It is not accidental that Kafka, who in his whole life made only two public appearances, devoted one of these occasions to reading passages from Heinrich Kleist's novella *Michael Kohlhaas*, a work which, in his own words, he could not even think of without being moved to tears and enthusiasm. That is the story of a man who is struggling for his rights and justice in the corrupt feudal system of Germany in the sixteenth century. As a defender of truth, he becomes a bandit and, having achieved his rights, self-righteously proceeds to his own execution, atoning for the evil that he did in his fight for justice. But this force of conviction and frenzied defense of justice was for Kafka only a tale. And if his contemporaries tirelessly spoke about the possibility and necessity of aiming at justice, Kafka, with the conviction of desperation, over and over repeated the opposite: that today in the world of capitalism such a struggle was worse than hopeless. The first chapter of the novel *America*, entitled "The Stoker," is devoted to an attempted struggle for justice. Here the struggle (the stoker on the ocean liner has been cheated of part of his pay) bears an almost comical character. The stoker, defending his rights before the legal authorities, lisps, falters, is choked with tears. Karl Rossmann, a sixteen-year-old boy, sent by his parents to America for his alleged "immorality," vainly tries to help. All Karl's efforts to direct the conversation in a reasonable vein provoke the anger of his "client" and deepen the confusion.

And Joseph K., the hero of *The Trial*, also tries at first to wage a struggle for justice and his human rights. But, as always with Kafka, the protest is tongue-tied and concerns private circumstances which derive from the general deprivation of justice. The "two" who early one morning come to tell the important bank official Joseph K. that he is under arrest themselves cut unseemly figures: they impudently eat up his breakfast. [. . .]

Upon Joseph K.'s complaint, the pasty-faced and stupid executors of a foreign will, for whom eating the breakfast of arrested people is their fundamental nourishment, are punished by the executioner's whip. And the aggrieved himself, seeing this retribution, feels himself to be a criminal, entangled in the general circle of suffering and fear of those two creatures who are not responsible for their actions. Even more bitter does the attempt to struggle for justice taste to the surveyor K., the hero of *The Castle*. K. tries to take on himself the responsibility for the fate of Frieda, his beloved, his fiancée, but the natural and logical effort to defend her human dignity and female honor leads not only to a moral catastrophe, but also to one in life, and forces the lovers to leave one another.

The society in the bosom of which Kafka's heroes reside resembles a morass more than anything else. The slightest effort at liberation, at making their existence more tolerable and sensible, only worsens their situation and brings them closer to ruin. The interrelationship between Kafka's heroes is truly a dialogue of the deaf; no exertion leads to where it was directed; every relationship is erected on the foundation of a false and tragic insanity; and this deeply pessimistic conception of the interrelationship of man and the world becomes deeper from year to year. It is not difficult to discover as early as *America*, the first novel Kafka worked on. It is true that this "Dickensian" novel (in the author's definition as well as in the objective essence) appears almost as an idyll against the background of his other work. And Karl Rossmann himself, thrown by his parents into the "sea of troubles" and all his adventures, very much recalls Dickens' youthful heroes and their fates. Even the vagabonds Robinson and Delamarche, clinging to him and hindering his progress in the "normal" bourgeois world, are almost Dickensian rogues—eliminate their irrationalism and demonism, and they are no more frightful than Mister Jingle and Job Trotter from the *Pickwick Papers*.

In *America*, the feeling of guilt, the feeling of being alien to the surrounding world, only steals up on the hero, but for all that, it has a real, living foundation. *America* remained unfinished, like all of Kafka's three novels. Max Brod on the one hand and the author's notebooks on the other hand give us directly contradictory versions of the ending. Brod, with Kafka's words, speaks of the ending of the novel as a happy one in Dickens' manner. Karl Rossmann finds the way to creative work, social and free. The theater—the Oklahoma Nature Theater, fantastic in its possibilities, undertakings, and creative accomplishments—gives the hero everything: happiness and freedom, and even brings back to him the family which had earlier dismissed him unjustly. However, Kafka's notebooks speak of an entirely different ending: not only the guilty K. of *The Trial*, but also the innocent Karl of *America* is put to death. Such a decision no doubt better fits the artist's whole sense of the world. The feeling of guilt, born as early as boyhood in the collisions with his family, "dissimilarity," inscrutable and later taken as a rule and a duty, led Kafka far on the road to metaphysical encoding of real historical and social evils and affixed a pathological and nightmarish appearance to what is unique and incomprehensible in the essence of capitalism. Loneliness and the hostility of the surrounding world pushed the artist to a "retreat into himself," to an individualistic self-isolation, to the attempt to find a refuge in the world of art, to creative activity. But let it be said in Kafka's honor that the attempt did not succeed. Constant self-observation again and again led him to the conclusion that he himself was some kind of germ cell of the whole frightful world, and this perception poisoned and cheapened his own creative labors for him. It is not accidental that not one of his novels is finished, that all his books are filled with words of repugnance toward his own works. It is not accidental that he ordered that all unprinted works be burned after his death and that none of the already published ones be reissued.

No, all of this is not "psychological explanation." The psychology of the artist is always a social category. Behind the feeling of "strangeness," "guilt," and "anxiety"—which is the basis of the relationship of the world to both Kafka and his autobiographical heroes—stand definite social laws. The "ghost in the trees" of his "frightening world" grew from a real seed.

The young traveling salesman Samsa from the story "The Metamorphosis," the obedient son of a well-to-do family that is greedily exploiting his labor, one fine morning turns into a huge insect—either a beetle or a cockroach. Samsa is both obedient to the family and dissimilar to it. And his "strangeness" assumes a countenance not consonant with his true essence, but with the way his essence is *treated* by the surroundings. [. . .]

Similarly, family and environment constantly take Karl Rossmann, the hero of *America*, for something other than what he is. This supremely honest and modest boy is banished by his parents for "debauchery," by his millionaire uncle for independence of will, and by the administration of the hotel where he works as an elevator operator for theft, scandals, and so forth. But of not one of these is Karl guilty. He is "strange" in the country, in America, in the big capitalist enterprise predicated on venality and exploitation which the hotel appears to him to be. But Karl Rossmann's misadventures are real enough (slandered and thrown out of his job). His "strangeness" is almost an idyll compared with the universal metaphysical strangeness which determines the fate of Joseph K., the hero of *The Trial*. It must be that someone slandered Joseph K., for one fine morning they came to arrest him. So begins the novel. The horror of this arrest—purely formally—is that the arrested person, retaining his freedom, that is, his work and all his family and business ties, finds himself at the same time in the situation of "one against everyone." The "court" which conducts the trial is the whole population of the city where Joseph K. resides. The "court," the court's spies and associates—these are Joseph K.'s landlady, neighbors, relatives, and the lawyers to whom he turns for help; and also the lawyers' mistresses, passers-by, street walkers, his co-workers at the bank and his superiors. [. . .]

The novel *The Trial* is, as it were, a "slow-motion" film about human ruin in the bowels of the bureaucratic machine. The "court" encounters the man at every turn, like the black jaws of the grave in the familiar tale. If the man lies down so as not to move toward it, the grave itself, finding mobility, crawls toward him.

In connection with this "strangeness" of Kafka's heroes in their surrounding world, one hears more and more frequently in the foreign press words about "alienation," about Kafka's figurative embodiment in his work (and especially in the three novels) of that phenomenon whose essence was defined by Marx. This concept, however, occasionally acquires quite a strange coloring. This term (just the term, not the sociohistorical essence of the concept) is interpreted extremely broadly. "Alienation" becomes the name for any form of "discomfort" in the relationship between the individual and society, independent of the social structures of the society and the class situation of the individual.

And if, according to Marx, "alienation" arises in a particular (late) stage in the development of capitalism and its essence appears as a "mystical encoding" of real socioeconomic relationships between exploiters and the exploited, then "alienation" soon starts to be the name for some eternal "metaphysical" category which wanders from one socioeconomic formation to the next. This concept "alienation," "alienated" from a concrete historical content, occasionally also influences those interpreters of Kafka's work who are not idealists.

And it sometimes becomes such a universal key to his whole creative work that occasionally, with its help, the metaphysical encoding begins with just those pages where actual reality is reflected with the greatest precision. In the novel *America* there is therefore the inserted novella, the hotel typist Theresa's story of her terrible youth and the death of her mother. This story, written with great emotion and passion, is doubtless tied to the traditions of critical realism in world—and above all in Russian—literature. In Ernst Fischer's work on Kafka, the destruction of the jobless woman helping out at the construction site is not explained by the fact that she is sick, homeless (her landlady has thrown her out of her apartment), hungry, and exhausted by the cold and aimless nocturnal wandering, but by the fact that on the scaffolding an "alienated" brick crumbles under her feet and that an "alienated" board covered it before her fall. I do not think that Kafka, feeling the suffering "of all flesh" with a burning force and shame, is guilty of *this* mystification.

Despite this, a tie between Kafka's work and the real, Marxist, historical, and class-related understanding of "alienation" undoubtedly does exist. At the bottom of the "strangeness" and "guilt feelings" of Kafka's heroes lies the real fear common to all the categories of the "little men" in bourgeois society at a late stage of its development, who are faced with the omnipotence of strong capitalism, ruin, and proletarization. This fear, when "mystified" and separated from man, becomes an independent force hostile to him. We must not forget that virtually "irrational" bureaucracy and corruption that characterized the work of the government apparatus in the Austro-Hungarian monarchy.

I think that actuality, the real socioeconomic foundation of universal "evil," is most clearly visible in the novel *The Castle*. Here all is fantastic, "as in a frightening dream—but a waking dream"—the heroes, their fates, the setting. But the land surveyor K., having arrived in the province, infinitely far from his native town, feels himself to be a stranger above all because he is not suited to that "idiotism" which pervades all the life of the village, rejecting the stranger and "urbanite" like a foreign body.

In his diary Kafka preserved some entries dealing with his stay in Zürau, a little estate surrounded by villages as dark as the one where fate has thrown the surveyor K. In his diary Kafka describes real people and their real fates with the iron exactness, almost aridity, which is generally peculiar to his style. And then the relationship which exists in Kafka's works between the living material and its artistic embodiment becomes particularly visible. This most exactly corresponds to the relationship of an object to its enormously enlarged shadow flickering on a wall.

[On the eighth and ninth of October, 1917, he made diary entries about his acquaintances in Zürau:

Feeding the goats, a field with mouse holes, potato picking ("How the wind blows at our behinds!"). Farmer F. (seven girls, one a tot, sweet eyes, white rabbit on her shoulder), in the room a picture, "Kaiser Franz Josef in the Capuchin Monastery." Farmer K. (powerful, condescending narration of the natural history of his farm, but friendly and good). General impression of the farmers: noblemen who have taken refuge in agriculture, in which they organized their work so wisely and humbly that it fits perfectly into the whole and they are protected against all pitching and sea-sickness until their blessed death. True citizens of the earth.

And on the following day:

At Farmer Lüftner's. The large hall. Everything theatrical. He nervous with Hee Hee and Ha Ha and pounding the table and raising his arms and shrugging his shoulders and lifting his beer glass like one of Wallenstein's men. Next to him the wife, an old woman whom he married ten years ago when he was her hired hand. A passionate hunter, neglects the farm. Two huge horses in the stall, Homeric creatures in the fleeting sunlight which came in through the stall window.

From these entries it follows that Kafka, a "stranger," an "urbanite," was greeted amicably and affably in the country village. And that, despite all his timidity, pride, and ulterior motives, he felt well among the people of Zürau and was delighted with the "true citizens of the earth."

The village in the novel *The Castle* does not appear that way. And it is not a question of the fact that the surveyor K.—one of Kafka's literary incarnations—is met with hostility by the villagers. It is a question of the objective essence of the village and its inhabitants as they appear in the novel.

In reading the diary entries one is involuntarily reminded of Blok's lines (not included in the canonical text of his poetry in *Poets*):

> Alongside was the noise of busy villages
> And peaceful people lived. . . .

But in the novel the faces of the "true citizens of the earth" are deformed in conformity with the principle of "continuous capitalism" of the unified class society that suffers in all of its parts.

From a few lines about the man, the former hired hand, and his wife, grew the portrait in the novel of the village innkeeper and her husband, a former hired hand.

But in the novel the innkeeper lost the living and socially specific traits of theatricality and hysteria which masked his shame at his mercenary marriage. Under Kafka's pen he became torpid and turned into an appendage of his wife, who truly decided their public fate.

The old lady who bought herself a young husband becomes, in the novel, an extremely energetic and imperious middle-aged woman who not only exploits those in a lower social situation but who with all her authority affirms the inevitability of slavery, the charm of slavery, practically the "divinity" of those who in one way or another are part of the "Castle" that rules the village. In "The Landlady" is embodied the abominable powers of servility and loutishness, and the perversion of a person who has come up from the bottom and is seized by the ideology of the exploiting classes. "The Landlady" is the surveyor K.'s evil genius: it is she who takes away his last refuge; it is she who poisons the mind of his bride Frieda with the venom of submission, of respect for the "divine" authority of the castle and its bureaucrats.

Understanding the essence of servility and an aversion to it are new characteristics of Kafka's work and special traits of the novel *The Castle*.

Other entries in the diary also found their reflection in the novel. But affability, tranquility, and goodness—all that disappears in the portrayal of the families into which the surveyor accidentally comes, not as a guest but as an irksome and burdensome stranger who had lost his way in the labyrinth of roads leading nowhere.]

The surveyor K. attempts to get into the "castle," the mysterious "state house" that rules over the fates of peasants, servants, the officials of enormous chancelleries, the personnel who serve them; the foundation of this whole universal bureaucracy. And in K.'s attempts to reach this faceless and amorphous power, his fate is mixed with the will to fight for his right to life and work, with his fear of "proletarization," fear of falling into the class of the "pariahs," the "renegades" despised equally by the village and the castle, such as the family of Barnabas, the "messenger" of one of the chancelleries. The figures of Barnabas, his parents, and sisters are extremely important for *The Castle* and for all of Kafka's work, and not only because the inserted novella which deals with this theme is written with great mastery. This novella is the story of Olga, Barnabas' sister, and about how all the members of her family turn into pariahs and renegades. Amalia, the second sister, defending her female honor, did not wish to become the mistress of one of the innumerable representatives of the Castle's authority, the bureaucrat Sortini. No, no charge is made against the family as a result of this, no official sanction is invoked against it, but slowly, sluggishly, gradually the family is ruined and expelled from the company of honored citizens, not at the hands of the authorities—God forbid!—but at the hands of their fellow citizens, acquaintances, and friends, who suddenly "get the scent" of where the wind is blowing from. The strangest thing in this novella and in Kafka's whole narration about Olga is that both she, priding herself on her sister's action, and he, a fellow who does not want to give up, at the same time are always looking for and finding arguments in favor not only of compromise, but of a direct appeal to the mercy of the victor. Thus, even in depicting the struggle (and, as it were, glorifying it), Kafka "between the lines" entertains the notion of its aimlessness. In this ambivalence in the relationship to "authority," to the existing form of social life, is manifested Kafka's whole "inseparability" from the old world, the whole ambivalent evaluation of his "strangeness" to it. Thomas Mann remarked on this ambivalence in his essay for the American edition of *The Castle*. K., in Mann's words, stubbornly tries to arrange his life in conformity with the decrees of the "castle" regardless of the fact that all the "castle bureaucrats" strongly repel him. "This leads him to extremely disrespectful opinions and utterances concerning the 'castle,' which he nevertheless admires in the depths of his spirit. And this establishes the creative atmosphere, the ironic atmosphere of the novel."

A mournful irony, half laughter and half weeping (in the opinion of Thomas Mann) truly pervades all of Kafka's works. And without doubt, that constant strife, those endless dialogues "pro" and "contra" which his heroes engage in, almost always colors the author's sad and hopeless irony. Max Brod and, following him, some other interpreters of Kafka's work, believe that the influence of Jewish religious literature—and above all of the Talmud—can be felt in the controversies of his heroes. I think that in Kafka's "pro's" and "contra's"—if one is to speak of influence—Dostoevsky and some of his heroes are much more obvious, especially Ivan Karamazov, whose shadow frequently appears not only in the purely literary writings of the journal, but also in Kafka's novels and stories.

Nevertheless, for all his awkwardness in overcoming obstacles, his reflections, his inseparability from the public order which disgusts him, the surveyor K. is different from the other heroes of Kafka's novels and stories. The heroes of Kafka's novels, by the way, are no doubt more acceptable to the reader than the heroes of the stories and sketches. Despite all the strangeness of the happenings, of their fates and their whole appearances, they are nevertheless people.

[. . .]

In Kafka's novellas, even in those cases when they speak, as it were, of real people and real events (for example in the cycle entitled *A Country Doctor*), one can feel more sharply the conviction that people exist in complete isolation, that it is a bitter impossibility not only to help one another, but even to decipher correctly the signals for help.

Returning to the novel *The Castle*, we must say that here too there is a list of figures of an almost hybrid character—for example, Arthur and Jeremias, the surveyor K.'s "assistants," sent to him by the "castle," flatterers and spies who poison his life, much too svelte, bowing much too smoothly. In their black clothes which closely fit their long bodies, they remind us suspiciously of vipers standing up on their tails.

But with all this, surveyor K.'s efforts to obtain his rights receive in *The Castle* the moral sanction which Kafka's other heroes do not all have. A lad, a dark-eyed schoolboy from an unusual village family, likewise wronged by the "castle," brings him friendship and the wish to help. The boy reaches out to the "foreigner" precisely because he is not like all the others around him. The village boy recognizes and perceives the true nature of what is "foreign" to the dead world of the "castle." For him it represents the true human norm.

This figure is tightly connected to one of the themes which recurs throughout all of Franz Kafka's journals: the theme of childhood. It does not come from a recollection of his own dreadful, dark, and Philistine childhood. Not without reason, in his "Letters on Education" Kafka demands above all careful attention and consideration for the child. For Kafka the theme of childhood counts for about as much as it does in Fellini's most recent film, *8½*, in which a happy, harmonious, poverty-stricken childhood in a working-class family is a radiant, lost paradise for the hero, who has entered the frightening world of bourgeois success and bourgeois profit.

Amid brutal self-condemnations, pathological or poetic dreams, and thoughts of suicide, mercilessly exact portraits in Kafka's journal suddenly gleam like a flash: the figures of children. There is not the slightest sentimentality in these notes. The children's portraits in the journal are terse and exact, as always. A village girl—soft eyes and little white rabbit sitting on her shoulder; a girl from the outskirts of a city—a spotted design in her dress, straight pigtails, a bag bigger than she is, sent to the store by her mother; two tots in dark blue jackets carrying armfuls of hay; Italian tots to whom he gives a coin on the piazza in Ravenna; bathing in the sea; his "little girl friend," four years old "with a little paunch still left over from the time she was sucking her mother's breast," strong as a bear cub, and who, wheezing, tries to push her older, tall friend from the boardwalk into the water. "Pathology," "dark thoughts," desperation, hopelessness—all of this is left behind on the threshold of the theme of children.

A trifle? I do not think so. These figures are fundamental to an understanding of the entire complexity and contradictory nature of Kafka's creative profile.

[It is no less essential how, in the diaries, his relationship to great art and literature is reflected.

It is not possible to say that Kafka was a "modernist" in his taste or proclivities. "Craftsmanship," as one now says, that is, the knowledge of how to write, style (in the narrow sense) he learned, in his words, from the masters of "exact and naked speech," from Flaubert, Pascal, and Heinrich von Kleist. Among contemporary German writers, as we have already said, he singled out Thomas Mann. He joyfully recorded every success—down to each well-turned page, image, line—of those who were working at the same time as he. His diaries and pronouncements and the memoirs of friends testify that his true love and inclinations were for the past (Goethe, Kleist) and for what lay outside of German culture (Strindberg, Pascal, Flaubert, Russian literature).

In the notebooks it is Goethe and Goethe again. The clear sound of the adolescent voice in *Iphigenia;* the harmonious, almost bucolic charm of *Dichtung und Wahrheit;* an entry in Goethe's diary—a completely trivial one, but after acquaintance with which it starts to seem to the reader that he has done nothing for his whole life; lines of Goethe's prose where in the usual, balanced rhythm suddenly a sharp intonation breaks through. Sometimes, as if from "within" this adoration, Kafka rebels against the equilibrium, against the Olympian character limited by the boundaries of provincial Weimar, even against the marmorial beauty of Goethe's outward appearance. But most clearly visible of all in Kafka's entries is the unusual liveliness of feeling—it is not a matter of the classical author, who had died many decades ago, but of the "old man," whose power could both help one to live and crush one.

I do not think that it was contemporary prose in general, but himself personally that Kafka was thinking about when he made the following entry in his diary:

Because of his power, Goethe truly hinders the development of the contemporary German language. And if German prose after his death frequently moves away from him, then in the end result, as it is happening now, with renewed vigor it again strives toward him and appropriates the old things we find in Goethe, although not those that directly define his manner, the phrases; and nevertheless it is ready joyfully to feel its unlimited dependency on him.

À propos the interrelationships of Kafka and Kleist it would be possible to fill whole mountains of paper. And that is obvious: the connection between these two artists is evident on the surface. Kleist's novelistic practice undoubtedly had a great influence not only on the very style and language of Kafka's works, but also on the conception of the "discord" between human will and the will of "suprahuman" forces that direct its fate, which lies at the foundation of all Kafka's work.

But it is necessary to say that Kleist was a greater optimist than his successor. Kohlhaas achieved justice, and was not afraid to pay with his life for it. And two participants of the "divine court" (in the novella "The Duel") in the end get their just deserts. For educational purposes God (so that people would not become conceited, affirming his will) gave "evil" the possibility of inflicting a fatal wound in the "good." But the good, through divine power, rose up from its deathbed, and evil rotted alive from an insignificant scratch. This patriarchal god of feudal times relinquished its place in Kafka's work to the pitiless, anonymous "condition of the world and mind" called capitalism.

In Kafka's appraisals of the artists and philosophers who were the potentates of the mind for Western European writers contemporary to him, one can naturally feel the influence of the time and milieu. So, for example, he estimated highly the nineteenth-century philosopher Kierkegaard, one of the supports of European reactionism and individualistic philosophy, one of the predecessors of contemporary existentialism.

[. . .]

But undoubtedly for the Russian reader the most curious pages in Kafka's notebooks are those on which he speaks of Russian literature. When we read them we again recall Tonio Kröger and his conversations about art with Lisaveta Ivanovna.

In confessing to his Russian friend, Tonio Kröger is very severe in his evaluation of his own work, the work of a "bourgeois gone astray," an individualist. In Kafka's notebooks it is not hard to find all the components of self-incrimination which make writing for Tonio Kröger the fruit of a curse and not of a vocation.

As to Kafka's Russian notes, it would be possible to use as an epigraph for them those words about the sacred and deserved admiration of Russian literature in which not only Tonio's voice is heard, but also the voice of Thomas Mann himself. Kafka's relationship to our classical literature testifies to a good knowledge and in many cases a true understanding of it. Kafka loved Gogol and Chekhov. He worshipped Tolstoy, his greatness, purity and power, as he also worshipped Goethe. It does not follow that from Dostoevsky Kafka borrowed only his psychological analysis of emotional instability [*dostoevshchina*], completely bypassing the writer's critical realism and humanism. Of course, in the "controversies" of his heroes we not infrequently hear a direct echo of the reasonings (which are now dead for us) of the heroes in the novel *The Possessed* or of some of the characters in *The Idiot*. But the first days the surveyor K. spends in the village, his attempts to find shelter, to get into the "castle" in order to find out about his fate, the roads that don't lead anywhere, the efforts that end in nothing—all this is not connected with *dostoevshchina* but with Dostoevsky. And if in the tortuous self-torment of the heroes it is often possible to see Dostoevsky's magnified *ghost*, Dostoevsky's reflection lies on the chapters of *The Castle* which narrate the fate of Amalia and her family, on the chapter of *America* dealing with Theresa's childhood, on the description of the day preceding Joseph K.'s meeting with the clergyman in the dark cathedral. Unquestionably, in all these episodes there is an artistic reminder of the tragic, absurd, and true-to-life attempt to find an escape and salvation, to which, in fateful hours, Mitenka Karamazov, and the hero of the novel *The Gambler,* and the "youth" Arkady Dolgoruky all abandon themselves.

And as for Ivan Karamazov, Kafka's diary constantly speaks of him.

Thus, defending his right—and, more than that, his duty—not to be happy, Kafka, a man of literature, had long since found allies among the "greats" and their heroes. There were two allies. One of them was Dostoevsky or, more truly, his hero Ivan Fyodorovich Karamazov. In December 1917 Kafka wrote in his diary: "Just read through that passage in Dostoevsky which reminds me so much of 'the inevitability of being unhappy.' " That would not be enough to guess at what is meant, if Ivan Karamazov's words, in quotes and without reference to Dostoevsky, did not come almost immediately thereafter: "deafening wail of the seraphim's rapture." From that it follows with complete certainty that the "passage" referred to is Ivan's conversation with his brother Alyosha in the inn, and that "the inevitability of being unhappy" is a variant of the hostility of the world and God's blessed future harmony, which leaves unavenged the "tears of the tortured child."

That in Dostoevsky Kafka found a kindred insurgent and theomachist is of course quite a noteworthy fact. But something else is much more curious: the bridge from "the inevitability of being unhappy" goes to a completely unexpected side. In the pages of the notebooks, the name of A. I. Herzen is recalled with particular fondness and respect, again not only as an artist, but as a "guide," a Virgil. In the feeling of guilt because of his inability to work, in despair, Kafka turns to Herzen: "perhaps he will somehow succeed in leading me on." And again on Herzen: "Sometimes the almost torturing feeling of my 'inevitability of being unhappy' and at the same time the assurance that this is right, that the end is inevitable, the passage precisely through unhappiness (just now this feeling arose through recollections of Herzen, but it occurs without that too)."]

[. . .]

The memory of the existence of the genuine, which lies on the periphery of Kafka's perception of the world and of his creative capacity, doubtless distinguished him from his contemporary admirers and disciples. But this private tragic fate does not change the fact that the road which Kafka took is a blind alley. And his vision, acquiring a more and more frightening countenance, today serves in the struggle against that "genuine" for which he darkly yearned.

No, Kafka did not open new paths for literature. Its vigorous stream, here and abroad, ran and runs in a completely different bed. But the inheritors and continuers of the great realistic, heroic, and popular tradition of art have equally little reason either to exalt him or to reject everything that is in his books.

Kafka is not the "father of a new Western Literature," as the modernists believe, not a "prophet," not a victor. He is a vanquished, a victim or—more truthfully—another material witness for the crimes of capitalism against human culture.

Kafka Untouched

DMITRI ZATONSKY

Kafka died forty years ago, but the raging controversies about his books have not yet abated. It is no accident that he became one of the objects of the ideological struggles of our time. People speak of a very complicated, very conflicted, but in his own way very great artist. And a great artist, even if he has such a sick talent as Kafka's, inevitably appears at the intersection of certain significant "lines of force" in human culture, becomes a phenomenon and leaves his mark in history—in the history of literature and of society. And the interest in such an artist is conditioned perhaps not only by *what* and *how* he portrays but, so to speak, by the very "phenomenon" of his existence—of his uniquely individual and at the same time his typical existence.

In the Albanian weekly *Drita*, indignation was expressed that at one of the scholarly conferences in Moscow, a speaker "dared" to analyze the works of decadent writers, and of Kafka in particular. Such callous sectarianism can only call a smile to the lips of every sensible person. In order to understand literature, in order to create literature, it is absolutely necessary to appraise its history in all its aspects, recent and distant, healthy and unhealthy.

Kafka hated that soulless, dehumanized world in which he lived; he hated it deeply and passionately. He expressed the bottomless horror of human existence in the "penal colony" of bourgeois civilization; he suffered for humanity and felt himself responsible for it. That cannot but arouse sympathy for his search and his suffering.

At the same time, sympathy ought not to conceal from us everything that Kafka was not given to understand—in the first place the contradictions that broke him. He did not believe in the world, did

Dmitri Zatonsky, "Kafka bez retushi," *Voprosy Literatury*, 8 (1964), No. 5, pp. 65-109. The two bracketed passages on pp. 234f. and 235f. I have inserted here from the expanded discussion of alienation in Zatonsky's *Frants Kafka i Problemy Modernizma* (Moscow: Vysshaya Shkola, 1965), pp. 55-57 *pass.* (Cf. pp. 257-67.)

not believe in man, did not believe even in the theoretical possibility of happiness and harmony.

[. . .]

I. VARIOUS OPINIONS

Contemporary Western "Kafkana," although essentially developed only within the past twenty years, are so colossal that no one can think of surveying them in the limits of one article. But let us look at least at some of the main tendencies.

Max Brod, Kafka's friend and executor, who despite Kafka's last will saw to the posthumous publication of his manuscripts, maintains a religious-zionist interpretation of the writer's work.[1] Brod sees in Kafka something like a medieval Jewish scholar educated in the grotesque mysticism of the Cabala and prostrate before the incomprehensible will of an angry God. In keeping with this, Brod interprets Kafka's novels as uniquely personal religious allegories.

There are, however, also attempts to interpret Kafka in the Christian spirit. In particular, he is frequently related to the Danish theologian Kierkegaard (1813-1855), and the images in his novels are regarded as Protestant symbols.

Erich Heller sharply rejects the fideistic understanding of Kafka, claiming that his works "appear to be religious allegories to the same extent as a photograph of the devil could be said to be an allegory of Evil."[2] According to Heller, Kafka's world is the world surrounding us, but one which recognizes that it is forever damned. Recognition of the "curse" is all the faith that Kafka has left.

Hans-Joachim Schoeps goes even further along the same line and thinks that Kafka is beyond good and evil, and in that way he leans toward a nihilistic evaluation of being.[3]

Max Bense reckons the writer to the surrealists and simultaneously to the representatives of "subjective sensibility" in the spirit of Husserl and Heidegger, that is, to the existentialists. Bense calls Kafka an "ab-

1. See the following works of Max Brod: *Franz Kafkas Glauben und Lehre* (St. Gallen, 1951), *Franz Kafka als wegweisende Gestalt* (St. Gallen, 1951), *Franz Kafka. Eine Biographie* (Berlin and Frankfurt am Main, 1954), as well as his many afterwords to Kafka's works.

2. Erich Heller, *Enterbter Geist* (Wiesbaden, 1954), p. 289.

3. Hans-Joachim Schoeps, "Franz Kafka und der Mensch unserer Tage," *Universitas*, 1961, No. 2.

surd writer," using the word in the same sense as Albert Camus (that is, referring to the unlimited aspirations of man and his factual impotence).[4]

Wilhelm Emrich, on the other hand, sees Kafka's work as a struggle to balance subjective and objective principles against one another. Emrich is inclined toward a more optimistic interpretation of Kafka's parables, albeit not on a religious foundation, but on the basis of "genetic links" with the classical German tradition, presupposing a philosophical identity of spirit and nature, subject and object.[5]

For Hermann Pongs, Kafka is an artist who portrays the exitlessness from the conceptual and psychic labyrinth in which humanity is locked; Kafka's characters are "ambivalents," that is, deprived of all inner wholeness, infinitely alone and hopeless individuals.[6]

There are also investigators who consider Kafka a madman—not an ordinary madman, however, but rather, so to speak, a "paranoid genius" who sees the world more clearly than the healthiest of the healthy. Such investigators usually steep themselves in Freudian psychoanalytic studies of the character and fate of the writer.

And there are still others who treat Kafka as a "misunderstood realist" who, for all his outward metaphorism, describes only objects, gestures, words actually spoken—they are important and significant only in themselves; no profound and mysterious content can be derived from them. Alain Robbe-Grillet, the representative of the "new novel" in France, takes this position.[7]

And the view has been expressed that Kafka generally "doesn't portray": "A work of art," writes Günter Blöcker with regard to Kafka's work, "does not mean anything; it exists." And further: "Its truthfulness consists exactly in the impossibility of interpretation."[8]

Such a kaleidoscopic variety of conclusions, it seems, is aided by the actual vagueness, haziness, and strangeness of Kafka's works. In the face of such an unusual phenomenon as these shadowy novels, novellas, parables, aphorisms, unfinished sketches, it seems we might as well give up.

And so, fallacies and mistakes are possible in investigating Kafka.

4. Max Bense, *Die Theorie Kafkas* (Köln and Berlin, 1952).
5. Wilhelm Emrich, *Franz Kafka* (Bonn, 1960).
6. Hermann Pongs, *Franz Kafka. Dichter des Labyrinths* (Heidelberg, 1960).
7. Alain Robbe-Grillet, "Kafka discredité par ses descendents," *Express*, January 31, 1956.
8. Günter Blöcker, *Die neuen Wirklichkeiten* (Berlin, 1957), pp. 298 and 300.

However, if we scrutinize everything that has been written about this artist in the bourgeois West, it is not hard to notice that almost all the researchers are in error, lose their way somehow or another in the channel of very specific tendencies.

Kafka is torn away from every possible concrete historical, social, national base. Very seldom, and reluctantly, is there some mention of the fact that he lived and worked in the epoch of the exacerbation of imperialistic contradictions, that as a writer he was formed in the specific atmosphere of the Austro-Hungarian monarchy. In studying the sources of his works, attention is preferably turned to European influences in general (Flaubert, Dickens, Dostoevsky) or to Germans (Kleist, Hoffmann), although Kafka, as a resident of the Bohemian capital, was tied above all to the Austrian and Czech literary events of his time.

In recent years, a number of literary scholars from Czechoslovakia, Poland, and the German Democratic Republic, and also some philosophers and communist critics from capitalist countries, have turned to Kafka's work. The aim they set themselves was to expose the reactionary legends regarding Kafka and, using Marxist methodology, to reveal the true face of the writer.

As early as 1938 the Czech-German publicist Rudolf Fuchs, reviewing the first edition of Brod's biography of Kafka (1937), charged its author with the desire to attribute to Kafka a "noble" pessimism of an extra-social character.[9]

In 1945 another Czech-German writer, the well-known progressive novelist and essayist Franz Weiskopf, wrote the article "Franz Kafka and the Consequences."[10] In this article he raised, for the first time, the question of the need for a concrete historical study of Kafka's legacy and pointed to his indisputable dependence on Prague and generally Czech themes. Weiskopf's article defined the direction of progressive foreign "Kafkology." The works of Paul Reimann, V. Dubský and M. Hrabek, Hugo Siebenschein, František Kautman, Eduard Goldstücker (Czechoslovakia), Klaus Hermsdorf, Helmut Richter (GDR), and Ernst Fischer (Austria) more or less follow his lead.

V. Dubský and M. Hrabek, not hiding the contradictions in Kafka's world view and creative method, nevertheless distinguish Kafka's

9. Rudolf Fuchs, "Franz Kafka," *Internationale Literatur*, 1938, No. 4.
10. "Kafka und die Folgen" in Franz Weisskopf, *Literarische Streifzüge* (Berlin, 1956).

symbolism from surrealism and point to the presence in his work of elements of social satire. They also record Kafka's proximity to the leftist circles of the Czech intelligentsia.[11]

Hugo Siebenschein divides Kafka's work into three periods, grouping them around the novels *America, The Trial,* and *The Castle.* The *America* group he regards as more or less realistic; the *Trial* group as metaphysical, but not yet colored by the mood of complete hopelessness; in the *Castle* group the characters find themselves finally defeated by the recognition of their bottomless although completely abstract "guilt." Siebenschein also underlines the social meaningfulness of Kafka's position in the period of the First World War, in particular his reluctance to join the Austrian chauvinist "Union of Artistic Workers," the members of which included even such writers as Stefan Zweig and Karl Kraus.[12]

Paul Reimann concentrates his attention on that criticism of capitalist reality which, in his opinion, is inherent in a range of Kafka's works, acknowledging at the same time that the writer saw only one side of capitalism, the blind spontaneity of its laws. Reimann criticizes Brod's book *Franz Kafka's Faith and Teachings* for its attempt to metamorphose the author of *The Castle* into a Zionist prophet. Reimann dwells in detail on Kafka's sympathies with the working people, his part in the meetings of leftist anarchists, and his acquaintance with later prominent supporters of the Communist Party of Czechoslovakia, such as Stanislav Kostka Neumann.[13]

In his dissertation on Kafka's work, Helmut Richter distinguishes between those of the author's works which were published during his lifetime and those which he bequeathed to Brod to destroy. On this basis, Richter speaks of the lack of uniformity in Kafka's work, of his inner contradictions.[14]

No doubt the highest appraisal of Kafka was given at the end of the fifties by Ernst Fischer. For Fischer, Kafka is a great artist, an outstanding master of fantastic satire who continues the great tradition begun by Aristophanes, Rabelais, Swift. The conditions of old Austria-Hungary created the presuppositions for Kafka's artistic generaliza-

11. V. Dubský and M. Hrabek, "O Franzi Kafkovi," *Nový Život*, 1957, No. 4.

12. Hugo Siebenschein, "Franz Kafka und sein Werk," *Wissenschaftliche Annalen*, 1957, No. 12.

13. Paul Reimann, "Společenska problematika v Kafovych romanech," *Nová mysl*, 1958, No. 1.

14. Helmut Richter, *Werk und Entwurf des Dichters Franz Kafka* (Leipzig, 1959).

tions, helped him to foresee the faults of "industrial civilization," and to foretell the horrors of fascism. Just that makes Kafka's work so relevant to our time. The picture of life which Kafka drew appears to be a reflection of the actual processes of capitalist "alienation," of the "reification" of man. Kafka, in Fischer's view, is not a pessimist but a humanist and a petty bourgeois insurgent who stood close to the workers' movement in Czechoslovakia.[15]

On the 27th and 28th of May, 1963, a conference took place in Prague to celebrate the eightieth anniversary of Kafka's birth. The conference was opened by the noted Czech scholar P. Reimann. He gave Kafka's great talent and sincerity its due. He called for separating Kafka from his bourgeois falsifiers and "inheritors" and also renounced sectarian and dogmatic appraisals of the writer. At the same time, Reimann warned against an excessively enthusiastic, uncritical approach to Kafka's legacy: "We do not believe, with Kafka," he said, "that the laws of life are unknowable. Nor do we believe in the insolubility of contradictions. All of life, and the experience of the decade of our struggles, convinces us that from the conflict of contradictions there regularly arise new and higher forms of life. The contradictions which broke Kafka belong mostly already to the past."

The principal papers at the conference were delivered by Roger Garaudy, František Kautman, and Eduard Goldstücker.

In attempting to restore the historical truth, falsified by bourgeois science, a number of speakers, in the course of their judgments, turned Kafka into a realist whose work is very relevant to our time: he foretold World War II, he anticipated the horrors of fascism, he foresaw the whole tragedy and drama of contemporary man. They regarded Kafka's work as the "experience" of the last war, experience of the postwar years of the capitalist world which more than ever before alienates man and prevents him from being master of his own fate. But, say these researchers, Kafka's experience is also "the experience of the socialist world," for the conquest of power by the proletariat does not mean the immediate and automatic liquidation of "alienation"—that is, a certain mystification, a perversion of the true relation between man and society or state is one of the typical manifestations of late capitalist development (about which Marx wrote). Kafka, some critics maintain, was a poet of "alienation"; capitalist alienation

---

15. Ernst Fischer, "Franz Kafka," *Sinn und Form*, 1962, No. 4.

is the leading theme of his works; he combatted "alienation" on every page of his books. That means that Kafka's work is related to reality not somehow accidentally, in individual areas, and so forth, but rather tightly and organically. Naturally, this relatedness does not appear straight and direct, lying, so to speak, on the surface, but it is not the less true for that. And the very presence of such relatedness is enough to make a work realistic.

[. . .]

2. "HE DOESN'T HAVE THE SLIGHTEST CONCEPTION OF FREEDOM."

[. . .]

America[16] is the story of a sixteen-year-old boy who, without a penny in his pocket and with a pitiful little suitcase in his hand, has been sent by his parents from Prague to the distant United States, banished as punishment for the fact that he has been corrupted by their hideous old servant. The boy—his name is Karl Rossmann—is a rare specimen of modesty, naiveté, kindness, and sympathy, full of willingness to help everyone in everything.

[. . .]

In this book, as in general in all of Kafka's works, man is set in opposition to the world, which is strange and hostile to him. In Kafka's view—and this is a characteristic of all his work, beginning with the "Description of a Struggle" (probably 1902-1903) and ending with the novella "The Burrow" (1932)—the world is evil, absurd, in principle imperfect or, at best, unknowable in its incomprehensible workings.

It is true that the world of *America* is a considerably more concrete world than that of *The Trial* or *The Castle*. Not without reason did Kafka say that in the period he worked on *America* he was under the influence of Charles Dickens. In the situations of the novel and in the descriptions of the stinking, putrid slums in which vice and poverty abound, and in the writer's feelings of fine compassion for the op-

---

16. This name, of course, is not Kafka's, but Brod's. Kafka's manuscript does not bear a title. In letters and oral statements the author most frequently called it *Der Verschollene*, which in translation means approximately "Lost Without a Trace."

pressed and hatred of the oppressors, there is indeed something of *Oliver Twist, David Copperfield*, and *Bleak House*.

Moreover, the world of *America* bears the imprint of the imperialist world contemporary to Kafka. In it there are millionaires who don't know what to do with their money, there are metal workers on strike, there is a woman who, tortured by unemployment, throws herself one night from a construction scaffold. There is even a scene in the novel which grotesquely and comically depicts an interparty struggle before the election of the regional judge.

Of course, the world of *America* (apart from the precise location of the action, which is unusual for Kafka) is not at all the "real" United States of the beginning of the century, as Klaus Hermsdorf, for example, has demonstrated. For Kafka (who, by the way, was never there) America is no more than an exotic, stylized and, consequently, abstract social background on which the writer constructs his universal tragic schemes. This background is not as abstract and not as totally gloomy as those in *The Trial* or *The Castle*. But it does with sufficient definitiveness express the "universal" depravity of the world.

So, from the point of view of Kafka's evolution, the world in the novel *America* is not so curious as is man pitted against it.

In his journal, Kafka wrote that Karl is an "innocent." That is, the reason for the misfortune and defeat of the hero appears not to be himself, but rather forces acting outside his will and cognizance. As a person, Karl deserves every respect. If the conditions surrounding him were to change (if that were only possible!), he would win in his life's struggle, he would bring reality into accordance with his noble ideals. He is better than the Delamarches, although, unfortunately, he is weaker than they. Therefore Karl must perish; but not as a criminal—rather as a gentle victim of his fate, which sympathizes with him but is powerless to set anything right.

So, while working on *America*, Kafka still believed in man. It was not a real humanistic faith, for it did not leave any real hope for victory. But it was a faith nevertheless, and its light illuminates the whole book.

In *The Trial*, the connection to reality is weaker. Not only because the time and place of the action are not specified (in the book everything is equally tied to the atmosphere of Prague at the beginning of the century), nor even by virtue of the strangeness of the story told (the story of Karl Rossmann was also strange). It is fundamental that this is part of the evolution of the relationship between man and the world and a change in Kafka's approach to man himself.

[. . .]

On the basis of the relations between Joseph K. and the court, bourgeois literary scholars have concluded that there is no arrest, no court, not even any trial; that is, no outward circumstances at all press the hero. Everything proceeds only from his own imagination, from his own tortured anxiety and his sense of remorse. Max Brod has even written with some indignation that there are people who find in *The Trial* elements of a satiric criticism of Austrian justice.[17]

Even further along the path of "purging" Kafka's work from any hint of social content is the American scholar Ingeborg Henel. In her opinion, the court in *The Trial* is not a "symbol of the depravity of the world," but only "a construction of human self-justification for weakness,"[18] that is, pure fiction, self-deception, mirage.

However, the text of the novel disproves philosophical speculations of that kind: "There is no doubt," says Joseph K. in his defense speech at the inquest,

that behind the manifestations of this court, in my case behind the arrest and today's interrogation, stands a powerful organization. [. . .] But the sense of this powerful organization, ladies and gentlemen? It consists in the fact that innocent people are subjected to arrest, and that senseless trials and, in my case, one without result, are conducted against them. How, given the senselessness of all this, can we avoid recognizing the abominable corruption in the midst of our officials?

The court, as it is characterized, is an entirely real and objectively existing power, a power which is hostile to man and which oppresses and enslaves him. This is the bourgeois world, as Kafka knew it and hated it.

Moreover, if in *America* Karl's interaction with the surrounding reality was limited by the fact that he was sharply opposed to it, that he was unlike all the others and had nothing in common with them, then in *The Trial* Joseph K. is related to the world in a particular way.

Throughout the whole novel the hero leads a double life: on one

17. Max Brod, "Nachwort" in Franz Kafka, *Das Schloss* (Frankfurt am Main, 1951), p. 482.

18. Ingeborg Henel, "Die Türhüterlegende und ihre Bedeutung für Kafkas *Prozess*," *Deutsche Vierteljahrsschrift für Literaturwissenshaft*, 1963, No. 1, p. 58.

hand he is "simply" a man driven and persecuted, and on the other he is an official, an important bureaucrat, protected (in this his official, public function) by a wall of secretaries from surprise and chance.

Consequently, Joseph K. himself appears to be part of that world which is inimical to him and to individuality and which I. Henel pronounces to be nonexistent or, at best, of which Kafka has not the slightest idea. Just this fact of belonging to the world makes the hero "unclean" in his own eyes. It is as if he were an accomplice to a crime committed against man by the surrounding reality. In front of the door to his office in the bank crowd just such hapless and lonely people as he himself appears to be when, in patient and timid anticipation, he sits out the court sessions in the corridors. And he is just as rude, arrogant, and indifferent in his treatment of those in the bank as the judiciary is rude, arrogant, and indifferent to him.

Hence comes that feeling of guilt which gradually develops in Joseph K. It is for this reason that he cannot leave the court, although the court does not keep him. But when two men in black appear in his apartment one dark night and lead him to the deserted stone quarry, in order to execute him there according to the court's sentence, he does not resist—although it would be easy to call for help and, apparently, he would be rescued. V. Dubský and M. Hrabek believe that this amounts to suicide. But to stop completely at this point of view means to simplify the situation, to make it more rational, logical, and consistent—but at the same time less Kafkian. As a person, Joseph K. accuses himself of being a petty official, and at the same time the world of "officialdom," as indistinguishable from the official world of Joseph K. as two peas in a pod, kills him as a person. That means the court is some high justice, an individual law which everyone creates for himself, the hostile world outside, in which one can discern the features of Kafka's contemporary capitalist society. All this is sick, relativistic "dialectic," a magic circle, a labyrinth without exit, but it is all Kafka without simplification, Kafka the way he was in reality.

I have already said that externally, even after the arrest, there is nothing that seems to change in Joseph K.'s life. But, just the same, had anything particularly important ever happened? Just exactly what? For the first time the hero perceived himself as an individual, looked at himself from the inside. Up to his arrest, Joseph K. was, to himself, simply an "official," that is, simply a function of his external duties—official, public, domestic—an "official" like all those around him. He did not distinguish himself from the others, because he saw himself only from the side—which means that he did not know himself, his loneliness, his fears, his powerlessness. But when something happened to wrench him from the faceless, gray multitude of "officials," he became a "person," a being thrown back on his individuality, and left alone with it. Now he is free—terribly, desperately, hopelessly free. Around him there is darkness and silence.

Joseph K. has been persuaded to renounce his freedom, in other words, his own "I" (lawyer Huld: "It is often better to live in chains than free"; the priest: "To be tied thanks to your duty to the entrance to the Law is incomparably more than to live free in the world"). However, the hero, notwithstanding all this, does not rise up against himself, but against the unjust reality which has revealed itself to him in this way.

"A lie turned into the foundation of world order," he says. He wants to struggle with the "conception of the court"; in his passive resistance there is much tragic value.

And nevertheless, finding his individuality, Joseph K. does not look directly at the world, but at it only within himself, only through himself. The world of *The Trial* is a subjectively colored world, a world seen through the prism of his own suffering, his own helplessness and sinfulness. For that reason it is misty, diffuse, capricious, symbolically fantastic, absolutely without a ray of hope.

But man in the novel *The Trial* is no better. Private truth for Kafka is a cruel and gloomy truth. In *The Trial* there is no mention of that faith in human possibilities which inspired and animated the figure of Karl Rossmann. To Joseph K., profaned by the feeling of guilt, there remains only one fate—stoic despair. And he submissively allows his throat to be cut.

Karl is distinguished by his winning human qualities; Joseph K. is distinguished by no qualities at all, neither winning nor repelling. It is possible that there is some contradiction here: it is just this Joseph K. who finds his identity! But, for Kafka, "identity" is not the same as individuality. All people are "identities," just as all people are "officials": they are all inwardly alone, alienated from one another, unhappy but eternally bound together by the cement of a depressing conformism.

[. . .]

Kafka's conception of man, as it presents itself to the reader of *The Castle*, is best illustrated by one of the stories inserted in the novel—Olga's tale of the misfortune of her family. Three years before they lived in comfort and plenty. And then the official Sortini invited Olga's sister Amalia to him. He demands that she give herself to him, but the girl sharply rejects the crude importunity of this "super-human."

Such unprecedented disobedience plunges the whole village into a holy terror: the customers begin to avoid the father's shoemaking workshop, the workers run away, acquaintances stop greeting. In the end, a former apprentice seizes the workshop and turns the old man and his daughters out of their home.

Very clearly, it seems that the "little man" in class society is completely in the power of the strong people in his world: the refusal to obey any of their whims inevitably brings uncounted disasters.

However, after only outlining the social conflict, Kafka withdraws it, for it turns out that Olga's family is its own enemy. The castle does not convene to punish the family; in any case it undertakes no steps in this direction. And when the first passions and the first fears have abated, there is still time to set everything right again. "A favorable decision in this matter," says Olga, "would be the best of all for the people. If we suddenly go to them with the information that everything seems to be in order . . . they will undoubtedly receive us again with open arms."

But instead of that, the unfortunate renegades who were led astray, who were frightened even by the obstinate and, as it seemed to them, threatening silence of the castle, begin feverishly to pray for forgiveness. For hours the father waits in the cold by the road which the sleighs of the officials use; Olga—when the insulted Sortini hides himself "in the most remote chancelleries"—attempts to gain pardon even through his servants. In order to find him, she makes her way every evening to the village inn, and there she sleeps in the stable with the official's servants.

The circle closes: what formerly Amalia had refused the great Sortini, her sister now gives freely to every contemptible servant.

Amalia, Olga, and their father struggle desperately for their place in the sun, but all of their actions are senseless, all their attempts to affirm themselves in the world are doomed beforehand to failure. And not because someone is hindering them or persecuting them. No! The aspirations of the heroes are unsuccessful because, like blind kittens, they nuzzle up to the solid wall of their *own* foolishness, their *own* helplessness!

Naturally, in this view the whole situation is only a reflection of the real absence of justice for the "little man" in the bourgeois world. Externally, however, something has been torn out of its cause-effect relationship, absolutized and turned into a delirious law.

In one of his notes the author wrote of man:

He feels himself to be a prisoner on this earth, he feels constrained; he is embraced by the feeling of sadness, weakness, illness; he is haunted by the insane visions of the prisoner; no consolations can comfort him . . . in the face of the fact of his unfreedom. But if you ask him what he, himself, really wants, he is not able to answer, for—and this is one of his weightiest reasons—he has not the slightest conception of freedom.

3. THE GREEN DRAGON COMES TO VISIT

The majority of Kafka scholars have turned their attention to the disparity inherent in his style between the "realistic method of portrayal and the absolutely unlikely central occurrence."

Indeed, it would be hard to name another writer who narrates the improbable, fantastic, and unthinkable in such a peaceful and matter-of-fact tone and in such drawn out, apparently colorless and flat phrases of "bureaucratese."

Let the reader recall just the first page of the Russian translation of the novella "The Metamorphosis":[19] A man has turned into an insect! It would be hard to contrive something wilder and at the same time it would be difficult to narrate this monstrous metamorphosis in a more everyday way than Kafka does. The hero, and with him the author, does not try despair or even astonishment. The world has not been turned on its head; the room has remained a room; samples of material are lying on the chair; the cheap little picture is hanging on the wall—it immediately attracts Samsa's attention.

He remains an insect. However, this insect is not a product of hell nor some deep-sea monster, but rather something ordinary (on the basis of Kafka's description, an entomologist might be able to determine its genus and species); only the size of this insect is much larger

19. See *Inostrannaya Literatura*, 1964, No. 1.

than normal. However, here some paradoxical logic enters the game—
if a man could turn into an insect, then certainly he would not turn
into a tiny little bug! That would be improbable and unnatural.

In the story "Blumfeld, an Older Bachelor," two celluloid balls
suddenly begin to dance in the hero's room. He tries to crush them to
have peace and quiet again. "He dismisses the objection that even the
fragments of the balls might continue their dance. *Even the improbable must have its limits.*" (My italics-D.Z.)

Kafka's language also is extremely telling. On the first page of "The
Metamorphosis" there is not one epithet, not one metaphor, not a single simile. The writer carefully avoids everything specifically artistic,
everything that could lend the narration even a semblance of emotional coloration. The adjectives are only definitions; the nouns are
only names of objects; the verbs are naked designations of actions.
Kafka informs, but he never evaluates.

Here, in the fitting definition of the West German scholar F. Beissner, "there is only (*paradox praeteritae*) the self-narrating event."[20]
And this applies equally to all the writer's works.

[. . .]

In a word, no one before Kafka had so closely joined the irrational
and the rational, the fantastic and the ordinary, nor had welded such
stylistically divergent elements into one indivisible whole. The coloration of "The Metamorphosis" is the coloration peculiar to Kafka.

Kafka constructs the edifice of his works from two kinds of bricks—
the unreal and the actual—cementing them together with the mortar
of a balanced and monotonous narration, a narration which is extremely subjective in essence and as "objective" as possible in form.
Here everything is equally meaningful—the little scene observed on
the street and the nightmarish sleep, the delirious vision and the unattainable daydream. Between them there is no antagonism, nor even
any noticeable transition; it is all "material"—palpable, ponderable,
visible.

[. . .]

Or another example:

The door opened, and in the room there appeared a flourishing, very
heavy-hipped, legless green dragon, shifting along thanks to the movement

20. Friedrich Beissner, *Der Erzähler Franz Kafka* (Stuttgart, 1952), p. 35.

of his hind parts. Exchange of greetings. I ask him to creep all the way in. He expresses regret that it is not possible to do so, for he is too long. The door therefore had to remain open, which was quite unpleasant. He smiles half confusedly and half maliciously and begins: "I am called by your longing and passionate wish; I have crept from far away; my belly is chafed and bleeding. But I do this willingly. I appear willingly before you, I willingly offer myself to you."[21]

He is an objectified vision, the body of a metaphor, this green dragon, a figure of domesticated, almost cozy horror. One may greet him politely, one might even hold out one's hand to him—if indeed he had a hand. He is not from a different dimension, but wholly of this world: the stones of the road are sharp to him too—he has scraped open his fat belly on them. It is truly a pity that he doesn't fit into the room—it is impossible to close the door; the neighbors will see him and suspect something strange.

However, it does not follow that the "domestication" of the marvelous, depriving it of its outward signs of the demonic and otherworldly, has anything at all in common with realism. On the contrary, the green dragon, taking part in the everyday just as much as a buffet service or a flowerpot on the windowsill, is a destruction of actuality, a declaration of war on everything spontaneous and authentically living. As a result of this contact with the fantastic, the buffet service and the flowerpot and even the men surrounded by these harmless objects begin to radiate a mysterious phosphorescent light, fall apart, cease to be themselves, become incorporeal, ambiguous symbols of something incomprehensible, dreadful, and inevitable.

But in order to create such a "magnetic pole" of unreality, it is not at all necessary for Kafka to have recourse to the medium of the unequivocally irrational.

In his novels and the stories there are not so many elements of the fantastic and, in any case, there are neither Hoffmannesque fairies and magicians, nor Meyrink's golems, nor the specters of Wilde. But at the same time, almost all the works of this writer are fantastic in their substance.

The residence of Count Westwest in the novel *The Castle* is situated on a low hill; it is not fenced. Naturally, it is not a real castle, but

---

21. Franz Kafka, *Hochzeitsvorbereitungen auf dem Lande und andere Prosa* (Frankfurt am Main, 1953), p. 282.

an ordinary manorial court, surrounded by a group of plain one-story structures. It is only a short distance to them, but K. is unable to reach them. It is as if in a dream, when for some reason one freezes to the spot—one is alarmed, feels awestruck and must flee, but cannot flee, for one's legs don't carry one.

The village under the jurisdiction of the "castle" is not large, but it is administered by countless hordes of bureaucrats. In fact, there are many more times the number of them than there are inhabitants, and all these bureaucrats are busy with work. Given the appearance of some insignificant reason, or if a modest complaint or innocent inquiry is received, then for years the gigantic bureaucratic machinery, for which there are neither big nor little, important nor unimportant matters, spins around. It creates stacks, pyramids of decisions and conclusions, which no one is given to read, and suddenly, when everything about the matter seems forgotten, some sort of completely delirious order is churned out. And the strange thing is that down there, in the village, no one is amazed at it; they take it as necessary, for granted. And if the order is not carried out (for there is nothing to carry out!), it is in any case respectfully received and accurately added to the archive of equally useless orders.

There is some coloration of the absurd that penetrates every word that Kafka wrote—an absurdity that precludes even the possibility of understanding anything that is happening and that appears as the basic method of Kafka's derealization of being. Everything runs through one's fingers like sand—things, words, houses, people, thoughts; there remains only fear in the face of the inanity and incomprehensibility of life.

[. . .]

All these are symbols—vague, elusive symbols of great significance. As for the symbolists, the outer meaning of symbols for Kafka does not lie in their dialectical relationship to their inner content. They are separate; and for this reason the outer meaning as a rule is only a "hieroglyph" which in itself is empty of content.

Many realists also use symbolic methods of expression. But with them, there always exists a direct kinship between the inside and the outside of the symbol. Moreover, for realistic writers the outer meaning of the symbol is not itself indifferent. It is not a single chiffre of an idea, but an artistic figure, valuable in itself, taken from reality, related to it, revealing it, and independent of its more general symbolic content.

Thus, for example, the central situation of Brecht's play *The Caucasian Chalk Circle* appears to be the dispute over the right to the child, a dispute between the biological mother who abandoned the child in the moment of danger and the foster mother who rescued and raised the child regardless of the danger. This whole story, including the judgment of the judge Azdak, which awards the child to the foster mother, has for Brecht above all the meaning of a symbolic parable that invokes confirmation of the socialist principle of property:

> Everything in the world belongs necessarily
> To those famous for good deeds, that is:
> Children to the maternal heart,
>   that they grow tall and manly;
> Carriages to good coachmen,
>   that they quickly roll;
> And the valley to him who waters it,
>   that it bring forth its fruit.

However, all this does not prevent a symbolic story from being a realistic story. By placing the action in medieval Georgia, the dramatist is able to draw a somewhat provisional but fundamentally faithful picture of feudal oppression and the poverty of the people. And it is not at all accidental that he has made the biological mother the wife of the governor, and the foster mother a poor servant girl. And finally, the judge too, who pronounces a just sentence, is an immigrant from the dregs of society.

Kafka's symbols are of an entirely different character. When he wishes to demonstrate human loneliness, an absolute, infinite loneliness which does not exist anywhere in nature, he transforms his hero into a centipede. He could have turned him into a pillar or a speechless human block, as for example the contemporary modernist Samuel Beckett did in his novel *The Unnamable*, and nothing decisive would have changed. The man-centipede is a "pure" symbol of loneliness, its "hieroglyph." And all of Samsa's personal "centipedal" actions—the disgusting stains which he leaves behind him on the white doors, his dislike of milk, his passing time on the ceiling or the walls of his room—these do not have the slightest potential to become the content of symbols. They are a completely different order of narration, merely pseudorealistic, "lifelike" accessories, not intended to reveal or elucidate anything, but rather to conceal, to veil. This break between the inner content and the outer meaning of the symbol with Kafka determines (apparently to a well-known degree) the previously examined disparity between the sense of the story and the character of the narration which is inherent in the style of the artist. This break contributes to the multiple meaning of Kafka's symbols.

"The man from the country" arrives at the gates of the Law. The man wants to enter, but the way is blocked by a guard. He declines to allow the man to enter. And the man waits, waits until his very death. But before his death he asks the guard a final question: How is it that for all these years no one else has tried to enter into the Law? And the guard answers: Because this entrance was intended only for this man. . . .

What kind of parable did the priest tell Joseph K. when they were conversing in the cathedral? What does all this mean? On one hand, the gate is open (as always!), on the other hand, there is a guard at the gate; on one hand, he promises to let the man enter later, on the other hand, he nevertheless does not admit him; on one hand the man does not enter, on the other hand the gate is intended for him alone. What kind of gate is this? What kind of guard? What man? What law? The Law—that probably is truth, perception, justice, grace, happiness. The man—he is man, persistent and yet powerless at the same time. The gate is the path to truth. The guard—he is the obstacle on the path.

All this becomes especially significant in the context of the whole novel *The Trial*, with its idea of the inaccessibility of truth and justice. It is not accidental that the authors of the French-American filming of the novel (scenarist Orson Wells, director Alexander Salkind) presented the parable of the Law as a "prologue" to the film: they saw in it the key to *The Trial*. But if we really try to understand what is bothering this person—the implacability of the guard or his own cowardice (that is, the outer or the inner obstacles), then we immediately find ourselves before such a number of the most various and equally probable decisions, that it does not appear possible to choose one of them. And, we may say, the most curious is that the difficulty, if not the complete impossibility of understanding the parable of the Man, the Guard, and the Law, is demonstrated to the reader by none other than Franz Kafka himself.

In recounting the parable, the priest also acquaints Joseph K. with some of its basic interpretations, but he does not subscribe to any of them. The priest treats the text of the parable just as the "church fathers" treated the Old and New Testaments which, as is well known, present themselves not so much to be understood as to be accepted. Concluding his commentary on the parable, he says, "It is not necessary to accept everything as true, one must only accept it as necessary."

As a result the foggy becomes even foggier. The form of the parable, that of the biblical or evangelical type, vague and at the same time specific in its vagueness, is so complete and so closed in on itself that it does not tolerate elucidation—it is a form unusually characteristic of Kafka's works. It is consonant to a high degree with his ahistorical, primitive-figurative, "naive" way of thinking. It is the way the religious fanatics of ancient Israel thought, or the holy monks of medieval monasteries. Kafka was not a philosopher, but only an artist.

[. . .]

In the night of the twenty-second to the twenty-third of September, 1912, in the darkness of five hours he wrote the novella "The Judgment," and he entered in his diary: *Only this way* can one write: only in one sitting, with such an open body and soul."

And on the eleventh of February, 1913, that is, almost five months later, he made the first attempt to comment on this story, which had become his favorite, recognizing that only now, working on the proofs, did he understand its meaning.

So it took five hours to write "The Judgment" and five months to understand it! Of course, it is not necessary to trust such a perception unconditionally; all the same, Kafka's work is intuitive to a great extent.

It is not the philosophical intuitivism of such refined erudites as Proust or Joyce, which derives from the teaching of Henri Bergson, that is, not a "cerebral" intuitivism, but rather an "internal," "naive" one. Here it is not so much a matter of Kafka's being less educated than those other two pillars of contemporary modernism (in any case, Kafka was not ignorant). It is rather that Kafka himself was a "sickness of the time"—that is, one of the symptoms of the decay of bourgeois consciousness—but he did not intentionally make this sickness into his "fortune." Just for this reason he is always inside his works—he fuses with them; they escape out of him.

In contrast to Kafka's, the symbolism of Proust and Joyce is "learned" and "rational." The author of *Ulysses* and of *Finnegan's Wake*, strictly speaking, does not create metaphors; he takes them ready-made from classical mythology, from the Irish epos, or from the teachings of ancient Indian mystics. And if Joyce's symbolism is not always accessible to decipherment, it is not because there is no key to it, but because the key has not been found. Joyce himself, regardless of whether or not he spoke the truth, always knew what he wanted to say.

Kafka did not always know that. He depended on his intuition and on that general impression which the picture he drew evokes in the reader.

[. . .]

The general idea of ["A Country Doctor"] is clear: man's life is senseless and horrible; the world around him is unjustly ordered; people are not capable of helping one another—acting with the best intentions, they only injure their fellow men. However, neither all this nor even the fact that there are very specific individual and biographical sources in the novella (Uncle Siegfried, the brother of Kafka's mother, had a practice as a country doctor) does not in the least help us to understand the particular symbols in the work.

What kind of horses and groom are these? Why does the groom fall upon Rosa? What is the wound on the young boy's body? Why do they put the doctor to bed next to the patient? There are no answers to these and many other questions, and it would be naive to look for them.

Just how ludicrous such a search is, is confirmed by the "individual examples" of the American critic Norman Holland, who attempts a definitive explication of all the symbols in Kafka's "Metamorphosis." Gregor Samsa's boss, according to Holland, is a symbol of God; the three roomers who come to the house after Gregor's metamorphosis are the gods of each of the family members; the clothing and dressing are symbols of "subordination"; Gregor's whole metamorphosis is a symbol of the transformation of God into man; Gregor's death is a symbol of Christ's death; and so forth, and so forth. Even in the fact that the family's servant calls Gregor an "old dung beetle" Holland sees an ambiguous allusion to the scarab, which was sacred in Egypt at the time of the Pharoahs.[22]

Holland's calculations are an example of the scholastic, academic treatment of artistic material characteristic of many bourgeois literary scholars. Holland obviously copies the "method" of Joyce's interpreters, in particular of his most famous commentator, S. Gilbert. But even if such a "method" is capable of yielding results when applied to Joyce (I have already said why), when turned to Kafka it has no perspective: it amounts only to a collection of completely arbitrary, totally subjective conclusions.

But is it possible, on this basis, to maintain that everything Kafka wrote generally has no sense? As I have already mentioned, many Western Kafka scholars incline to that deduction. Lothar Fitz, in looking at the novel *The Castle*, says that "it is impossible to understand [it] more directly than Kafka did himself. The interpretor must not be less modest than the author; he cannot strive to do the impossible, namely to elucidate the meaning of the castle in all its objectivity."[23] But to take Kafka "in all his objectivity" and not to try even to place something above it, that means tearing the writer out of the historical and social conditions that formed him, a goal toward which the bourgeois literary scholars strive. Fitz and Holland come together in this tendency.

Kafka was not a "spontaneous phenomenon." Everything, even the "uninterpretability" of his symbolism, the absurdity of his system of images, is the result of a disease-stricken writer of a "sick time."

4. THE GLASS WALL OF HIS LONELINESS

Kafka's political views and his public positions remain at first glance in clear contradiction to his creative work. Turning to this side of the Kafka problem is like falling into a completely different world—a normal and clear one far from pathological equivocation.

As a sixteen-year-old gymnasium student, Kafka, together with his

---

22. Norman Holland, "Realism and Unrealism: Kafka's 'Metamorphosis,'" *Modern Fiction Studies*, 4 (1958), No. 2.

23. L. Fitz, "Möglichkeiten und Grenzen einer Deutung von Kafkas Schlossroman," *Deutsche Vierteljahrsschrift für Literaturwissenschaft*, 1963, No. 1, p. 77.

fellow students Pollak and Hecht, joined the anticlerical club "Free School"; he read Haeckel and Darwin and was in fact an atheist.

During the Anglo-Boer War, Kafka openly displayed his sympathy with the tiny, heroic people that had the courage to resist the might of the greatest colonial power in the world. Not less openly, Kafka condemned Pan-German chauvinism; one day in the company of an ill-tempered mob of nationalists, this quiet, shy man of frail build stubbornly refused to rise when the orchestra struck up "Die Wacht am Rhein."

Thanks to his service in the insurance companies—"Generali" (1907-1908) and especially the "Workers' Accident Insurance" (1908-1923), which wrote insurance for on-the-job injuries—Kafka was well acquainted with the disastrous and legally unprotected situation of the Czech proletariat. In conflicts between the workers and the industrialists, he took the side of the former, which is witnessed by his article "Manufacturing Insurance and the Entrepreneurs," published (without the author's name) in the *Tetschen-Bodenbacher Zeitung* of November 4, 1911.

Kafka believed that the workers have a right to much more than they in fact receive, for "the luxury of the rich is paid for by the misery of the poor"[24] and that the workers are too passive in their demands. Once he said to Max Brod: "How modest these people are; they come to us with requests. Instead of storming our offices and smashing everything to pieces, they come with requests."[25]

According to G. Janouch, a man who knew him well and respected him highly, Kafka repeatedly criticized the system of capitalist exploitation and "Taylorism" in particular. He was actively interested in revolutionary and socialist teachings, studied Saint-Simon, Herzen, and Kropotkin. He also wrote a fragment of a project for organizing a socialist colony of the Owen type.

[. . .]

Through his friend at the gymnasium, Rudolf Illowý, Kafka became acquainted with some leftist anarchists[26] and in the prewar years

24. Gustav Janouch, *Gespräche mit Kafka. Erinnerungen und Aufzeichnungen* (Frankfurt am Main, 1951), p. 78.
25. Max Brod, *Franz Kafka. Eine Biographie* (Berlin, Frankfurt am Main, 1954), p. 102.
26. The leftist anarchist circles in Prague later became the nucleus from which the Communist Party of Czechoslovakia was formed.

he frequently visited their meetings, as well as the meetings of the
"Klub mladých" and of the political union "Vilem Körber," which
set as its goal the struggle with the exploiters of the working class.

Michal Mareš, a progressive Czech poet and acquaintance of
Kafka's, was arrested during one of these meetings because he resisted
the police. Kafka, who was also present, followed him to the police
station and tried to help him and others detained, suggesting that he
pay their fines.

The same Mareš introduced Kafka in 1910 to a circle of Czech
artists who met at the cabaret "Vulcan" [Mareš calls the cabaret
"Balkan." *Ed.*] and there Kafka became acquainted with Jaroslav
Hašek and some other Czech writers: S. K. Neumann, Karel Toman,
Franja Šrámek, Gellner.[27]

Some of Kafka's statements on the place of art in public life concur
with the views we have just examined. "The artist," he told Gustav
Janouch, "tries to give people different eyes, in order by this means to
change reality. For that reason artists naturally appear to be subver-
sive elements, because they want to change. But the state, with all its
faithful servants, only wants to conserve."

As an addition to these thoughts of Kafka's we may refer to his
evaluation of one of the works of contemporary Soviet literature,
Aleksandr Neverov's *Tashkent, City of Bread* (1923): "All true art is
a document, a testimony. A people with such young men as the book
portrays cannot suffer defeat."[28]

Kafka rejected the contemporary decadent and "demonic" writers
Huysmans, Wilde, Wedekind, Meyrink. He also did not care for the
expressionists, although he had much in common with them.

Kafka's progressive public and political position found specific expression in his creative work also.

I have already said that the early novel *America* not only bears the
stamp of the imperialist world contemporary to Kafka, but also contains a direct critique of its conditions. We can cite further examples.

The unfinished story "Recollections of the Railroad in Kalda"
(1914), written in a completely realistic way, depicts the utterly
gloomy existence of a signalman who, in order not to lose his job, is
obliged to entertain the inspector with vodka on his monthly visits.

27. See Michal Mareš, "Wie ich Franz Kafka kennenlernte" in Klaus Wagenbach,
Franz Kafka. Eine Biographie seiner Jugend, 1883-1912 (Anhang) (Bern, 1958).
28. Gustav Janouch, *Gespräche mit Kafka*, pp. 87, 60.

In the story "Report to an Academy," the problem of "bourgeois freedom" is subjected to criticism. The method which Kafka uses here—an appraisal of everyday reality through the eyes of an astonished observer—has a precedent in Voltaire's *Candide*, for Kafka has the report to the academy rendered by a humanized ape.

And finally one more example. Among the diary entries for 1914 there is a fragment of the beginning of a story about the director of the insurance company "Progress," to whom some poor wretch comes looking for a job as an attendant:

"How receding your forehead is," the director says to him, "strange. Where have you been working until now? What? You haven't worked for a whole year? And why? Because of pneumonia? You don't say! Well, that doesn't say much in your favor, does it? Naturally, we can only use healthy people. . . . Oh—you have recovered now? You don't say! Of course, that is possible. If you would only speak a little louder! You get on my nerves with your whispering. As I see, you are married and have four children. And you still haven't worked for a whole year? Well, you know, dear fellow. Oh, your wife is a washerwoman? You don't say! Well, of course. . . ."

Here the writer conceals neither his hatred for the insolent rich man nor his sympathy and compassion for the unfortunate man out of work. Just the social side of the contrast between them is uncovered, and put in the sharpest possible relief. Kafka undoubtedly took the scene from life, possibly even from his professional practice. But he turned it into a satirical indictment of bourgeois heartlessness. This is aided by the name of the insurance company ("Progress") and by the reader's hearing only the self-assured falsetto of the Herr Direktor.

But no complex of world view, of feeling about the world, is complete in the political sympathies alone of any man—much less of an artist—no matter how important they are in themselves. It is necessary to keep this truth firmly in mind when we have to do with a writer like Kafka.

Emil Utitz, a friend of Kafka's at the gymnasium, wrote: "We all loved and respected him very much, but none of us knew him intimately; it was always as if he were surrounded by a glass wall. Through his soft, affable smile he revealed himself to the world, but *vis-à-vis* the world he was a closed circle."[29]

29. Emil Utitz, "Erinnerungen an Franz Kafka" in Klaus Wagenbach, *Franz Kafka* (Anhang), p. 269.

Kafka was only a passive observer, a contemplator. On August 29, 1907 he wrote to Hedwig W., one of the women close to him: "I still do not have that interest in people which you demand of me."[30]

Kafka took part in antimilitary demonstrations, and he really hated war. But when World War I broke out, he did not "notice" it, or if he did, then only in connection with himself.

On July 31, 1914 he wrote in his diary: "General mobilization. K. and P. called up. Now will begin a time of loneliness for me." On August 2, 1914: "Germany has declared war on Russia." And the following phrase is: "Went to the public pool after dinner." But after 1914 and to the end of the war, there is not a single further entry in Kafka's diary that bears directly on the war.

Kafka's diary is in general a very curious human and literary document. It lays bare to our eyes how Kafka really lived. In it there are a great many unfinished literary fragments and variants of things later written; there are detailed recountings of dreams and even of waking visions; many pages devoted to complaints about the state of his health, to the vague "disquietude" torturing the writer, to the impossibility or inability of creating; much attention is paid to the relationship with his father, his position in the family, and so forth. However, we search in vain in the diary for detailed reports about the writer's *external connections*. True, there are realistic and clear appraisals, portraits of different people, and so on. But such entries bear an obviously sporadic character. Much more frequently the writer speaks of his relations with other people in a "telegram style": "Was at Baum's"; "Went to the theater"; "Conversation with Max" (Brod), and it is usually that way when he refers to the people closest to him. There are almost no entries relating to Kafka's official duties or to his public positions. If we did not have the testimony of his contemporaries, we would know almost nothing of the writer's socialist sympathies, of his visits at the meetings of progressive organizations, and so forth.

One can object that in his conversations with Max Brod or Gustav Janouch Kafka did speak about revolution, capitalism, and the exploitation of men by men. Yes, he did speak about these, but they nevertheless remained secondary problems. Mostly he spoke about himself.

That was not egoism or indifference to his fellows. In no way did

30. Franz Kafka, *Briefe 1902-1924* (Frankfurt am Main, 1958), p. 40.

Kafka admire or overestimate himself. Rather, he was closer to underestimating himself. "You yearn for the impossible, but for me even the possible is impossible," he wrote to Max Brod on January 31, 1921.

He recognized many of his deficiencies, in particular the one he mentioned to Emil Utitz: "I am cut off from everything by a kind of empty space, even to the edge of which I cannot aspire."

But he could not get out of himself, master or overcome himself. "There is nothing but the world of the spirit," he wrote, "that which we call the sensory world is the evil in the spiritual one."[31]

This is not solipsism, which bourgeois literary scholarship has imputed to Kafka. It is only evidence of his enormous inner loneliness, "loneliness among people," in comparison with which "Robinson's island" was "full of the life of a strange land."

However, the outer world—as idea, possibility and goal—continued to have significance for Kafka. But, not having any alternative, he contemplated this world less than he projected on it his own weakness, indecisiveness, and passivity. In observed reality he distinguishes only that which is like himself, and he omits everything foreign, dissimilar, and incomprehensible. Because of that, the world becomes merely senseless and impenetrable, for only consequences are left; causes, however, and motivations vanish.

"Everything which jumps into my eyes strikes my field of vision starting not at the base, but only somewhere in the middle," Kafka recognized as early as 1910.

But the whole outer world, being thus fully identical with the inner, is able, it seems, to find room in Kafka's head, as it can in the head of every man in general: "There is no need to leave the house. Stay at your desk and listen. Don't even listen; wait. Don't even wait; be immobile and alone. And the world will be opened for you; it can do nothing else. . . ." (*Hochzeitsvorbereitungen*).

Kafka sympathized with the socialists, but he did not believe in them, for, starting from his subjective conception of being, he thought that "there is a goal but no path; everything that we call a path is simply hesistation" (*Hochzeitsvorbereitungen*).

And thus his skeptical attitude toward any and all changes, among them revolutions: "At the end of every truly revolutionary development appears Napoleon Bonaparte," he said to Janouch, "and the more

31. See Erich Heller, *Enterbter Geist* (Wiesbaden, 1954), p. 324.

extensive the flood, the stiller and thicker the water. The wave of revolution recedes, leaving behind the sludge of a new bureaucracy."[32]

Possibly, it was just this that Kafka was thinking about as he sat modestly in the corner at the meetings of the leftist anarchists.

5. STRANGE, EVERYWHERE STRANGE

Kafka's contradictions are contradictions rather typical of the Western intelligentsia in the first half of the century. But with Kafka they assume grotesque, absurd forms: on one hand he is "almost" a socialist, on the other an irrationalist and mystic; on one hand he unmasks the crimes of the bourgeois world, and on the other he is an antirealist.

For this reason it is particularly interesting to take a look at the conditions that formed Kafka. There were three factors, the same three factors which made each of us too: the historical epoch, the country with all its peculiarities and traditions, and, finally, the family. But the combination of these three factors in the given, concrete case was particularly unfavorable, capricious, and willful.

He was born in 1883 and thus lived at the same time as Heinrich and Thomas Mann, Romain Rolland, and Roger Martin du Gard, John Galsworthy and James Joyce, Theodore Dreiser and Upton Sinclair— although he died earlier than all the others, in 1924. This was a time of change, a time of imperialistic wars and proletarian revolutions, a time of powerful social displacements and weighty human decisions, a complicated time which set up a whole series of difficult destinies for writers. But it was the *same time* for all the artists enumerated here, and nevertheless, each of them, with the possible exception of Joyce, pursued a path which was completely different from Kafka's. However, I will not begin to speak in detail of the influence of the era (since, it is necessary to assume, we will not find the key to Kafka's uniqueness in it alone), but will stop at the problem, throwing some light on the originality of this writer's perception of the capitalist reality surrounding him.

There is a point of view that says Kafka was able to reflect one of the noteworthy aspects of life in bourgeois society—the "alienation" of man inherent in it.

32. Gustav Janouch, *Gespräche mit Kafka*, p. 71.

The worker in large capitalist enterprises who, in contrast to the craftsman, executes only one (often extremely undemanding) productive operation, is to that extent "alienated" from the product of his labor; the thing ceases, as it were, to be a matter of human hands and acquires a certain independence in the eyes of its maker. It seems to him to be something which has ceased to obey him, which has been consigned its own, incomprehensible and even almost mystical meaning. Things in such an "industrialized society" become, so to speak, the masters of man and suppress him. Moreover, in the bourgeois state, where all the former—and clearly perceived—feudal hierarchial ties are broken, man feels himself to be "alienated" from his surroundings and alone. He is completely without laws and at the same time is not personally subordinate to anyone, for above him there is no sovereign ordained by god, no margrave appointed by the sovereign, not even a burgomaster or a shop steward; everything is regulated by a faceless bureaucratic mechanism. The feeling comes to people that they themselves are no more than things among other things, are drawn along by some blind, elemental current of life. That is the true situation of man in the bourgeois world, where labor power indeed does become a ware among other wares in the capitalist marketplace and gets tangled up with man's wrong, mystified idea of his situation in life.

All this is really present in Kafka's feeling about the world, to the limits of his naked vision.

Milena Jesenská, who knew Kafka better than all his friends—because it was she alone, it seems, whom he really loved—wrote of him:

For him life seemed to be something different than for everyone else. Above all money, the stock market, currency exchange, typewriters—all these things were absolutely mysterious (and they really are, only we, the others, do not see it), for him they were the most amazing puzzles . . . He had no shelter, no roof over his head. For that reason he was completely in the power of everything that we are protected from. He was like a naked man among the fully dressed.[33]

Kafka himself remarked about the phenomenon of alienation: "The conveyor belt of life moves us along somewhere—we don't know where. We appear to be more a thing than a living being."[34]

33. Quoted in Max Brod, *Franz Kafka. Eine Biographie* (Frankfurt am Main, 1954), p. 68.
34. Gustav Janouch, *Gespräche mit Kafka*, p. 68.

And such a perception of reality is reflected in the writer's creative work:

I was told that all the walls of his room were covered with piled up columns of large portfolios of files; they are the same files that Sortini is working on at the present moment, and since these files are always being taken out of the pile or being put back, and all of this happens with great haste, the pillars of papers are always falling, and just that unending noise, repeating itself in short intervals of time, became characteristic of the worker in Sortini's rooms,

just as, in the novel *The Castle*, is described the activity of the eager bureaucrat, who is choked by the papers and turned into their empty appendages.

In the story "Blumfeld, an Older Bachelor" the celluloid balls dancing around in the room at first amuse the hero but then begin to annoy and finally to frighten him. He is chased by them, climbs under the bed, clambers onto the dresser. But the balls are elusive. As if mocking him, they jump around in front of old Blumfeld's very nose. These are things which are emancipating themselves, "rising in mutiny." We encounter such people-objects in Kafka, something midway between living and non-living orders. Such, for example, is Odradek, the hero of the fragment of the same name.

However, it is not a matter of a concrete, that is to say palpable-figurative, embodiment of the psychological process of "alienation." The whole absurd, alogical, grotesquely distorted world of Kafka's narration is the map of the "alienated" world, as the writer saw and understood it.

[Thus, Roger Garaudy (both in his presentation at the Prague conference and in his book *D'un réalisme sans rivages* he examines the problem of Kafka's "alienation" in great detail) seems to be right. But really he is right in only one point: in his observation that Kafka was a "poet of alienation" (or a "poet of the absurd," as we would prefer). But what follows from that? That Kafka fathomed some profound truths? That he discovered the essence of the age? Not at all!

Alfred Kurella [. . .] polemicized against Garaudy's term "alienation," objecting to the excessive broadening of its application: "Since the time when the existentialists of clerical, agnostic, or atheistic shades discovered the 'early Marx' and armed themselves with his pseudo-philosophical concept of 'alienation,' some Marxist thinkers have similarly tried to broaden this concept and make it the point of departure for demanding that orthodox Marxism be enriched and broadened under the sign of 'alienation.' Thus they begin to label as 'alienation' everything that someone doesn't like in society, everything that doesn't accommodate him in it."]

Nevertheless it seems to me that the term "alienation" is sometimes too broadly applied to Kafka. "Alienation" is a concrete historical concept; even more, it is a political and class concept connected with a specific means of production, that is, the capitalist means; it derives above all from private property and an antagonistic division of labor, which in turn leads to a distorted relation between the producer and the product. There is no need to go further into the way in which socialism (even simply economically!) is completely opposed to capitalism. But let us underline once again the logical deduction which evidently and necessarily follows from this: "alienation" does not have and cannot have any relation to socialist society. In the course of the construction of socialism, there arise (or may arise) difficulties, miscalculations, and infractions. But to call them "alienation" is completely without foundation. And it is not only a question of terminology. For "alienation" is a completely specific term with a completely specific content. In the sphere of this content—if one gives up the concrete historical application of the term—is surely involved the negation of every regulation in general as something foreign and hostile—in principle.

But once, with the beginning of socialism, "alienation" no longer has any sway, then the question of the "direct educational meaning" of Kafka's work for people of the new revolutionary world disappears.

[Kafka and the bourgeois world is another matter. And when Kurella touches this side of the question, it is not possible to agree with all of his theses. For instance, he doubts that "Kafka's works reveal in an artistic form what Marx, criticizing contemporary bourgeois society, generalized under the concept of 'alienation.'" But he doubts this not because he has not found in Kafka's novels and stories anything resembling a picture of alienation. No! Rather, it seems, because Kafka did not read Marx and was not acquainted with Hegel's and Feuerbach's points of view. But "alienation" exists objectively in capitalist society, and not only in connection with Marx's theory.

Hegel, Feuerbach, and Marx did not think up "alienation"; they discovered it. That means that it is possible to express the laws of capitalism in an artistic form without having read Marx!

It seems to us that one must view the problem of "alienation" from a completely different side. It is not important whether or not Kafka was able to grasp and express the essence of "alienation"; what is important is whether or not he in fact expressed this essence.]

Sometimes Kafka is compared to Bertolt Brecht and it is said that, like Brecht, he unmasked capitalist "alienation" and fought it with the power of his art. But that is not so. Brecht depicted the "alienation" of man in bourgeois society; in his play, *A Man's a Man*, he represented man's transformation into a "human fighting machine," and in *The Good Woman of Sezuan* into a heartless money-maker. But Brecht knew well that the "alienated" world is the unjust, untrue, historically doomed world. And he not only knew it, but also, sharpening the evident contradictions to the point of a monstrous grotesque, he led his theater audience to recognize the necessity of tearing down and abolishing that artificial world of marionettes dancing their horrifying tragicomic dance.

For Kafka, on the other hand, the "alienated" world was the true, actual world which, with all its abominable and appalling abnormality, was still virtually "normal." For the situation of Joseph K. after his arrest, or the situation of Gregor Samsa after his metamorphosis into a centipede, is precisely the situation of "alienation" and, at the same time, the situation of recovering one's sight, of a beginning self-knowledge.

The "alienated world," the unmanageable world, the world without rudder or sail—that, for Kafka, is our only world and will forever remain our only world, for we ourselves are not suited for any better one. "It was suggested to them that they make a choice"—so reads one of Kafka's parables—"between becoming kings or kings' messengers. Following the example of children, they chose to become messengers. For this reason, there exist only messengers; they rush around all over the world calling out to one another—since there exist no kings—the most senseless information; they would gladly quit their poor existence, but they cannot decide to do it on principle" (*Hochzeitsvorbereitungen*). No, the writer Kafka was sooner the victim of capitalistic "alienation" than an artist who could interpret the phenomenon.

Franz Kafka was a subject of the Austro-Hungarian monarchy. He was one, it appears, at the very moment when it was dissolving itself, when the corrupt feudal trunk and its consumptive imperialist off-shoots were crumbling under the blows of war and revolution.

Austria-Hungary, wrote Robert Musil in his novel *The Man Without Qualities*, "according to its constitution appeared to be a liberal state, but it was ruled by the clerics. It was ruled by the clerics, while the population was free-thinking. Before the law, all citizens were equal; but not all were citizens."

That is not at all a map of its inner contrasts, because they are already satirically exaggerated by the novelist. But it is the very essence of the contradictions in this huge, feeble, historically already almost unthinkable empire, in which the corroded medieval evil of a rusty age aggravated the new evil of the bourgeois downfall, in which, under a handful of German officials and Hungarian agricultural magnates, pined the masses of the Slavic millions: Czechs, Poles, Ukrainians, Ruthenians, Croatians.

Engels remarked as early as 1848 that "not in any other country did feudalism, patriarchy, and a slavishly servile petty bourgeoisie, guarding its native stupidities, preserve itself nearly so inviolably and totally as in Austria."[35]

And in this sense, the Austria-Hungary of 1918—that was the last year of its existence—was little different from the Austria of the time about which Engels was speaking.

If on the border between the nineteenth and twentieth centuries this unstable dual unity, coming apart at the seams and fraught with rebellions and insurrection, was still able to preserve some illusory semblance of equilibrium, then it was not thanks to the army (many faced and speechless, it was astonishingly weak), nor to the police (which was corrupt), nor to the administrative apparatus (which was rotting), but, apparently, only by dint of a thousand-year-old "habit," in the name of the idea of "Habsburg power."

So, at least, thought many people. In Vienna—the residence of the "Roman Emperors of the German Nation" and formerly the first capital of the civilized world—sat the old monarch, who had ruled over even the grandfathers of Kafka's contemporaries, old enough to have succeeded in becoming a legend, a myth, the shadow of his own power. Between the monarch and his subjects stood the bureaucratic

35. Karl Marx and Friedrich Engels, *Collected Works*, IV, 471.

institutions—the bureaus, chancelleries, offices, ministries—clumsy, slack, and immense, acting only in the name of the monarch but in fact sovereign, consisting of subordinate officials who were accountable to no one. The impression grew that there was no power, but that no one had any rights; that everyone was free, but for some reason did not wish to make use of his freedom.

And in Kafka's work too at every step we run into the shades of significant and at the same time unbeatable powers. In *The Castle*, where chancellors dispose in behalf of the elusive Count Westwest; in *The Trial*, where the powerful court has not the slightest sovereign leadership; even in *America*, where the crown of the hierarchy in the provincial hotel "Occidental" loses itself in altitudes beyond the clouds. All of this, no doubt, Kafka compiled from specific Austrian historical conditions.

But in this respect the most illustrative work of the writer is the story "The Chinese Wall" (1918-1919): "Our people thinks of the emperor with hope and hopelessness. It does not know which emperor is reigning at present; there is even doubt as to the name of the dynasty" (*Beschreibung eines Kampfes*, 1946, p. 79).

But nevertheless the Great Wall of China got built. It has no sense, for no one is protected by it. And it protects from no one. The barbarians on the borders are weak. And possibly they are not there at all? No one knows, can know or wants to know. . . .

It is not accidental that Kafka transports the action into some legendary country, in this case China. He creates the story "along Austrian motifs." But it is not a simple allegory. It is a metaphor imbued with the presentiment of a near end, a catastrophe, universal ruin.

In Western Europe and America at the moment an object of special attention is a group of German writers of old Austria-Hungary: Karl Kraus, Stefan Zweig, Georg Trakl, Joseph Roth, Robert Musil, Hermann Broch, Rainer Maria Rilke, Franz Kafka. The secret of their popularity seems to be this: by virtue of their Austrian provenance, these artists sensed sooner than others that "this world is threatened by the abyss and the end," and this feeling is allied to the accelerating process of the decline of their common Austro-Hungarian birthplace.

But the Austrian writers named—the majority of them in any case—were certainly not purposeful opponents of capitalism; they are regarded in the West not at all for their social criticism but because they (primarily Hermann Broch and Franz Kafka) interpreted concrete historical phenomena as "generally human" and not socially conditioned. And that is understandable.

Austrian backwardness did not contribute to clarifying the fact that the decay of the monarchy was already a consequence of imperialist decline. And this decline did not appear purely imperialistic: on the same stinking, rotting heap of remainders of absolutism were the survivals of the even older feudal relations. It did not contribute to clarifying the accelerating process: Austria was the first "victim" of epochal changes, and because of that the reasons for her approaching ruin were generally not sought where they really lay.

Recognition of the senselessness of the present without any faith in the future—that is the condition for the use of "class-bound" decadent literature. And the Austrian situation at the end of the last era and the beginning of ours produced such a musky, sickly, mystical literature. And, to a notorious extent, Kafka was educated in the traditions of this literature: however negatively he felt toward Gustav Meyrink, a connection between these two writers does exist. Kafka was the unhappy child of Austria—her son and stepson simultaneously.

Kafka lived in Prague. If we don't count the short journeys to Austria, Italy, and France or several months in tuberculosis sanatoria and the year-and-a-half-long "flight" to Berlin, then he lived there for his whole life.

In the rate of industrial growth, Prague was the second city (after Vienna) in Austria-Hungary. Nevertheless, Prague was the center of Czechoslovakia, economically the most developed part of the empire. For this reason, the interest which the Praguer Kafka had in the workers' movement and progressive ideas was not casual; the spirit of proletarian Prague was forming such German communist writers as the "furious reporter" Egon Erwin Kisch (Kisch's brother was a schoolmate of Kafka's), Rudolf Fuchs, and the younger Franz Weiskopf. But all the same, proletarian Prague was not Kafka's Prague.

This city was everything for him. Here he was born and grew up; here he attended the gymnasium and later the university; here he served in the capacity of a petty, inconspicuous official overburdened by work and prevented from devoting himself fully to his one passion in life—literary creativity. Here lived his family—father, mother, sisters—and his small circle of friends: Oskar Pollak, Max Brod, Oskar Baum, Felix Weltsch. And with Prague his novels and stories are very tightly connected. But Kafka's Prague is only the gloomy, shabby, "homeless" Prague, for he himself was homeless there.

Kafka came from a Jewish family and wrote in German. The Jews were a community in Prague, the Germans were a colony, and the Czechs were the people. "As a Jew," writes the West German critic Günther Anders,

he was not himself in the Christian world. As an indifferent Jew—for such Kafka was at first—he was not himself among the Jews. As one who spoke German, he was not himself among Czechs. As a Jew speaking German, he was not himself among Germans. As a Bohemian, he was not quite Austrian. As an employee of the workman's insurance office, he did not fully belong to the bourgeoisie; as the son of a solid burgher, not fully to the workers. And he was not at home at work, because he felt himself to be a writer. But he was not a writer, because he devoted all his strength to the family. "I live in this family stranger than the strangest foreigner."[36]

Everywhere Kafka was *strange*, superfluous; in addition to the general process of capitalist "alienation" in his private life, he felt himself to be a man without a country, without a people.

Describing the situation of a man without a country and a home, he wrote to Milena Jesenská:

You have your homeland and for that reason you can do without it—and that surely is the best thing one can do with one's homeland, especially since one cannot dispense with what is indispensable in it. He, however ["he"—that is Kafka himself—D.Z.] has no homeland and so he can never dispense with it and must constantly think about seeking it or constructing it, constantly, whenever he takes his hat from the peg or lies in the sun at the swimming pool or works on the book which you are going to translate.[37]

Kafka's individual "alienation" was aggravated by his relationship to the family, primarily to his father. Hermann Kafka was the son of a half-impoverished village butcher. He had made his Philistine happiness with the work of his own hands and had opened an extremely prosperous store in Prague. This "life-success" developed in him an unusual self-confidence and self-satisfaction—traits that were organi-

36. Günther Anders, *Kafka. Pro und Contra* (Munich, 1951), p. 118. The words in the last phrase of the quotation are borrowed from the rough draft of a letter from Kafka to his fiancée's father.
37. Franz Kafka, *Briefe an Milena* (Frankfurt am Main, 1946), p. 173.

cally foreign to Franz. The son and the father were completely different people, incapable of understanding one another: "I am gaunt, weak, lanky," Kafka wrote in the *Letter to his Father* (1919), which he never made up his mind to send, "you are strong, big and broad."

The father demanded gratitude, adoration, and absolute obedience. He was a household tyrant, crushing his son's will from childhood, depriving him of trust in himself. Franz was not in a position to rebel against this tyranny. The only thing he was capable of were timid attempts at "emancipation," leading to his stubborn refusal to study business, to his thirst for self-affirmation through his literary work.

Traces of Kafka's hostility toward his father are very noticeable in his works. The cruel parents of the chief hero of the novel *America*, Karl Rossmann, ship the boy out to sea. The father of Georg Bendemann (in the story "The Judgment") accuses his son of indifference and sentences him to death; obedient to his father's will, Georg throws himself into the water. The insect Gregor is hated and mistreated by his father, and the father even appears guilty of his death—the reason for it being the apple which the old man threw and which lodged in the insect's soft back. A series of sketches which we find in Kafka's diaries is devoted to similar themes.

This circumstance suggests a connection between Kafka and German and Austrian expressionism, for a general characteristic of that tendency is the occupation with problems of the hostility between generations. Kafka's first explicators related him in a general way to expressionism.[38] However, in contrast to Walter Hasenclever, Georg Kaiser, Franz Werfel, and others, Kafka is far from any attempt to decide such questions on a social plane. There is no conflict of ideas between his heroes and their fathers. Kafka's sons do not rebel against their fathers; they are passive and obedient, even inclined to attribute all guilt to themselves.

In short, the conflict between father and son in Kafka's works is a personal problem. By virtue of the fact that Kafka was "alienated" from the world, left so to speak to his own devices, his work is generally extraordinarily autobiographical.

The affair with the maid, which serves as an excuse to banish Karl Rossmann, comes from the boyhood of the writer himself. The Samsa

38. See, for example, Walter Rehm, *Geschichte des deutschen Romans* (Berlin and Leipzig, 1927).

family is modeled to a significant degree on the Kafka family. Frieda in *The Castle* is Kafka's second fiancée, and so forth.

[. . .]

6. "HIS" AND "NOT HIS"

Why did Kafka request that Max Brod burn his manuscripts? Critical opinion is divided on this matter.

For Kafka, creative work was not only the chief passion, but the sole passion of his life. For the sake of being able to write in peace he was ready to sacrifice everything else, especially since nothing else interested him. "Everything that is not related to literature is hateful to me," he wrote in his journal.

Even his dream of marriage he was willing to lay on the alter of art. But we must say that family and children meant much more to Kafka than to many other people. "To marry, to found a family," we read in the *Letter to his Father*, "that is in my opinion the highest thing that a man can strive for."

But whenever it actually came to marrying (three times he was engaged, and twice to the same woman), then doubts began to overwhelm Kafka: "And would that not distract me from my work? Not that! Not that!" (*Tagebücher*). And as a result, he remained a bachelor.

Certainly, writing was for Kafka not simply a means of "emancipation" from his father, as he repeatedly asserted. Writing was for him the only possibility of asserting himself in life, of feeling himself to be a genuine, competent person, useful to others and significant in his own eyes. For that reason he was capable of speaking only about it, writing only about it. To it he devoted all the free time he could wrest from his hated job, sitting at night over his manuscripts, fighting off headaches and attacks of fatigue, weakness, and despair.

[. . .]

The reasons for his dissatisfaction with his writings and his fear of their publication become understandable thanks to an entry in his journal which he made upon returning home from a party at Baum's, at which Max Brod had read some of his stories: "If sometime I were able to write something full and whole, well organized from beginning to end, then . . . I would feel as if I had the right, peacefully and with open eyes, as a blood relative of a completely healthy work of art, to listen to it being read" (*Tagebücher*).

Thus, Kafka sees and understands that his art is disorderly, capricious, and sickly, and this torments and distresses him. True, after 1912 (that is, after publication of the *Reflection* collection) there appears to be something of a change in his mood. Kafka actively corresponds with his new publisher Kurt Wolff, sends his manuscripts and corrections punctually, makes plans of various kinds to republish already printed works.

[. . .]

Of course, such ups and downs are one of the manifestations of those innumerable contradictions which are characteristic of Kafka in general. However, these ups and downs have their own remarkable consistency. In the first place, the happiness of creating each time appears temporary and unstable, and the feeling of dissatisfaction always stays, even in the midst of happiness.

"Great satisfaction," Kafka wrote in his journal, "I can get from works like 'A Country Doctor,' provided that nothing like that has ever been done successfully before (highly unlikely). Happiness, however, would be accessible to me only if I were able to exalt the world as something pure, true, and permanent."

In the second place, the "ups" came only when Kafka succeeded in creating something which, in his view, was worthy of attention.

It is interesting that Kafka never—not in his journal nor in letters nor in conversations with Brod or Janouch—mentions any of his works that were not published during his lifetime (excepting only the novels and if, naturally, we do not count scant mentions like "working on 'The Young Procurist' "; "in 1914 I wrote 'The Schoolteacher,' " and so forth). Apparently he considered these works completely unsuccessful. But he also considered the novels unsuccessful. "Why should I shake the dust off these useless efforts?" he wrote to Max Brod, "Just because up to now I haven't burned them?"

Kafka wrote and spoke more—although again not too often—about the novellas he himself put into print. And he also has a different attitude toward them: he loved "The Judgment"; "The Stoker" and "A Country Doctor" pleased him, although not without reservations; "The Metamorphosis" and "In The Penal Colony" he did not like.

And nevertheless, Kafka felt it possible to publish these. He did not do it without vacillation, nor without pressure from Max Brod, but he did it nevertheless. And certain other works, including completely finished ones like "The Description of a Struggle" and the "Investigations of a Dog," as well as a series of little stories, parables, and aphorisms he did not consent to publish under any circumstances. Why?

It is extremely difficult to draw any sharp line in character between those works which were published by Kafka himself and those which Max Brod prepared for printing. It is difficult because all of Kafka is like—Kafka; and because he not infrequently paid tribute to his momentary mood. But one thing is clear: on the whole the selection which Kafka made was not accidental. Nor did the publishers dictate this choice. The author's reputation during his lifetime was not wide, but it was high. Both Rowohlt and Kurt Wolff would have taken everything that he wanted to give them. But he did not want to give everything.

If one were to picture Kafka only as the author of slender books of short stories which the artist agreed seriously to consider "his"—that is, if we imagine him without *The Trial*, without *The Castle*, without "The Burrow" (1922), without the journal and letters—then against that background the writer would appear strange and sick, but not so gloomy and desperate as we now know him.

I imagine that, when Kafka gave his final instructions to Brod, it was his wish to weaken that utterly gloomy atmosphere which he himself hated and which his work in general creates. He knew that he was at an impasse; he knew that life had not turned out well, that the most important and weightiest thing in it he did not catch sight of and failed to capture: "On Balzac's cane was drawn: 'I break all obstacles.' On mine: 'All obstacles break me.' We have only the little word 'all' in common" (*Hochzeitsvorbereitungen*).

He tried to save whatever could still be saved—"to pretend that nothing has happened," that there was no writer Kafka and never had been.

In the history of literature it is almost impossible to find a tragedy of an artist that is more desperate than the tragedy of Franz Kafka. And it follows that we must respect the pitiless honesty with which he condemned and crucified himself. In 1922 he wrote to Brod:

Creating is such a sweet, wonderful reward, but for what? Tonight it was clear to me . . . that it is a reward for serving the devil. This descent to the dark powers, this releasing of spirits from their naturally confined condition, these dubious embraces and everything else that transpires down below and which one cannot see when one sits in the sun above and writes his stories. [. . .]

Whoever has read Thomas Mann's *Doctor Faustus* is struck by the unusual resemblance of this admission to the composer Adrian Leverkühn's final confession:

Item, my desperate heart ruined it for me. Had surely a good, quick mind and talent vouchsafed me generously from above, which I could have used modestly and in probity; but I felt all too well: now is a time when no work can be accomplished piously, soberly, and honestly, when art is become impossible without the Devil's help and hellfire under the pot. . . . Indeed, that art stagnates and is become too heavy and mocks itself . . . is surely the fault of the time. But if one invokes the Devil, one betrays one's soul and takes on one's own back the guilt of the time and is damned.

Like Kafka, Adrian Leverkühn is speaking of himself here. In one of the fantastic-allegorical scenes of the novel, the composer (whose brain is already afflicted by his serious illness) gives his soul to the devil, receiving in exchange—as a "sweet, wonderful reward"—twenty-four years of creative ecstasy, an icy loneliness thawed only by the hellfire of "vanity and voluptuousness."

Leverkühn has altogether much in common with Kafka. He too is torn by contradictions. And he writes cursed, dark, barbarously cruel works, dreaming at the same time of a "happy and modest" art, from which "fall the scales of a melancholy ambitiousness and a new purity, a new serenity constitutes his life."

No, Thomas Mann did not write his Leverkühn with Kafka in mind, although he knew and in his own way loved this writer, as he also loved his own Adrian. The immediate prototype of the main protagonist in *Doctor Faustus* was Friedrich Nietzsche. But Thomas Mann would not have been a great master of realism if he had merely drawn a portrait of Nietzsche, without typifying in him the characteristic features of the decadent modernist artist and thinker as well.

Leverkühn's pact with the Devil is a metaphor for that kind of artist's betrayal of his relationship with a pure, healthy, truthful, realistic art; it is a symbol of decline, decay, dehumanization.

Thomas Mann was far from underestimating the enormous difficulties which rise up on the path of the artist in the contemporary bourgeois world. He himself knew the tenacious power of the dreadful and blissful embrace of despair, hopelessness, sympathy with death. Therefore he could be extremely forebearing with Leverkühn; he recognizes his great talent and his subjective honesty and the whole depth of his human suffering. However, Thomas Mann is able to separate the subjective from the objective. He sees the unquestionable bond between Leverkühn's art and ideological reaction, the spirit of fascism; and he judges Leverkühn, judges him more harshly than Leverkühn had ever judged himself. And in judging Leverkühn, Thomas Mann judges Kafka too—condemns him, of course, without thinking of him personally at that moment. Surely, Kafka is talented. But his talent, like Leverkühn's, is gnawed by the worm of doubt, darkened by the black clouds of disbelief, despair, and loneliness. That which Thomas Mann depicts, explains, and censures, Kafka merely relived.

Franz Kafka was not the founder of any literary direction; there did not develop any school after him, in the usual sense of the term. One can point to several attempts to imitate him, chiefly in Austrian, German, and Swiss literature. For example, such attempts seem to be Hermann Kasack's novel *The City Beyond the River* (*Die Stadt hinter dem Strom*, 1947), Ilse Aichinger's story collection *The Bound Man* (*Der Gefesselte*, 1953), Friedrich Dürrenmatt's radio play *The Double* (*Der Doppelgänger*, 1960). However, not one of these works became or could become eminent, or even noteworthy.

Dürrenmatt is an artist of great and original talent, of a sharply expressive satirical tendency. But in the play *The Double*, which deals with a man who has become a murderer as a result of his terrible powerlessness and absolute loneliness, and who is sentenced by a nonexisting court, neither talent nor satirical tendency is visible. The play is unique in the dramatist's work and is essentially foreign to him. Aside from the fact that Dürrenmatt's interest in Kafka is not accidental, he even tried to launch his literary career with a comedy "in Kafka's manner" (1943), for which he could not devise a title or find a producer. Kafka is simply impossible to imitate; he is impossible to follow. The world of his works is too subjective; his creative style is too individualistic; as an artist he is too closely tied to the errors, faults, and maladies of a specific historical epoch, an epoch which, although relatively close to ours in time, is already irrevocably sinking into the past.

However, for the twenty and more years of the "Kafka boom" in the West, we have heard only: this writer has "the greatest influence on the English novel" in the twentieth century; he was "the precursor of the French existentialists"; contemporary American literature is "unthinkable without him," and so forth.

Maja Goth in her book *Franz Kafka and French Literature* enumerates the writers who are his disciples. There is Henri Michaux, Maurice Blanchot, Georges Bataille, Samuel Beckett, Albert Camus, Jean-Paul Sartre—that is, every color of French modernism and then some.[39]

And not only the critics have treated Kafka as a teacher of other writers; many writers too have considered themselves his disciples—French, English, American, West German, Swiss, and Dutch writers.

Even if we peel off the layer of sensational hubbub, and make allowances for the wish of certain writers to cling to "Kafka's fame," then it is impossible not to recognize that there is some truth in the statement of modernist critics and artists: Kafka really does have a unique value for them.

But does this perception not contradict the thought expressed above, that Kafka cannot be copied or followed? No, it does not.

The truth is that in the first case I was regarding Kafka as an artist, and in the second case as a phenomenon. And it is possible, and necessary, to differentiate between these. Let us see what contemporary modernists look for and what they find in Kafka.

The existentialists (this can be seen primarily in the early Albert Camus) are interested in Kafka's problem of the relationship between the solitary individual and the society which is alien to him—or, more exactly, the absence of any connection whatever between them—and also in questions of human freedom or unfreedom. The solutions to these problems, say in *The Myth of Sisyphus*, are related to although not identical to Kafka's (Kafka, by the way, also mentions Sisyphus; for him Sisyphus was a "bachelor," that is, an "outsider").

The proponents of the "new novel" concentrate their attention on

---

39. See Maja Goth, *Franz Kafka et les lettres françaises 1928-1955* (Paris, 1957).

the human gesture or subject which has lost contact with its roots, and which Kafka did not cease to wonder at—just because this gesture or subject was an end in itself, a "thing in itself" devoid of all content. The description of the picture on the wall of Samsa's room, in its absolute gratuitousness, its complete indifference to the fundamental content of the story, recalls the analogous descriptions of the picture in Robbe-Grillet's novel *In the Labyrinth;* just as the description of the port of New York in *The Trial* [sic; obviously, *America* is meant. *Ed.*] recalls the description of the port in Robbe-Grillet's *Voyeur.*

The founders of "a-literature," such as Samuel Beckett, Henri Michaux, and William Burroughs are attracted above all to the "grand disorder" of Kafka's composition, the principled "uninterpretability" of his symbols, the general grotesquesness of his picture of the world.

The dramatists of the "absurd theatre" see in Kafka an "unsurpassed master" of the destruction of reality who reaches the path to a mixture, an amalgam, of the irrational and the everyday. Every farce of Eugène Ionesco is, in this sense (and *only* in this sense), a repetition of Kafka.

And finally, religious writers of every faith borrow from Kafka the motif of unfathomable human guilt, which they interpret in the sense of "original sin."

In this way, Kafka is—in my opinion, clearly despite his wish which, although not expressed, was quite definite—received as a deeply decadent phenomenon of crisis, foreign to all truth of art and life. And the more the sickness of bourgeois society progresses, the more actively modernists of this sort turn their attention to this writer.

But all these reactionary ideas, disfigured forms and distorted shapes, which are now interpreted and assimilated as "Kafkaesque," are blowing in the wind, as it were, in the poisoned mind of the imperialist world. They belong to no one—and they belong to everyone who is sufficiently blind, or perverse, or self-serving to take advantage of them. Not Kafka created them; not Kafka was the first to put them in circulation, for he had no relation to many of them.

Nevertheless, the heirs of Kafka pull him to pieces. Each of them, being occupied only with himself, attempts to see in this complicated writer that side which impresses him personally. This side is absolutized at the expense of the others. Actually, the successors do not follow Kafka but invent him, each for himself. Only on one point do they all miraculously agree: in paying not the slightest attention to his sincere sickness at this world, to his despair and tragic self-negation.

In this connection it seems to me appropriate to touch on the question of the so-called "Kakfa tradition." [. . .] The writer Alain Robbe-Grillet and several other participants at the Leningrad session of the European Writers' Union in August 1963 regarded Kafka as entirely the "father" of the contemporary novel; they asserted that there is no tradition but that of Kafka or Joyce which appears viable today. But even if we take Kafka as what he was, that is, removing the falsifications and misinterpretations—even then it is unthinkable to imagine him as the beginner of a full-blooded and triumphant artistic tradition. Up to now the history of literature has known not a single progressive tradition founded on pessimism, weakness, or despair, on an open recognition of its inability to know the world and to aid its reconstruction. The foundation of every progressive artistic tradition is a deep and unshaken faith in man, the conviction of those who struggle and create that they are capable of making the world happy. That has always been so—in Dante's time, in Cervantes' time, in Goethe's time, in Tolstoy's time. And even more importantly, it is the optimistic foundation of art in our era—the era of the decline of the old world and the affirmation of a new world. And the tradition of Kafka lies away from the mainstream of artistic development in our age.

Kafka's strange and sad fate, to an extent truly greater than his creative work, is evidence against the contemporary bourgeois world, against contemporary bourgeois culture. In itself this fate is both a lesson and a warning.

The World and Man in Kafka

VLADIMIR DNEPROV

[. . .]

At the center of his works Kafka places an idea which is horrifying and intolerable for the poet: the idea of the *expedient unreasonable-ness* of the world, of its ultimate incongruity with everything that is really human. In place of a preestablished harmony there is preestablished disharmony. A cosmic bureaucratism became the natural embodiment of a highly organized absurdity, an artful senselessness of being. The irrational has rushed out of the social sphere and shifted to the center of the artistic universe; everything revolves around the irrational with the same lawful regularity with which the planets revolve around the sun. The metaphor of the "celestial chancellery"—in everyday life it means that man gets no answer from fate to his entreaty—grew in Kafka's work to an illusory and at the same time unalterable reality, and was systematized in a literary image worthy of occupying a place among the greatest images of world literature.

Proceeding from *America*, Kafka's first novel, to *The Trial* and *The Castle*, we can recognize the direction in which the artist's novels developed. In *America* the relationships and forms of human life are still tied to their historical base in modern capitalism, the peculiarities of which Kafka felt with astonishing sharpness. But already in this work the constitution of society imperceptibly blends with the universe, and the hotel, in which the novel's hero works as an elevator operator, grows into something infinite. The bourgeois relations, in all their irrationality, brutality, and indifferent stagnation, threaten to encompass and engulf the whole universe.

In *The Trial*, ordinary bourgeois reality and the general laws governing this reality are represented as two worlds existing side by side. The ruling world is located, as it were, on the back of the real world,

"Mir i chelovek u Kafki," From Vladimir Dneprov, *Cherty romana XX veka* [*Characteristics of the Twentieth Century Novel*] (Moscow-Leningrad: Sovetskii Pisatel', 1965), pp. 199-207.

quartered in stuffy attics (Kafka's heaven!), in deserted corners, in seedy and insignificant houses; it is represented by endless strings of officials, each of whom knows his little piece of the "law" and in his turn depends on the mysterious supreme hierarchy that loses itself in the vague distance. This world is infinitely miserable, corrupt, petty and at the same time omnipotent; its content is alien to all that is human even though it directs people's fates. The forms of bourgeois relations, in acquiring independent existence, become the universal lot. The gigantic bureaucratic machinery with its countless little wheels, purposeless units, absurdity, irresponsibility, with all its negligence and strictness, anonymous coldness and mercilessness, becomes an evil and sad caricature of world expediency and providence. In this world man is doomed. The "law" ruling over life hangs like a noose around men's necks and matter-of-factly, unhurriedly, strangles them—in this consists the sense of *The Trial*. In the seventeenth century, an optimistic metaphysics spoke of the earth as the best of all possible worlds; Kafka in the twentieth century came to speak of it as the worst of all possible.

In *The Castle*, the last ties of empirical reality are broken. Before the eyes of the reader rises a strange, archaically simplified reality similar to a mirage, and furnished at the same time with the most precise details and characterized with the help of extremely real psychological dynamics. Kafka's purpose is to depict the genuine essence of the world order, in contrast to the temporal and deceptive forms of its appearance. For that reason, the writer is not interested in similarities with available observations of contemporary life. The scenes no longer reconstruct a picture of life as it comes to the surface and as we see it; they directly express the moral meaning of existence, its ultimate tendencies. In the "village" about which *The Castle* narrates, the sun never shines. A short, dull-white winter day quickly turns to twilight, and then falls into darkness—the natural condition of Kafka's hypothetical world. Light and darkness are not used in the novel in their primary function of pictorial imagery; on the contrary, they acquire sharp pictorial qualities and expressive graphic character thanks to their obvious symbolic significance. Darkness directly fuses with the image of life's own existence in the shadows.

And at the same time within the borders defined by this moral sense, Kafka strives to reproduce the scene with all the fullness of authenticity—the harsh effects of his verbal graphics are remembered for a long time, as before our eyes rise rooms plunged into pitch darkness from which shines a little scarp of barely visible yellow light from a lamp or candle.

The people inhabiting the "village" (the allegorical village) are similarly shown in their direct connections to the ultimate results of the moral world order. It is not enough that these people are as submissive as sheep, and obedient to all worldly and heavenly authority (the table of official ranks accords with the topography marked in *The Castle*—ascending to the very skies so that the heavenly power becomes an extension, and the crowning, of the temporal power), servile and compliant; they even adopt in their view of themselves the perspective of the bureaucrats dominating them. In contrast to the oppressed people of Dostoevsky, they do not feel themselves at all insulted or humiliated, and in this self-righteousness concerning their fall is expressed most clearly the finality of their degeneration. And perhaps the last gleam of the human appears in them as fear, envy, a contemptuous respect, a malevolent esteem in their attitude toward the newcomer who is intent—just think of such impudence!—on being equal to the authorities and who, to the end, persists in his hopeless attempts to realize his design. Their manner of avoiding the newcomer expresses not only the cowardice which penetrates their flesh and blood, but also the secret uncertainty in the hope of their souls for immunity against the feeling of human dignity.

That is the way, thought Kafka, people must be if they are adapting themselves to an all-powerful necessity, expressing it through their moral conscience, humbling themselves to the invincibility of worldly evil. Absolutely alien to the writer was the thought of the utilization of historical necessity for the benefit of human freedom. In Kafka, objective laws receive a specific moral character—they are insidious, ominous, and hostile to all that is ideally human. Man can become accustomed to objectivity only in conditions of spiritual growth. But when the subject demands to assert his rights in the world order, he is indeed a voice crying in the wilderness.

In transposing social injustice to the scale of the universe, Kafka becomes a mystic. But from that one cannot conclude that his "world" is governed by a god of any sort. (If anyone does command Kafka's "world," then surely it is the devil.) Necessity for Kafka is faceless and blind; it slips off into vagueness. The persons who embody it are merely executors, merely instruments that do not comprehend the sense or the aim of what they are doing. Their ranks fill up the whole universe, forming an evil, monotonous, tedious infinity. We know of only a few steps ascending the hierarchy, and there is no end that follows on them: "and so on." In this "and so on" the whole essence resides, and it means that only the senselessness of life is revealed to us, but never its sense and never its goal.

The injustice which Kafka depicted in *The Castle* summarizes in itself the traits of slavish, feudal, and capitalist oppression. This extract, the essence of injustice, its prototype, reminds one of Plato's prototypical ideas.

The masters of the Castle are representatives of a universal power. They fulfill the function of the state and the function of fate. They set limits, forbid, provide, humiliate, regulate, deceive, procrastinate. They guarantee the normal functioning of the system of lawlessness and at the same time they form through their activities the structure of time, as it were, for the oppressed. The "peasants" appeal to the authorities, petition, hope, wait; they are denied, promises are made to them—as time passes, so also passes life. In the end, they receive nothing, having become entangled in a labyrinth of hopes and delays; whereas "time passes," they never catch a glimpse of the dim and hopeless truth. All the constant activity of the authorities, in its fine and witty way, is organized so as to be completely fruitless. Those wielding power are base, wanton, brutal, proud, whimsical, ugly. They are the instruments of evil and of a senseless world order and are necessary to it; their inane activity accomplishes the movement that Hegel would have called "from nothing to nothing."

The universal "to nothing" dissolves in itself the sense of everything happening on our little planet. Relationships created by history are removed from history and become ahistorical.

With perfect aim, Kafka hits the irrationality of capitalist reality. This irrational was not thought up by Kafka; it in fact comprises a necessary moment and form of the phenomenon of capitalist contradictions. In *Capital* Marx at every step of the way remarks on this irrationality and the apparent senselessness of bourgeois relations: "production for the sake of production," "money giving birth to money," "the price of the earth," and so on. Everywhere Marx depicts the mystique of bourgeois reality. But in Kafka, the irrational display of mystified forms becomes an end in itself and the substance of the life process. The forms of living appearances are abstracted and then assume the completeness of an independent life—such is, in the majority of cases, the manner of artistic generalization in Kafka's works. The predicate becomes the subject, and the subject becomes the predicate.

Man moves in complete darkness, gropingly, trying to guess at the road; now here, now there little lights flare up, enchanting and seductive: man dreams among deceptive flashes of hope and illusion, all is in vain, all is sad and baleful. And in his *Castle*, Kafka creates an artistic model of an exemplary vicious reality. Why does one people oppress and torment another? For nothing. To what do the suffering of people and their resistance to it lead? To nothing. On the world's throne sits an endless absurdity.

But how difficult it was for the writer to put such a conception of the world into the flesh! Moreover, Kafka was a man nobly sympathetic, humanely educated, feeling his loneliness as a broken attachment, capable of experiencing an ideal feeling in a powerful, spectacular soul.

For the writer apparently regarded his own image of the world as the expression not only of a peculiar understanding of life: to no small extent he saw in this image the mirror of his incomprehension, the artistic portrayal of life in its incomprehensibility.

This is expressed particularly in the fact that the conception of the world and the conception of man in Kafka find themselves in complete disharmony with one another. More than that—they absolutely contradict one another. Destiny is fruitless, barren, pernicious, tedious and merciless; but man, regardless of for what, regardless of his infinitely sad experience, continues to hope and to aspire toward the ideal, continues to struggle and, in his longing to be up against a blank wall, stubbornly to dream and to strive for harmony between himself and the world. Whence springs the ideal in man? How does it arise in him who lives in the despondently bureaucratic, colorless world, if God did not send down to him a spark of spirituality?

Kafka raises all the similar questions; they touch on the basic mystery which makes up the ultimate essence of being. An artist does not have to possess an inner right to create the semblance of approaching an understanding of life's mystery; his task, on the contrary, consists in reproducing the mysterious that lurks behind the appearances, clearly, as it were.

And everything in the collision between the incomprehensible world and searching-reasonable man, between real desperation and the tenacity of hope, between oppressive objectivity and the ineradicability of the ideal aspirations of the spirit, between the absurdity of being and human esteem for the reasonable and intelligent, between loneliness and love, between the dim subconscious nature of mental processes and the classical transparency and reasoned precision of narrative speech—in all this and much that is similar the struggle between the modernist and the classical sources which define the artistic order of Kafka's works is manifest.

The hero of *The Castle* is doomed, but he does not say: I give up. He is convinced of the domination of evil, but he does not enter into an agreement with it, does not betray his birthright for a mess of pottage, and he rejects his warm little places, offering them in exchange for human dignity. He is terribly alone, infinitely weak in comparison to the necessity so hostile to him, but he does not fear it and tries to penetrate to its very belly, acts and fusses like a little bug, looking for paths and exits. He is inclined to be petty, he yields to temptation, easily becomes a toy of his appetites, dodges about with trivialities, but he does not fawn, does not play the lackey, behaves toward the personified temporal powers as an equal, not as one enslaved. He does not achieve anything, but he does not shrink from himself. He did not come on his own into this world, the village; he was called to it. But because of the indifference of the "heavenly chancellery," because of departmental confusion in the structure of this world, because of the bureaucratic errors, he finds himself completely useless—even though he has been received. The hero himself does not want to perceive himself as useless; he demands his rights; he is ready to repeat his demand an infinite number of times: the world called me, so let it now give me my place. The bureaucratic machine can easily perplex him, lead him astray, weaken and ruin him; but it cannot force him to say: Have it your own way.

We see the nothingness of the hero, but we cannot deny our respect for him. He is a lonely man, subject to passions, but he is a tenacious man and does not betray himself. We see the vanity of his struggles; with pain and sympathy we watch his tossings and deeply feel the tragedy of his destruction.

The artistic world of Kafka is torn by the dualism of the world and man.

The picture of reality which the writer himself drew oppressed and stifled him, but he would consider every other picture a falsehood and deception. Having written the first line of a new composition, he simultaneously thrust a steel blade into his heart, and with every passing page the blade sank deeper, and the pain increased, becoming unbearable.

And then Kafka broke off writing, almost never returning to the rejected work. Everyone who has in any way followed the history of Kafka's works in his diaries and letters, has immediately noticed the feeling of dissatisfaction with himself which is inherent in that artist, going as far as a perception of the most complete artistic failure at the very moment when the end of the work was in sight. In Kafka's author's soul there lived an active force of self-negation—it was unable to force him to alter his creative path, but it forced him to repudiate the results secured on this path. His finished works were exceptions, the unfinished ones the rule. The final act of self-negation was Kafka's last will, enjoining his executor to destroy—unread—all of the writer's manuscripts, the largest and most important part of his creations.

Kafka and Problems of Modernism

DMITRI ZATONSKY

I. KAFKA'S OPTICAL PERSPECTIVE

Klaus Hermsdorf made a very interesting and important observation. In analyzing the first preparatory sketch of *The Castle* (as we have already mentioned, it goes back to around 1914), he called attention to the fact that here the narration takes place from the point of view of one of the village residents. This enables us to look at K.'s actions and behavior *from the side*, to maintain in relation to him a specific spatial and psychological distance.

There is nothing unusual in this fact itself. The history of literature is acquainted with epic and lyric and, so to speak, "mixed" forms of narration. What is striking is something else: the change in the situation itself. The village at which K. arrived seemed at first an ordinary village, and Count Westwest seemed a typical landlord. It was K. himself and his efforts and aims that seemed abnormal, incomprehensible, and mysterious.

"Maybe he wants to get a place at the estate," an anonymous villager wonders. "No, he doesn't want that; he's rich enough himself and has a carefree life." "Maybe he's in love with the landlord's daughter? No, no, he's free of that suspicion too."

That fragment was written at least six or seven years before the basic text of *The Castle*. After that Kafka's views changed somewhat. But nevertheless it is not so much a question of the evolution of the writer's views as it is of his *optical perspective*. Kafka always (both before and after 1914) suspected that his heroes and he himself were to a certain degree "abnormal"; he suspected that nothing could be

From Dmitri Zatonsky, *Frants Kafka i problemy modernizma* [Franz Kafka and Problems of Modernism] (Moscow: Vysshaya Shkola, 1965), pp. 67-74 and 84-89. The passage from H. G. Wells is from *The Time Machine and Other Stories* (New York: Scholastic Book Services, 1963), p. 215.

done with himself or his heroes. And whenever he began to write, speak, or think, then from the point of view of his "inner truth" it almost always seemed that the outer world was abnormal, incomprehensible, mysterious.

Therefore the early draft of *The Castle* is curious not as an example of the artist's insight [*prozrenie*], but as a narrative experiment which breaks sharply with the principles of Kafka's writing and yet helps us understand these principles better. For the rare exception always underlines and sets off the rule.

If we approach Kafka's work from the angle of his style, then it appears that the strangeness of the situations, the illogical activities of the characters, the complexity of the collisions, the fogginess of the whole sociohistorical background—all this results primarily from the lack of distance between the author and the central figure, that is, it is an aspect of composition.

Neither in *America* nor in *The Trial* nor in *The Castle* nor in the majority of Kafka's novellas does anything happen in the absence of Karl Rossmann, Joseph K., K., Gregor Samsa, Georg Bendemann, and so on. It is as if the author understands no more of what is happening than his hero and sees reality only through his hero's eyes. What is going to happen on the next page is hidden from him by just as thick a curtain as hides it from the characters.

Kafka followed this principle with such strictness that, in cases when he was obliged to disclose something happening outside the limits of the hero's competence, he had recourse to the help of inserted stories. Such inserted stories are Theresa's tale of the ruin of her mother in *America*, the information about the court's organization which the lawyer Huld and the painter Titorelli provide in *The Trial*, and Olga's confession pertaining to the conflict between her sister Amalie and the bureaucrat Sortini in *The Castle*.

All of this unexpectedly reminds one of Cervantes' *Don Quixote*, Smollet's *Peregrine Pickle*, or Fielding's *Joseph Andrews*, and raises a question as to the "old-fashioned" and "traditional" nature of Kafka's novels. In reality Kafka does not and cannot have anything in common with the realism of the seventeenth and eighteenth centuries, nor with the realism of the nineteenth century. The inserted story in Cervantes is a technically somewhat naive but nevertheless ideologically perfectly justified means of widening the real and living sphere of the novel. The great novelist resorts to such devices not because of any limitations in his authorial powers and responsibilities; on the contrary, in Cervantes, as in Fielding and Sterne, the author stands above the hero and constantly intervenes in the action; he is an active propagandist for his own ideas.

But the author's hiding behind the backs of his heroes is not Kafka's own invention: it is connected with a certain significantly older tradition.

In France Gustave Flaubert and in Germany Friedrich Spielhagen were the founders of the "objective method" and the "objective novel." The author, they said, should not interfere in the course of the narration, should make no commentary directly from himself; his task is to analyze reality strictly "scientifically," with no emotional participation. From here lead two paths: to *contemporary psychological* realism of the Hemingway type, that is, to the writer who is able to see the world through his hero's eyes and at the same time to remain above him, knowing and seeing more than he; and to naturalism, chronologically closer to Flaubert, but in fact farther from him.

The author of the naturalist novel does not elevate himself above his hero's horizon. In the spirit of positivism, he merely wants to accumulate facts, to content himself with an immediate vision, neither explaining nor delving deeper.

The Swiss writer Carl Spitteler was not a "pure" naturalist. But in the foreword to his story *Conrad, der Leutnant* he expounded the naturalist's point of view on the role of the author:

The main character is introduced in the very first phrase of the story, and from that moment until the very end he does not leave the scene for a moment. Only what he perceived is narrated, and it is narrated as it is reflected in his mind. Finally, the chain of events is painstakingly unfolded hour by hour; the narrator does not allow himself to jump over any interval of time that may seem to him empty of significance.[1]

It is astonishing to what an extent this theoretical program coincides with Kafka's artistic practice. With him too (apart from everything else), the development of the action "is painstakingly unfolded hour by hour." In the example of *The Castle* (Kafka sustains this novel in the most well-regulated manner) it is not difficult to see that the continuity of the narration is broken only for relatively short in-

1. Carl Spitteler, *Conrad, der Leutnant. Eine Darstellung* (Vorbemerkung) (Jena, 1906), p. 1.

tervals of time when K. is asleep, that is, when his consciousness is switched off.

It might seem that Kafka, the creator of symbolic parables and fantastic visions, might have something in common with naturalism, the tendency to tie literature to the empirical "method" of investigation foreign to all conditional character. But there is not such a big difference between a photographic reproduction of the external "given" and an equally undiscriminating registration of a disorderly "stream of consciousness." At the bottom of each lies the refusal to make a selection from life's facts and to generalize and typify them. [. . .]

Naturally, in his destruction of reality, Kafka goes significantly farther than the old naturalism. Spitteler says nothing about the character of a hero in whose mind the represented reality is to be refracted. And if that aspect does not appear decisive, it is nevertheless very important. With such naturalists as Spitteler or the Goncourts (not to speak of Zola or Hauptmann, artists who were connected more with the naturalist school than with naturalist methods), the hero was not only a typical phenomenon of the epoch, but frequently also the enunciator of a progressive world view. And therefore he was sometimes capable of truly evaluating the environment.

Kafka's hero, as we already know, is absolutely subjective in his evaluations. He is pettily prejudiced and blindly tendentious, and in addition his vision is perverse. The world is reflected in his mind as if in a curved mirror, a bewitched world enchanted by an evil and cruel sorcerer. It is possible that not everything in this world is as dark, hopeless, and senseless as it seems to the hero.

"Always, sir," says a young man in the "Description of a Struggle," "I have wanted to see things the way they are before they appear to me. Then they are probably beautiful and peaceful. That must be so, because I have frequently heard people speaking about them in that way."

But what does all that mean if the hero is not in a condition to see the world as more beautiful and peaceful than he actually sees it?

Moreover, Kafka's deformation of the world does not end there. The author departs behind the scenes or hides behind the backs of his characters; the author does not maintain the slightest distance between himself and them. But just in such a case there remains the possibility of hinting, if not showing, that the curved mirror of narration is simply the fruit of the hero's individual feelings. As a rule, Kafka stops up even this last vent.

He began to write *The Castle* in the first person. Such a narrative form is just one of the vents mentioned. If a person narrates about himself, that means he is *recollecting*. A break between the time of narration and the time of action becomes inevitable, and it follows that the hero-narrator's *knowledge* of how the whole story ends also becomes inevitable. That in itself—even independently of the writer's wishes—creates something similar to a distance: the narrative "I" stands willy-nilly above its own active "I," even if only because the first "I" is compelled to construct his story dispensing, as it were, with the ending, with the unknown active "I." Moreover, narration on the part of the hero is an undisguised, frankly subjective narration. It makes no claim to the reader's absolute credence: the reader knows from the beginning that it is the hero, but not necessarily the author himself who thinks thus, sees thus, and evaluates thus what he has seen. Finally, first-person narration obliges the writer to illuminate the hero's inner world in all its depth, to know everything about him that a man can know about himself.

But before finishing even the first few chapters, Kafka discarded this narrative form, changed the "I" to "he" in all places, and continued *The Castle* in the third person. And what was the result of this? A lyric novel became an epic novel? Not at all! *The Castle* remained what it had been, that is, a subjective confession. Only what was subjective in it became "objectified," without, however, becoming more truthful. To the extent that the author did not appear as any kind of active factor, the last hope that he might reserve for himself an opinion apart from the hero's views evaporated. In all ways the author and the hero became identical with one another; the story of K. turned into the story of Franz Kafka, and in connection with that its ending became impossibly problematical and lost itself in the fog of the future. Strictly speaking, now the novel could end only with the end of the writer himself; and that is the way it actually happened. But at the same time the author and the hero did not merge (after all, the narration is in the third person). K. (and that means Franz Kafka too) is just "he" for Franz Kafka—a foreigner, a stranger, an uncomprehended and unsolved mystery. K.'s actions (that is Kafka's) are not motivated, not located in any kind of causal chain; in the novel they are not seen as "beginning from their roots," but from "somewhere in the middle." Why does K. live with Frieda? Why does he at first reject the position of school janitor and then gratefully accept it? How did he get the idea of representing himself as a surveyor? All these and many other questions remain unanswered.

And the final point. Having become "objectified," the story of K. (of Franz Kafka) starts to lay claim to be the story of man "in general" and of the world "in general," that is, to be a universal, unalterable, and authoritative story. Whether or not the writer wanted to, he placed a weapon, a dangerous weapon, in the hands of his bourgeois commentators.

Wolfgang Kayser writes correctly that "The death of the narrator is the death of the novel."[2] It would be hard to find a better example than *The Castle* to illustrate Kayser's point.

Of course, Kafka did not always decamp so radically as author. In *America*, for example, we clearly feel his authorial sympathy with Karl Rossmann. In "A Report to an Academy" the narration, which is by an ape, creates an extremely marked authorial distance from what is portrayed. The story "In the Penal Colony" has a double perspective: on the one hand the scholar-traveler's view of the world (with which the author is in agreement), and on the other hand the conception of the same reality given in the judge's story (to which the author is in sharp opposition). Moreover, just in this story—for the only time in Kafka's works—the author tries to fathom the thoughts of a secondary character, of the soldier who has been condemned to torture, and he does that at the moment when the judge unties him in order that he may lay himself down under the machine's needles: "Probably the foreign traveler had given the order. So that was revenge. Without having himself suffered to the end, he would be avenged to the end. A broad, silent laughter now appeared on his face and no longer disappeared."

But these are rare, although not completely accidental, exceptions. Ultimately, the *optical perspective* of Kafka's novels and stories is foreign to realism. Not only as a man, but also as an artist he does not resist imperialist reality; he recognizes himself defeated by it and unconditionally accepts it in the most "alienated," mystified forms in

---

2. *Entstehung und Krise des modernen Romans,* p. 34.

which it appears to him, and he presents the reader with a naturalistic photograph of his own thoroughly subjective, sickly-perverse view of things.

[. . .]

2. IT IS NOT A MATTER OF LITERARY DEVICES

We have already said that the images of the offices in *The Castle* and of the judicial proceedings in *The Trial* were suggested to the author to one extent or another by the reality of the Austro-Hungarian monarchy. But these images are not a satire on bureaucracy. And here it is not at all a question of whether the pictures Kafka sketched were fantastic. In Swift's *Gulliver* or Saltykov-Shchedrin's *Story of a City*, in France's *Island of the Penguins* or Capek's *War with the Salamanders*, there is much more of the fantastic. But that does not prevent those novels from being realistic works in the sense of realistic satirical allegories. Each of these books aims at a completely specific historical reality. The fantastic in them is a method of sharpening, of "defamiliarizing" [*ostranenie*] and consequently of exposing the baseness, stupidity, and brutality of a concrete, exploitative order.

Kafka's satire is an atemporal satire, a satire on the world and man "in general." But that is not all.

"Kafka," Walter Benjamin writes, "never tired of confirming the pure gesture. But that never happens except with amazement. [. . .] He separated the human grimace from its cause and in that way obtained an object for infinite reflection."[3]

The offices of *The Castle* are such a "human grimace" separated "from its cause," a "pure gesture," so amazing and frightening to Kafka that he was prompted to search for an innumerable multitude of explanations, in the midst of which only one is missing: the true historically and socially stipulated one.

In order to demonstrate graphically the essential qualitative distinction in the use of the fantastic in realist and non-realist works of art, let us compare H. G. Wells's story "The Man Who Could Work Miracles" and Kafka's novella "The Metamorphosis."

George McWhirter Fotheringay, a minor clerk, sitting one evening in the Long Dragon bar, in an argument with Mr. Toddy Beam-

3. *Schriften*, II (Frankfurt am Main, 1956), 226.

ish denies the possibility of miracles. And just in that moment he unexpectedly discovers in himself the ability to command the elements.

Having quickly exhausted his scant fantasy on the little trick, Fotheringay turns for help and advice to the parish pastor. They experiment enthusiastically deep into the night until it occurs to the minister to stop the moon, like Joshua. The world turns into a pile of ruins. Turning somersaults, Fotheringay still manages to give his last command: let everything become the way it was and he will give up his miraculous powers. And George McWhirter Fotheringay once again is sitting in the Long Dragon and arguing with Toddy Beamish. That, in a few words, is the story's plot.

We find something similar in Kafka's story. Having been turned into a centipede, Samsa with difficulty leaves his bed (he awakens lying on his back). The centipede-Gregor creeps up the door, opens it with his jaws, and appears in the Samsa family's dining room. He rushes to gulp down his breakfast in order to rush to the railroad station, where a messenger from his firm is already waiting for him with samples of new wares.

But in a fit of disgust his father drives the transformed Gregor back into his room. From now on, desired by no one and infinitely lonely, he does not leave it any more, crawls along the walls and ceiling, lies for a long time on the window sill and grieves. And when his sister or the maid comes in to put his dish of food down in the corner, Gregor spares their aesthetic feelings and hides under the couch.

One day the father throws an apple at his son and injures his soft back. Gregor dies from the consequences of this wound. They throw out his body like an old useless thing.

Before us we have two works constructed on apparently similar principles. At the bottom of each there is an unbelievable, fantastic event. But having once accomplished the miraculous transformations of their heroes (Fotheringay into a magician, and Samsa into something like a centipede), the authors leave them in the very same usual, completely real, and even scrupulously authentic surroundings in which they have lived and acted until then: Fotheringay in the provincial life of a little English town and Samsa in his humdrum home. And even the heroes do not change in essence. Fotheringay, the commander of the elements, the most powerful man on earth, is the same little clerk, shy, dull, insignificant. Samsa-centipede is the same loving son and diligent employee: even his new and terrible situation does not stop him from going to breakfast as usual.

In the story "The Man Who Could Work Miracles," apart from the absurdity of the initial position, the natural laws of nature continue to exert their force. Moreover, the author gives them a completely scientific explanation!

Why, in stopping the moon or, more accurately, in stopping the earth's rotation, does Fotheringay create a universal catastrophe? Because "he had made no stipulation concerning the trifling movables upon its surface. And the earth spins so fast that the surface at its equator is traveling at rather more than a thousand miles an hour, and in these latitudes at more than half that pace. So that the village, and Mr. Maydig [the pastor—D.M.] and Mr. Fotheringay, and everybody, and everything had been jerked violently forward at about nine miles per second," and so forth.[4]

In this point Mr. Fotheringay's miracle is decidedly different from Joshua's Biblical miracle: there everything came off perfectly, and the battle of the triumphant Israelites against the Amorites could be concluded during daylight.

In "The Metamorphosis" and "The Man Who Could Work Miracles," the events develop along a "natural" course. If for a moment we allow that the transformation of a man into a centipede is really possible, then we are forced to admit that everything that happens after that clearly has to appear the way that Kafka has portrayed it.

All of that is very similar; but nevertheless the works are different!

The basic idea of Wells's story consists in the following: power in the hands of a dolt gripped by messianism is an evil and insidious force; it threatens humanity with countless disasters. This idea grew out of the author's observation of life and his concrete experience of Europe in the age of imperialism. The political adventurer who makes no reckoning of the catastrophic consequences of his actions or, worse yet, is absolutely indifferent to them, is a typical figure in our time.

The ironic and farcical nature of the plot only underscores the seriousness of Wells's warning, and the fantastic aspect of the narration is only a means for maximum satirical generalization.

4. H. Wells, *Izbrannoe*, II (Moscow, 1957), 680.

The story "The Man Who Could Work Miracles" is allegorical, but allegory sometimes admits of several interpretations. It is possible that Wells was trying to develop another thought here, alongside the one we have mentioned: that the level of technological progress does not coincide with the moral state of society. But then the story is social and true to reality, for, without regard to the subjective illusion, Wells is posing the question of the durability of the capitalist mode of production.

And how does all this look in Kafka? In transforming Gregor Samsa into a centipede, the writer is striving to demonstrate that the true situation of man in the world is distinguished by his tragic and insurmountable *loneliness*. The individual exists in some kind of surroundings, some society. He goes to work and feels himself to be a small, but necessary, wheel in his firm or establishment. He communicates with those close to him—his father, mother, sisters, brothers, and friends—and considers himself dear to them. But all that is an error, a blind illusion. In reality man lives in a desert or, more accurately, in a vacuum, in a glass retort, and therefore he does not see the walls of his frightful prison.

Of course, such a theory (which, by the way, later lay at the bottom of the existentialists' ideas) was also suggested to Kafka by reality. In his mind were refracted the specific, historically concrete processes of the "atomization" of bourgeois society, but they were refracted in a fantastic, disfigured form: such a fundamental and absolute loneliness as that which appeared dimly to the writer *does not exist and has never existed*.

Precisely for this reason Kafka turns to a theoretical situation: he transforms Samsa into a centipede, that is, he artistically breaks all social, moral, and even purely biological ties between the hero and his surroundings.

A man-insect is no longer a generalization from reality (even though it may possibly have seemed so to the author himself); a man-insect is a departure from reality.

So, if we do not view these two works as self-contained "aesthetic phenomena," but correlate them with the truth of life, it appears that the conditional character in each of them plays a completely different role.

The same thing may be said about some more particular artistic devices [*priëmy*] of Wells and Kafka which may at first look quite similar. Let us look at both authors' tendency, already mentioned above, to place the miraculous in the context of the most ordinary and realistic details.

On the recommendation of Pastor Maydig, Fotheringay repeats Joshua's "experiment" with stopping the moon. But although the abilities of Wells's hero are not less significant than those of the Biblical leader, the results turn out rather unexpectedly: the laws of nature, which Fotheringay scorns, go into action independently of his will, and what happens then we already know!

In the atmosphere of the Old Testament myth, Joshua's miraculous powers are completely "normal"; they don't contradict either human or divine laws. But in the conditions of the reality which Wells reflects in the mediated forms of his art, Fotheringay's enormous powers come into conflict with the natural lawfulness of life [*estestvennye zhiznennye zakonomernosti*]. The world "rebels" against these powers, because here they are alien, lawless and, consequently, in some higher sense "unreal."

Thanks to that, by the way, the purely *metaphorical* sense of Wells's whole story is once again emphasized, the more so as at the end the author "takes back" the claim to verisimilitude and returns all the people and objects to their initial positions.

Such loneliness as Kafka ascribes to Samsa does not exist—we already mentioned that—and for that reason the writer could not confirm it through whatever real examples. But, like Gustav Meyrink in *The Golem*, he also could not simply brush reality aside and transport his hero into the sphere of unclear dreams and somnambulistic visions. He couldn't, because human loneliness is a relative quality: to measure it one must have an appropriate reference, that is, other people, society.

The only escape for Kafka was to "destroy" actual reality and at the same time stay within its limits. And so he cut all the threads tying Samsa to the world (by turning him into an insect) but left him in his family circle.

Consequently, the "similarity" in Wells's and Kafka's devices is the purest fiction: the former strives to "neutralize" the conditional character by polishing it on the grinding stone of reality, while Kafka "destroys" reality by means of the fantastic.

Remarks on Kafka's Journals

DMITRI ZATONSKY

When we want to learn more about a writer and understand him better, we try to read not only his creative works, but also his rough drafts, letters, and journals. However, there are writers whose creative work speaks completely for itself—everything else, although it may augment and expand our conception of the creative work, does not change anything substantial in our understanding of it. And there are writers to whose works we need a key. One of these is Franz Kafka. He has been much disputed and variously interpreted. Some reject him unconditionally; others just as unreservedly accept him. Some proclaim him a gloomy misanthrope; others an ardent humanist. Some see a realist in him; and others a decadent. He is connected with the aesthetics of expressionism, surrealism, naturalism. And it is true that in his novels, stories, and parables one may discover observations on all the circumstances of life.

The novel *The Trial* and some of Kafka's stories and parables are translated into Russian, so that the Soviet reader may form his own idea of the "mysterious" Kafka, of his very clear but sickly talent.

The journals are one of the keys to this talent, this work, to the personality of the writer. But to the same extent that Kafka is contradictory, ambiguous, and unique, so is this key to him.

They seem somehow to open the door to his work, to the meaning of Kafka's grotesques, his symbols, his terrifying riddles. But that is not the important thing here. The important thing is that the journals narrate the causes of Kafka's tragedy—as an artist and a man. They are journeys to the sources of his fears and despair, to where were born the fissures and breaks in the writer's spiritual life. The journals

Excerpted from D. Zatonsky, "Iz dnevnikov Frantsa Kafki: Neskol'ko predvaritel'-nykh zamechanii" [From the Diaries of Franz Kafka: Some Preliminary Remarks], *Voprosy literatury*, 12 (1968), No. 2, 131-35.

support what has already been presumed by the reader of the novels, stories, and parables but which he perhaps did not ultimately believe.

Let us say he has read the story "In the Penal Colony" and considered it surely something satirical. The author, he said, intentionally exaggerated the social relations around him in order to expose them all the more mercilessly.

But the journals correct such a point of view. Kafka did not do anything intentionally with a pedagogical aim or in the interest of social criticism. He saw the world this way. This and no other way. And therefore his view was dark and distorted. He was not exposing; he was suffering. The feeling of hopelessness in him results chiefly not from a fatal collision with reality (indeed, with the frightening bourgeois reality), but from the far more deadly collision with his own "I."

Every writer's journal is a story about himself. But also about others. It is an artist's story about his encounters with the real world. Commentaries on them, explanations and interpretations. Kafka's journals are primarily the story of his encounters with himself. They contain many incomplete literary sketches or variants of things written later. Detailed recountings of dreams or even of waking visions. Whole pages are devoted to complaints about his health, about a vague unrest or feeling of guilt torturing the writer, about the impossibility or inability to work creatively. No little attention is paid to the relationship with his father and his situation in the family.

But it would be useless to search in Kafka's journals for equally detailed accounts of his external connections. If he does speak at all of them, then he does so only rather offhandedly: "Was at Baum's," "Went to the theater," "Conversation with Max" (Brod).

Although in the journals there are realistic sketches of scenes or portraits of various people, notations of things observed or overheard, they are all presented in relation to the "private person." There are hardly any notes dealing with Kafka's occupational reality (if, of course, one does not count the complaints that his official duties are keeping him from literary work). And there are even fewer entries which reflect the social position of the writer. If we did not have at our disposal the testimonies of his contemporaries, we would not even know about Kafka's socialist sympathies, about his participation at the meetings of progressive organizations, and so forth.

The journals are hundreds of pages of small handwriting. And here we have reproduced perhaps the least part of them. [1] The editor concentrated his attention on Kafka's relation to life, to his own creative work, to other writers, and to art in general. And it may appear that he has passed over Kafka's political and ideological adherences. But that is not so.

Let no one think that among the notations omitted from 1914-1918, for example, there are many that deal with the First World War, the most important event of the era. Not all of them are presented here, but there are few of them, and they are very private.

But this is remarkable. In his correspondence or in conversations with his friends (later written down by Max Brod, Gustav Janouch, and others) he did touch on various social, political, and cultural problems. That is, he was ready to answer questions which others put to him. In the journals he asks questions and answers them himself. In essence, only here was he completely himself. And here he speaks about himself. For, strictly speaking, he lived thus too: completely within himself, perceiving the world only in and through himself.

And this is not egoism. Rather, a perpetual egocentric blind alley. See how intensely Kafka looks into and listens to himself, how scrupulously he notices the slightest displacement in his interrelationship with what exists—these are the unceasing oscillations of a pendulum, changes in tone, vacillations between complete hopelessness and frantic hope, ultimate disbelief in himself and feverish self-assurance. Look closely, and you will notice that there is nothing before you but a desperate struggle, a battle with his own shadow, which falls over the whole world. And this battle lost in advance saps too much strength. In the end, it breaks Kafka.

He was a contemporary of great changes. And, even, their subjectively honest witness. He saw the frightful inhumanity of the capitalist system, its soulless, mechanical, alienated civilization. But he was not only a witness; he was also a victim—hence the image, frequently repeated in his journals, of the knife thrust into the body. He even understood that he was not simply the victim of unsuccessfully resolved personal circumstances: of physical and mental illness, the tyranny of his father, a repulsive job, of the situation of the *déclassé* German Jew in the midst of Slavic Prague. He suspected that deeper, more difficult and contradictory social circumstances had formed him.

[1. These remarks were the preface to a selection from Kafka's journals. *Ed.*]

This is attested to by the journal entry of July 19, 1910, which begins the selection presented here.

He knew, understood, suspected . . . and, nevertheless, he could not do a thing with himself. He was completely defenseless in the face of his feeling of the fatal inescapability of his own as well as of general human agony. "Everything is fantasy," he wrote on October 21, 1921, "family, job, friends, the street; all is fantasy, farther or nearer—and woman; but the nearest truth is simply that you are beating your head against the wall of a room without windows or doors."

In this Kafka was completely incapable of looking at himself and at what was happening around him from the side, so to speak, from a distance. He was within the circle of this distorted black shadow, which he himself cast on the world. And he did not reconstruct the world, but this shadow. "The wish to portray my fantastic inner life," he wrote in the journal on August 6, 1914, "renders inessential everything else, which faded away and continues to fade in a terrible way."

He found himself in a river—a madly raging and galloping stream constantly changing its course. And in fact he was able to distinguish only what was carried along beside him, what the stream happened to snatch up. A horrible, mysterious, phantasmagorical "something." And in this "something" there is neither beginning nor end, neither present nor future nor even a past. Therefore he got this feeling only in maximal proximity to himself, with fluid, runny contours. He got it essentially only when he entered into himself, when he became his own transfigured, disfigured, incessantly torn spiritual flesh. And to carry, to preserve all of this horror in himself became indeed unthinkable. "What a monstrous world is squeezed into my head!" he wrote on June 21, 1913, "But how can I free myself from it, or free it itself, without destroying it? And it is a thousand times better to destroy all this than to keep or to bury it in oneself." And Kafka "destroyed the world," that is, recreated it as something not only contradictory, but also aimless, chaotic, primordially senseless.

He found himself in a river. . . . But at the same time he was consumed by the desire to "free himself," to separate himself from a frightening reality, to get out from under the power of the laws of life. "Thirst for the most infinite loneliness. To be eye-to-eye with myself," we read in the entry for July 1, 1913.

But when he succeeded in that—purely artificially, of course, for the reason that he was, so to speak, a fundamentally alienated individual—then he found himself in a yawning emptiness screaming with silence. Here is his perception in this regard: "Nothing, nothing. Emptiness, boredom, no, not boredom; only emptiness, senselessness, weakness . . ." (May 3, 1915). And on November 19, 1913, he complains: "I am like a sheep lost at night in the mountains, or a sheep running after that sheep. To be so lost and not have the strength to bemoan it!"

Kafka had no idea what to do with these antagonistic tendencies of his. They ate at him, robbed him of his last strength, pushed him into the embrace of the blackest pessimism. "I have arrived at the conclusion," he wrote (July 29, 1914), "that I avoid people not in order to live peacefully, but in order to die peacefully." In moments of despair the escape lay in a unique capitulation before the world, just as it was, with all its sins, imperfections, and brutality. For the only world which he knew and saw was the capitalist world.

If I examine my ultimate goal, it turns out that I do not actually strive to become a good man and to satisfy some highest court, but rather, quite to the contrary, to survey the whole community of men and animals, to recognize their fundamental predilections, wishes, and moral ideals, to reduce them to simple rules and to develop myself in accordance with them as quickly as possible, so that I become completely pleasing to all— so pleasing in fact (here comes the trick) that, without losing the general love, I may finally, as the only sinner who is not burned, openly, before everyone's eyes, reveal the vileness within me. In short, I am interested only in the human court, which I moreover want to deceive—but of course without deception.

That was written on September 28, 1917, that is, while Kafka was working intensively on *The Castle*. And that is the program that the alleged surveyor K., its hero, tries to realize with such amazing tenacity. He appears in a village subject to the judicial bureaucracy of a certain Count Westwest, tries to get into the immense chancelleries of the Count's castle in order to obtain from these hateful offices the right to settle in the village and to find a home, family, and work. In other words, to obtain the right to be like everyone else. He rebels. He rebels merely for the opportunity to become an obedient "subject" of the castle.

True, neither the "surveyor" K. nor Kafka himself can accomplish this. Their hatred, their turmoil is too strong. Thus the attempt of some Western interpreters to connect Kafka with a Nietzschean ideology is the fruit of an error, if not a conscious perversion.

Kafka's attitude toward the world is a decadent one typical of a crisis situation. He didn't believe in society and didn't believe in man. He did not even believe in the theoretical possibility of harmony between them. Not with the world as it is did he believe in them.

I have already said that he was a contemporary of great changes. But he did not scrutinize them and did not see that out of the ruins of the old society a new society was being born. And so he took world historical upheavals to be a universal catastrophe. Such an agony of the living, such a horror, could be expressed only in the language of mystical chiffres. In this sense Kafka is a bourgeois writer in the era of its decline.

But that does not mean that he was almost blind. Sometimes he saw truths that were hidden to his confreres. He did not accept the soulless, dehumanizing bourgeois civilization. Precisely because he lived in Austria-Hungary, a state in which the contradictions of this civilization appeared particularly sharply, Kafka felt earlier than many others that the capitalist world was plunging into the abyss. And he expressed the inescapable horror of human existence in its collapsing, but still pernicious, "penal colony."

But Kafka always saw only one side of the phenomenon. He always perceived life only through himself, irrevocably torn within himself.

His work is above all intuitive and impulsive; it is a result of "nocturnal" ecstasies. In a letter to Max Brod he one day said:

My work is a sweet, wonderful reward, but for what? Last night it became very clear to me . . . that it is a reward for serving the Devil. This descent to the dark powers, this disentangling of the soul tied to its own natural conditions, these doubtful embraces and all the rest settles down, and you do not see anything above when in the sunlight you write your story. Perhaps another kind of work exists; I know only this one: at night, when fear keeps me awake, I know only this one. And I see very clearly the diabolical element in it.

Let us turn our attention to the note of September 23, 1912, which tells how "The Judgment," Kafka's favorite story, arose. It is not as if he thought the story up, but, frightening the author and transporting him to raptures, it arose by itself from the subconscious depths of his soul. And only four and a half months later, already working on the proofs of "The Judgment," Kafka for the first time tried to comprehend consciously what had come out of his pen, and gave a commentary on his story (Feb. 11, 1913). Apparently his only self-commentary, by the way. In any case, the only recorded and published one.

On principle Kafka eschewed interpreting his images and symbols. For this did not lead to their clarification. On the contrary, the image became even more vague and unstable. A case in point is the journal entry of January 24, 1915. To his fiancée F., Kafka read the passage from *The Trial* about the guard at the Door to the Law ("Türhüterlegende"). In reading, he himself better understood what he had written, and it appeared that she understood. But it was worth it to him to start the discussion of the episode when everything was irretrievably ruined. And Kafka sadly summarizes:

The difficulties I have in speaking with people, which are certainly unbelievable to others, have their foundation in the fact that my thinking— or, better, the content of my consciousness—is very foggy, that, so far as I alone am concerned, I rest undisturbed and sometimes self-satisfied in it; but a human conversation needs pointedness, firmness, and constant connectedness: things that do not exist in me. No one will want to lie in clouds of fog with me; and even if he wanted to, I cannot drive the fog out of my head; between two people it dissolves and is nothing.

Kafka is speaking here not only of the impossibility of human communication, but also of the extraordinary difficulty of the reader's communication with his work. Not with creative work in general, but specifically with Kafka's. For that work is encoded. Not premeditatedly, but, because of that, all the more difficult.

And let us now look at the following: the entries of October 26, 1913 and of June 11, 1914, rough drafts of literary projects which Kafka never carried out; and the entry of April 20, 1916, which is the recounting of a dream. But between them—the artistic work of the writer and his nightmares—there is no essential difference. The same alogicality of the situations, the same fractured nature of all the projects. The dream looks, in plot, even more finished. In general, all Kafka's dreams are finished Kafkaesque stories, at least in their reproduction. Kafka's art is a dream-work art.

But Kafka dreamed (this is apparent from his journal) of another art, a healthy, normal, and inwardly whole one. But he knew also that reality cannot appear to us in the same way that it seemed to him in reveries. Hence his constant feeling of dissatisfaction with everything he wrote, hence his frightful discord with himself, his dividedness, his conflictedness.

He was attracted to people and feared people. For him nothing but literary work existed, and he cancelled out his literary work. Now he wants to be published by Rowohlt, now he muses that Rowohlt will reject his manuscripts, and he can see himself "just as unhappy as before."

Kafka's statements on literature and art, contained in the selection published here, are interesting in many ways. Especially his thoughts on the drama and the differences between it and the novel (entry of October 28, 1911), and also the numerous references to Dostoevsky.

But I will not stop there. For I see my task above all as the elucidation of what is necessary to an elucidation. And then the journals are instructive not primarily for his theoretical-literary judgments. They are a stunning document in themselves: the testimony to the frightful tragedy of a man ruined by bourgeois society and not finding in himself the strength to protest. To protest neither in the name of others, nor for his own sake.

Kafka's Alienation

AVNER ZIS

Ionesco presents an undeniably powerful picture of the dehumanization of life under capitalism in his works, but he does not apprehend the forces capable of transforming the world in keeping with humanist principles. One-sided reproduction of reality inevitably means its distortion. In the works of modernists we find reflections of inhuman reality, but it is presented in distorted form as a result of their mistaken view of the world.

To a large extent this even applies to such considerable and talented writers as Kafka and Camus. Their vivid writings not only bear the mark of true talent but are also permeated by a sincere sense of pain and revulsion at the inhumanity of the bourgeois world. Yet for our purposes what is important is not their particular subjective intentions, but the way in which their false view of the world left its mark on their writing. In *The Trial* and *The Penal Colony* and some other works, Kafka succeeded in depicting in his imaginary world certain aspects of the terrible and forbidding reality, into whose abyss mankind was hurled by fascism. Yet he was no prophet: he had neither knowledge of, nor faith in, the possibility of overcoming those inhumane conditions. His artistic imagination is antihistorical and, viewed objectively, his ideas play into the hands of reactionary forces, whose interests would stand to suffer if any radical changes in the world were brought about.

Marxist aestheticians find it impossible to accept the point of view of those writers who do not see the artist as bound to disclose the sources of alienation and work out ways for overcoming it, but consider it sufficient that he should indicate its existence. The artist is a student of life, its main trends, its profound nature, and he cannot

1. Karl Marx and Frederick Engels, *Collected Works*, III (Moscow: Progress Publishers, 1975), 176.

confine himself merely to confirming that alienation exists. Marx held
that the "immediate *task of philosophy*, which is at the service of history, once the *holy form* of human self-estrangement has been unmasked, is to unmask self-estrangement in its unholy forms."[1] Yet
does not this also constitute the task of art, not all art of course, but
that art which "is at the service of history," in other words, realist art
that is passionately concerned with the future of mankind? The artist's task is not merely to diagnose; he cannot stand outside good and
evil.

1. Karl Marx and Frederick Engels, *Collected Works,* III (Moscow: Progress
Publishers, 1975), 176.

Decadence and Alienation

YURI BARABASH

In the opinion of certain authors the art which we usually regard as decadent is not decadent at all. Really decadent art is the sort which, while pretending to be realistic and optimistic, adorns and embellishes the rotting capitalist system, if not to perpetuate it indefinitely, then at least to prolong its existence. "Our enemy in art," writes one of those who support this conception, "is certainly not Kafka or others who display similar tendencies which have been vindicated in their art, but *above all* [italics mine—*Y.B.*] various forms of pseudo-realism and naturalism which, in contrast to Kafka, try to preserve fidelity in details and affirm falsehood in general."[1]

No doubt of it, bourgeois pseudo-realism, false naturalism and mass culture really are our enemies. But a question arises: why should we not set *genuinely* realistic, *genuinely* truthful rather than decadent art in opposition to this pseudo-realistic art? Would it not be more accurate to say that both decadent art and the sort that embellishes are in essence two sides of the same coin, two hypostases of one phenomenon—the crisis of bourgeois consciousness in the artistic sphere? [. . .]

The view of decadence cited above is usually defended on the grounds that decadent art, while not being "consciously socialist," nonetheless emerges from a rejection of capitalism, from a tragic, though perhaps subjective, pessimistic sense of its inevitable destruction. It is in this particular respect that the supporters of decadent art see its objective, potentially revolutionary force. "In this very rejection," we read in one dissertation abstract, "we find the potential seed

From Yuri Barabash, *Aesthetics and Poetics* (Moscow: Progress Publishers, 1977), pp. 63-67.

1. G. Kunitsyn, "Klassovost v literature. Statya vtoraya" [Class Character in Literature. Second Essay], *Znamya*, No. 2 (1968), p. 217.

of historical optimism, for *before one accepts the socialist position one must understand that capitalism is doomed."*[2]

I do not think that one could acknowledge this as a convincing argument. The rejection of capitalism which is brought about by a tragic recognition of its hopelessness is, as a rule, incapable of nurturing wholesome art; more often it results in the rejection of human civilization as a whole, in that sort of all-encompassing scepticism which consumes the artist's creative powers. Historical optimism is not born of petty-bourgeois individualistic rebellion or of a lack of faith in the revolutionary potential and creative powers of the masses.

One of the most typical and most complex writers in this respect is Kafka, whose work, not without reason, has provoked most intense discussion in recent years. It would be worthwhile to look into this matter in greater detail here.

Garaudy not only includes Kafka without reservation in the sphere of "realism without bounds" (which is no cause for surprise when one considers that this "realism" is "without bounds" precisely in order to encompass *everything*); he also views the works of this author as a fundamental argument in favor of his conception. In his opinion the main reason for regarding Kafka as a realist is the fact that he shows us the world of alienation and conveys an atmosphere of "anxiety and impending catastrophe."

One has to acknowledge, of course, that Kafka "does not see the immanent movement, in the course of which the transition is accomplished from one world to another," that he "does not answer (or claim to answer) our questions." But for Garaudy it is enough that the writer "forces us to pose" these questions. In Kafka's ability to re-create the inhuman world of alienation, a world that on the surface of things is quite ordinary, a smooth-running machine, but at the same time is phantasmagoric, mysterious and hostile to man—in this ability, Garaudy believes, one can discern some sort of primordial impulse, the incentive to search for a way out. "In describing reality as it is, without any superfluous additions, that is, as a well-oiled machine, but one which constantly implies a threat, which oppresses and stifles man, which engenders panic and irony and rebellion in the mind and

2. G. I. Kunitsyn, *Puti i formy vozdeistviya politiki na razvitiye khudozhestvennoi literatury* [Forms and Ways in Which Politics Influences the Development of Literature] (Moscow, 1968), p. 18.

heart, Kafka suggests by virtue of this description alone the idea and demands of another world. . . ."

And we already feel, asserts the critic, that "this world is not tightly closed," that we are "awakened from the torpor of these habits, obligations and conventions, and are called to give an account"; "we desire to find some justification for our acts. . . ."[3] In an atmosphere of all-consuming negation, at first imperceptibly, then little by little, a feeling of horror spontaneously arises, followed by irony, and later by the seeds of rebellion. This, indeed, is what constitutes the "mission of arousing" which Kafka ostensibly took upon himself.

But is this really the case? Is it true in fact that the *depiction* of alienation almost automatically gives rise to an *awareness* of this alienation? And is it true that Kafka shows us "the light at the end of the interminable tunnel"?

The response of Marxist criticism is not excessively blunt, but it is nonetheless negative. Say what you will, the constant effort to find some revolutionary principle in Kafka's negation, the attempts to discern prophetic utterances connected with the rise of the Third Reich and the inception of the "atomic age," bear the clear imprint of oversimplification, if not pure speculation. It is true, as Evgenia Knipovich rightly notes, that "the feelings of 'alienation,' 'guilt' and 'fear' which characterize the attitude of Kafka and his autobiographical heroes to the world are based on certain social laws,"[4] but for the writer the essence of these laws remained a sealed book. Subjectively, it is true, Kafka was anti-bourgeois, and he, together with other writers akin in spirit and method, impressively conveyed the feeling that their society was doomed, that its decline and fall were inevitable, their fear before the impending cataclysms; but for them this was equivalent to the end of the world, the destruction of human civilization and mankind in general. Hence their "apocalyptic mood," their "pessimism and lack of faith in man's creative potential, his ability to tear the chains of slavery asunder and free himself from those forces which hold him captive."[5] To ascribe the "mission of arousing" to art which is permeated with decadent attitudes and to see in it the seed of his-

---

3. Roger Garaudy, *D'un réalisme sans rivages* (Paris, 1963), pp. 235, 236f., 238.
4. E. Knipovich, *Khudozhnik i istoriya* [The Artist and History] (Moscow, 1968), p. 414f.
5. Boris Suchkov, *Liki vremeni. F. Kafka, S. Tsveig, G. Fallada, L. Feikhtvanger, T. Mann* [Images of the Age: F. Kafka, S. Zweig, H. Fallada, L. Feuchtwanger, T. Mann] (Moscow, 1969), p. 21. [Cf. this anthology, p. 125ff.]

torical optimism is little more than wishful thinking, though undoubtedly a thoughtful, differentiated approach is imperative here.

One can find interesting thoughts on this problem in *Reflection and Action*, a book by the German (GDR) aesthetician and critic Horst Redeker. He analyzes the views of those who consider Kafka a realist because in some way or another reality is reflected in his works, and above all the alienation of the individual in bourgeois society (Garaudy, Fischer, Enzensberger), and shows how unconvincing their arguments are. The fact that the characteristic historical state of the individual in society becomes the subject of literary works does not mean that these works are realistic. Redeker says, "The reflection of alienation in and of itself is a manifestation neither of decadence nor of realism; it may be realistic, as, for example, in the works of Thomas Mann and others, or it may be decadent, as it is for Joyce or Beckett." The deciding factor is not what is being reflected, but rather the artist's attitude toward it, his position and perspective on the subject. Redeker underscores that realism declines and decadence begins when alienation is represented from the position of an individual who is himself alienated. "An awareness of one's loneliness, the feeling that one does not fit in anywhere, the impossibility of loving or being loved and of feeling like a member of human society—these are the basic emotions which many contemporary bourgeois authors claim to feel."

For Kafka these feelings are manifested in the extreme. "The conveyer-belt of life carries man along toward an unknown destination. Man is more like a thing, an object, than a living being." That is how Kafka felt in his world, and that is how he felt in his art—like a thing, an object, a victim, a little splinter tossed about in the turbulent sea of life and society.[6]

Alienation depicted in this way possesses particular authenticity and force, and this depiction, says Leo Kofler (as quoted by Redeker), "is often successful to such an astonishing degree that some literary critics are overpowered by the vivid sketch of the alienated individual and falsely attribute a critical, denunciatory function to this art."

True, in expressing the view that the artist who "assumes the guilt

6. In his book *Mera istiny* [The Yardstick of Truth] (Moscow, 1971, p. 35f.), Yuri Kuzmenko draws an interesting comparison between sentiments of this sort in Kafka (with reference to his diaries and his "Letter to My Father") and Tatyana's "decadent disposition" in Gorky's *The Petty Bourgeois*.

of his age is transformed, not only into a victim, but also into a participant," Redeker is being a little too categorical, in my opinion. He himself engages in polemics (and convincingly so) with Geörgy Lukács, who was inclined to view expressionism merely as an ideological defence of capitalism. A simplistic approach of this sort is just as inapplicable in dealing with complex phenomena like Kafka. But when the author of *Reflection and Action* says that "Kafka depicted alienation on the basis of his own alienated position," and that the school to which Kafka belongs "is not in the realist line," we would be hardput to argue with him.[7]

We are not dealing only with Kafka here. We are speaking of decadence as a phenomenon. It is a complex and contradictory phenomenon with many transitional forms and opposing tendencies; it cannot be schematized simply along an "either-or" axis. But by its very nature this phenomenon is alien to realism and to a revolutionary world view, and we must bear this in mind particularly when we are evaluating literary non-conformism in imperialist countries.

7. Horst Redeker, *Abbildung und Aktion. Versuch über die Dialektik des Realismus* (Halle, 1966), pp. 133, 152, 156, 148, 151f., 154, 145, 146.

CONTRIBUTORS

HANNAH ARENDT (1906–1977) was born in Hanover and took her Ph.D. at the University of Heidelberg. She emigrated to the United States in 1941 and taught at Berkeley, Princeton, Columbia and Chicago before becoming University Professor at the New School for Social Research in 1967. Her major works are *Origins of Totalitarianism* (1951), *The Human Condition* (1958), *Eichmann in Jerusalem* (1963), *On Revolution* (1963), and *On Violence* (1972).

YURI YAKOVLEVICH BARABASH (b. 1931) is professor and director of the Gorky Institute of World Literature in Moscow where he specializes in Soviet literature and questions of literary theory. Among his chief publications are *Dovzhenko* (1968), *On Popular-National Values in Literature* (1968), and *Aesthetics and Poetics* (1973; 1979).

VLADIMIR DAVIDOVICH DNEPROV (i.e., Vladimir Davidovich Reznik, b. 1903), the Soviet critic, has written many essays on Freudianism and modern literature, and especially on Thomas Mann. His major concern has been to connect aesthetic problems with issues of ideology and the propagandistic principles of socialist realism. His most important books are *Problems of Realism* (1960), *Characteristics of the 20th Century Novel* (1965), *Literature and Man's Moral Experience* (1970), and *Dostoevsky's Artistic Expression* (1978).

HOWARD FAST (b. 1914) was a member of the Communist Party of the United States from 1943 to 1956. In 1950 he served a prison term for refusing to cooperate with the House Un-American Activities Committee and in 1953 was awarded the Stalin Peace Prize. His best known novels include *Citizen Tom Payne* (1943), *My Glorious Brothers* (1948), and *Torquemada* (1966). He wrote an account of his political experiences in *The Naked God* (1957).

ERNST FISCHER (1899–1972) began his career as a poet, playwright, and journalist. In 1934 he broke with the Social Democrats, joined the Communist Party, and left Austria for Prague and then Moscow. He was founder and editor of *Neues Österreich* and from 1945 to 1959 a Communist member of the Austrian national assembly. After passionate support of the Czech reforms of 1968, he was expelled from the Austrian Communist Party, of which he was a Central Committee member, in 1970. Apart from his political writings and memoires, he has also written several studies of literary figures and three important studies in aesthetics: *The Necessity of Art* (1959), *Art and Coexistence* (1966), and *Art Against Ideology* (1969).

ROGER GARAUDY (b. 1913), professor of philosophy at the University of Poitiers, is one of the leading Marxist theoreticians in France. He holds a Doctor of Letters from the Sorbonne and a Doctor of Science from the Academy of Sciences of the U.S.S.R. From 1960 to 1970 he was Director of the Center for Marxist Studies and Research; from 1956 to 1970 he was the chief ideologist of the politburo of the French Communist Party, from which he was expelled in 1970. He has written extensively on twentieth-century philosophy and is well known in this country through translations of his books *The Crisis in Communism: The Turning Point of Socialism* (1969), *Marxism in the Twentieth Century* (1970), and *The Alternative Future: A Vision of Christian Marxism* (1972).

EDUARD GOLDSTUCKER (b. 1913) held diplomatic posts in England and Israel and later became professor of German and chairman of the Department of German at Charles University in Prague. He was principally responsible for organizing the Kafka conference at Liblice in 1963. In January 1968 he was elected president of the Czechoslovak Writers' Union, and he remained its spokesman throughout the reform period, for which he was bitterly denounced by the Soviet and German Democratic Republic press. After the Soviet suppression of the reform movement, he emigrated to England and is currently on the faculty of the University of Sussex.

JIRI HAJEK, Czech literary critic and journalist, was editor of the literary review *Plamen*.

KLAUS HERMSDORF is a leading literary scholar in the German Democratic Republic, who has specialized in twentieth-century literature, especially Kafka. His book *Kafka: Weltbild und Roman* (1961; 1966) was one of the first studies of Kafka in the German Democratic Republic.

EVGENIYA FEDOROVNA KNIPOVICH (b. 1898) is a distinguished Soviet literary scholar who has specialized in nineteenth- and twentieth-century German and Russian literature and in the relationship of the artist and society. Among her books are *Heinrich Heine* (1931), *Heine as Political Lyricist* (1932), *In Defense of Life* (1958), *Fadeev's "Young Guard"* (1964), *The Force of Truth* (1965), *The Artist and History* (1968), and *The Courage to Choose* (1975). She was awarded the Dobrolyubov Prize of the Academy of Sciences of the U.S.S.R.

ALEXEJ KUSAK is a Czech journalist and translator.

PAUL REIMANN, an influential Czech historian, is a corresponding member of the Czechoslovak Academy of Sciences and director of the Institute of the History of the Communist Party of Czechoslovakia.

HELMUT RICHTER, a literary historian in the German Democratic Republic, has specialized in the work of Franz Kafka since he wrote his doctoral dissertation under the direction of Hans Mayer in 1959. It has been subsequently published under the title *Franz Kafka: Werk und Entwurf* (1962).

BORIS LEONTIEVICH SUCHKOV (b. 1917) is a well known Soviet literary critic and scholar, member of the editorial boards of *Foreign Literature* and *Questions of Literature*, and a member of the Communist Party of the Soviet Union since 1941. Suchkov has devoted most of his voluminous writing to defining the problems and development of realism and socialist realism. He has edited the Soviet editions of the works of Thomas Mann, Stefan Zweig, Lion Feuchtwanger, and Franz Kafka. His major recent works are *The Historical Fate of Realism* (1967) and *Images of the Age* (1969). He was awarded the Lunacharsky Prize in 1964.

DMITRI VLADIMIROVICH ZATONSKY (b. 1922), Soviet critic and literary scholar, specializes in twentieth-century Western European literature and problems of literary theory. He is a corresponding member of the Academy of Sciences of the Ukrainian SSR and a member of the International Association of Literary Critics. His major books are *The Twentieth Century: Literary Form in the West* (1961), *Franz Kafka and Problems of Modernism* (1965), *The Search for Life's Meaning: Contemporary Literature in the West* (1966), *The Art of the Novel in the Twentieth Century* (1973), and *The Mirror of Art* (1975).

AVNER YAKOVLEVICH ZIS is a Soviet theater critic whose extensive writings on aesthetics have been collected in several volumes: *Lectures on Marxist-Leninist Aesthetics* (1960), *Epigones in Bourgeois Aesthetics* (1974), *Art and Aesthetics* (1975), and *The Aspects of Art* (1979). He is a Merited Scientist of the R.S.F.S.R.

INDEX

Italic numbers refer to articles appearing in this anthology.

LIBRARY OF CONGRESS CATALOGING IN PUBLICATION DATA
Main entry under title:

Franz Kafka: an anthology of Marxist criticism.

Includes bibliographical references and index.
1. Kafka, Franz, 1883-1924–Criticism and
interpretation–Addresses, essays, lectures.
I. Hughes, Kenneth Robert. II. Title: Marxist
criticism.
PT2621.A26Z7167   833'.912   81-51611
ISBN 0-87451-206-9   AACR2